Legal and Economic Aspects of State Control Over Compliance With Labor Legislation

Galina Ognqnova Yolova
University of Economics - Varna, Bulgaria

Andriyana Andreeva
University of Economics - Varna, Bulgaria

Darina Nedelcheva Dimitrova
University of Economics - Varna, Bulgaria

Hristina Vilhelm Blagoycheva
University of Economics - Varna, Bulgaria

Plamena Nedyalkova
University of Economics - Varna, Bulgaria

Hristosko Bogdanov
University of Economics - Varna, Bulgaria

IGI Global
PUBLISHER of TIMELY KNOWLEDGE

A volume in the Advances in Public Policy and Administration (APPA) Book Series

Published in the United States of America by
IGI Global
Information Science Reference (an imprint of IGI Global)
701 E. Chocolate Avenue
Hershey PA, USA 17033
Tel: 717-533-8845
Fax: 717-533-8661
E-mail: cust@igi-global.com
Web site: http://www.igi-global.com

Library of Congress Cataloging-in-Publication Data

Names: Yolova, Galina, 1973- contributor.
Title: Legal and economic aspects of state control over compliance with labor legislation / authored by: Galina Ognqnova Yolova, Andriyana Andreeva, Darina Nedelcheva Dimitrova, Hristina Vilhelm Blagoycheva, Plamena Nedyalkova, Hristosko Bogdanov.
Description: Hershey, PA : Information Science Reference, [2023] | Includes bibliographical references and index. | Summary: "In this sense, the aim of the study is to comprehensively - both doctrinally and theoretically - analyze and study the control mechanisms for compliance with labor legislation, viewed through the prism of normative systematics and in the aspect of their economic effects on traditional and alternative forms of employment"-- Provided by publisher.
Identifiers: LCCN 2023003380 (print) | LCCN 2023003381 (ebook) | ISBN 9781668490679 (hardcover) | ISBN 9781668490716 (paperback) | ISBN 9781668490686 (ebook)
Subjects: LCSH: Labor laws and legislation--Bulgaria.
Classification: LCC KJM1270 .L44 2023 (print) | LCC KJM1270 (ebook) | DDC 344.49901--dc23/eng/20230728
LC record available at https://lccn.loc.gov/2023003380
LC ebook record available at https://lccn.loc.gov/2023003381

This book is published in the IGI Global book series Advances in Public Policy and Administration (APPA) (ISSN: 2475-6644; eISSN: 2475-6652)

British Cataloguing in Publication Data
A Cataloguing in Publication record for this book is available from the British Library.

Advances in Public Policy and Administration (APPA) Book Series

ISSN:2475-6644
EISSN:2475-6652

MISSION

Proper management of the public sphere is necessary in order to maintain order in modern society. Research developments in the field of public policy and administration can assist in uncovering the latest tools, practices, and methodologies for governing societies around the world.

The **Advances in Public Policy and Administration (APPA) Book Series** aims to publish scholarly publications focused on topics pertaining to the governance of the public domain. APPA's focus on timely topics relating to government, public funding, politics, public safety, policy, and law enforcement is particularly relevant to academicians, government officials, and upper-level students seeking the most up-to-date research in their field.

COVERAGE

- Government
- Law Enforcement
- Political Economy
- Politics
- Public Administration
- Public Funding
- Public Policy
- Resource Allocation
- Urban Planning

IGI Global is currently accepting manuscripts for publication within this series. To submit a proposal for a volume in this series, please contact our Acquisition Editors at Acquisitions@igi-global.com or visit: http://www.igi-global.com/publish/.

The Advances in Public Policy and Administration (APPA) Book Series (ISSN 2475-6644) is published by IGI Global, 701 E. Chocolate Avenue, Hershey, PA 17033-1240, USA, www.igi-global.com. This series is composed of titles available for purchase individually; each title is edited to be contextually exclusive from any other title within the series. For pricing and ordering information please visit http://www.igi-global.com/book-series/advances-public-policy-administration/97862. Postmaster: Send all address changes to above address.

Titles in this Series

For a list of additional titles in this series, please visit:
www.igi-global.com/book-series/advances-public-policy-administration/97862

Reimagining Systems Thinking in a Post-Pandemic World
Mary Elizabeth Azukas (East Stroudsburg University, USA) and Minkyoung Kim (University of West Florida, USA)
Information Science Reference • © 2023 • 330pp • H/C (ISBN: 9781668472859) • US $215.00

Government Response to Disruptive Innovation Perspectives and Examinations
Sam B. Edwards, III (Quinnipiac University, USA) and James R. Masterson (Morehead State University, USA)
Information Science Reference • © 2023 • 371pp • H/C (ISBN: 9781668464298) • US $215.00

Examining Colonial Wars and Their Impact on Contemporary Military History
Miguel Madueño (Rey Juan Carlos University, Spain) and Alberto Guerrero (Universidad de Granada, Spain)
Information Science Reference • © 2023 • 311pp • H/C (ISBN: 9781668470404) • US $215.00

Governance as a Catalyst for Public Sector Sustainability
Neeta Baporikar (Namibia University of Science and Technology, Namibia & SP Pune University, India)
Information Science Reference • © 2023 • 392pp • H/C (ISBN: 9781668469668) • US $250.00

Acceleration of the Biopsychosocial Model in Public Health
Simon George Taukeni (University of Namibia, Namibia)
Medical Information Science Reference • © 2023 • 347pp • H/C (ISBN: 9781668464960) • US $325.00

For an entire list of titles in this series, please visit:
www.igi-global.com/book-series/advances-public-policy-administration/97862

IGI Global
PUBLISHER of TIMELY KNOWLEDGE

701 East Chocolate Avenue, Hershey, PA 17033, USA
Tel: 717-533-8845 x100 • Fax: 717-533-8661
E-Mail: cust@igi-global.com • www.igi-global.com

Editorial Advisory Board

Table of Contents

Detailed Table of Contents

In pursuit of the stated aim, the author set the following tasks: 1) To examine the nature of the control powers of the executive agency "general labour inspectorate"; 2) To examine the legal means for exercising control over compliance with the labour legislation, analyzing in detail the types of compulsory administrative measures under Art. 1 of the Labour Code; 3) To outline current legislative trends in the field of monitoring compliance with labour rights after Bulgaria's accession to the European Union.

Part of the newly appeared, over the last 25 years, non-standard forms of work do not fall within the scope of labor and social security legislation, while the rest are covered to a certain extent. Therefore, the purpose of the present work is to examine the challenges for the national governments in adapting labor legislation to the new conditions of the labor market and to propose possible measures in this direction. In pursuit of the set goal, the author sets himself the following tasks: 1) To investigate the preconditions that led to the appearance and rapid spread of non-standard forms of employment; 2) To point out the factors complicating the regulation of labor standards and the insurance protection of persons engaged in non-standard employment; 3) To look for and propose opportunities for regulatory and control measures in non-standard forms of employment, as well as to present some good examples of government initiatives.

In this part of the study, attention is paid to the need to determine the effectiveness and efficiency of the control activity of the labor control agency. The approach that was used is related to the binding of the results of the control activity of the agency and the resources that it uses to carry out its activity. Indicators for the period 2017-2021 have been calculated, which can be used to determine how effective and efficient the agency's activity is. Of primary importance for exercising control over compliance with labor legislation, according to the legislation in force in the Republic of Bulgaria, is the Executive Agency "Main Labor Inspection" (EA MLI).

Foreword

The work submitted to me for review has a total length of 297 pages. Structurally, it consists of an introduction, an outline, divided into two parts with three chapters each, a conclusion, literature used and an appendix (questionnaire). A total of 185 sources, including websites, were surveyed and cited in good faith in the development of the topic.

The adopted structural plan and methodology of the study are well chosen and appropriate for achieving the goals and objectives of the monographic work in the context of the research problem. An in-depth theoretical analysis of a wide range of literary sources of Bulgarian and foreign authors relevant to the topic of the monographic study has been carried out. They are correctly cited in the text. This fact illustrates the authors' very good knowledge of the available and accessible literature. Argumented opinions and conclusions are drawn on the formulated problems, novelties are highlighted.

The authors explore a scientific problem of current importance for theory and practice - the control of the observance of rights arising from work. Title One is devoted to the legal aspects and Title Two to the economic aspects of the control of compliance with labour legislation. In relation to each other, the legal and economic aspects of the monographic work serve legal and economic science, while being valuable for the practice of control institutions and for the subjects of the employment relationship.

As the most prominent positive aspects of the monographic study should be mentioned:

First, the study enriches both legal and economic doctrine on state control of labour law compliance and the practical impact of its enforcement.

Second, the monographic work is applicable to legal and economic practitioners, as well as employers and supervisory authorities.

The applicability and usefulness of the results obtained in the monographic work is evident both in theoretical and practical aspects. In conclusion and on the basis of the legal and economic analysis carried out in the individual parts, justified conclusions, specific legislative proposals and recommendations for control institutions are drawn. In this sense, the scientific objective of the monographic study has been achieved.

In view of this, I propose that the monographic work on "Legal and economic aspects of state control of compliance with labor legislation" with authors Assoc. Yolova, Assoc. Andreeva, Assoc. Prof. D. Andreyeva, Ph. D. Blagoycheva, Assoc. D. Dimitarova, prof. as. P. Nedyalkova, as. Dr. H. Bogdanov to be published in the Science and Economics Publishing House of the University of Economics - Varna.

Desislava Serafimova
University of Economics – Varna, Bulgaria

Preface

The realization of the constitutionally guaranteed right to work and related subjective labour rights has been and will always be a serious challenge for legislation and legal doctrine. Finding a balance in the interests and rights of the subjects in employment relations is the subject and task of the legislative endeavour to establish lasting stability on the one hand, and normative certainty in the countervailing and functionally bound rights and obligations of individuals on the other. In this sense, the development of a durable and guaranteed system of methods and means of control is sought and reflected in the establishment of an institutional and centralized mechanism for the assertion of labour rights, such as state control over compliance with labour legislation. Permanently established, but also built upon with timely and relevant mechanisms, it should be a guarantee of the legislative tendency to protect the right to work and its exercise in a dignified, socially acceptable and fair normative order.

At the same time, the contemporary forms of digitalization of labour and the increasingly aggressive use of artificial intelligence in labour relations pose both legislation and doctrine qualitatively different challenges, necessitating the introduction of new, adaptive to the new social realities normative means to protect the interests of workers. Over the last twenty-five years, in response to the economic trends of digitalization and globalization, new non-standard forms of work have emerged, significantly changing concepts and standards in terms of work position, social security, organization, location and working time periods. For some workers they offer desirable flexibility and reconciliation of personal and professional life. For others, however, non-standard employment is increasingly proving to be a source of precarious work, low earnings and lack of social protection. The traditional employment relationship is undergoing major transformations, directly affecting basic labour rights that are proving extremely vulnerable in the qualitatively different labour environment.

The European Foundation for the Improvement of Living and Working Conditions (Eurofound) mapping exercise identifies nine new forms of employment (ICT-based mobile work, platform work, casual work, co-working, job sharing, temporary management, employee sharing, portfolio work and voucher-based work) and documents their increasing prevalence in the EU, Norwegian and UK labour markets. Three of them (platform work, portfolio work and this joint employment organised by self-employed workers) are not covered by labour law, while the others are partially covered. In this sense, the current regulatory frameworks of governments, tax systems and social protection systems cannot be so quickly transformed to respond to all emerging and diverse forms of employment and to provide adequate income and social welfare protection for employees. Initiatives and regulatory measures to curb unfair practices are already being taken in many countries, but they are still sporadic, partial, for individual activities or professions.

At the same time, the classic forms of labour practices implemented through different models of teleworking are proving to seriously affect the rights of workers guaranteed and upheld by the traditions of labour law - including the right to rest, to leave, to privacy and to detachment from the working environment.

The new culture of "permanent connected persons" existing as a permanent state of affairs already leads to latent overtime, violated right to leave and rest, permanent and serious absence of work-life balance. In this sense, the need to build a qualitatively different and adaptive comprehensive labour legislation in the field of control, which would provide adequate protection and support to persons with non-standard employment, is becoming increasingly clear.

The necessity to study all aspects of the control mechanisms and their role or impact in the protection of subjective labour rights provoked the interest of the authors to a complex interdisciplinary study, combining legal and economic parts, studying in their entirety and with the methods of the respective scientific fields the specifics of state control over compliance with labour legislation. Such a study has not been conducted so far and in this sense its **relevance and contribution to the legal and economic doctrine is more than indisputable.** The combination of a legal and an economic approach to the study of the nature and aspects of control provides a comprehensive study, not carried out in the literature and doctrine, which clearly outlines the meaning, nature and, above all, the effectiveness and efficiency of the control mechanism. In this sense, and on the other hand, the authors' aim is to reinforce the understanding of the need to perceive control as a scientific discipline and, related to this, the increased validation of control activity in practice.

In these aspects, the study has not only theoretical, but also important prescriptive and practical - applied significance - by using quantitative indicators based on the theory of fuzzy sets to measure the effectiveness of the control are established, on the one hand, applicable models for future efficiency, combined, on the other - with doctrinal analytical - legal conclusions and proposals de lege ferenda, also outlined in the light of new, alternative forms of employment.

Given the interdisciplinary nature of the research, it is focused around two axes - legal and economic, to which the parts of the work correspond in structural terms. Accordingly, they are presented by the authors in their interrelation in view of the complex and comprehensive study of the subject.

In this sense, **the aim of the study** is to comprehensively - both doctrinally and theoretically - analyze and study the control mechanisms for compliance with labor legislation, viewed through the prism of normative systematics and in the aspect of their economic effects on traditional and alternative forms of employment.

Subordinated to this general objective, the legal study aims at a comprehensive and complex analysis - historical, topical and comparative - of the national legislation on the control of compliance with labour legislation, as well as to examine the new moments in the legal regulation on the transposition of European norms in the field of control. In this sense are also the tasks set by the authors, namely:

- Historical tracing, in systematics and periodicity, of the development of the institutional mechanism for the control of compliance with labour legislation;
- Comprehensive systematization and analysis of the relevant, establishing the tools and mechanisms of control general and special normative acts, as well as in the light of the analysis of the Draft Statutory Regulations of the Executive Agency "General Labour Inspectorate", through the prism of the new trends for updating the mechanisms of impact and capacity of the control bodies;
- Study of the nature of the control powers of the Executive Agency "General Labour Inspectorate" ;
- Analyzing the legal means for exercising control over compliance with labour legislation, through a detailed analysis of the types of compulsory administrative measures under Art. 404, para.

Analysis of the administrative procedures under Article 404(1) of the Labour Code;

- Outlining the current legislative trends in the field of control of compliance with labour rights after Bulgaria's accession to the European Union.

In this sense, a comprehensive systematics of the existing normative acts in the sphere of control is brought out, giving their respective analysis in the directions of the nature, competences and control powers of the Executive Agency General Labour Inspectorate, methods and means of control influence, nature, meaning and essence of the imposed compulsory administrative measures and administrative penalties.

In the economic part of the study, the directions of the analysis are in the aspects of studying, on the one hand, the measures for exercising control in non-standard forms of employment and, on the other hand, conducting an empirical study of the effectiveness of control over compliance with labor legislation through a proposed system of indicators, which is built on the basis of testing the direct and indirect resources and costs incurred, expressing the resource- and cost-absorption (capacity) of the control activity. Here, the relevance of the analysis is based on the dynamic changes in the normative framework of control mechanisms, the possibility of applying different quantitative methods and approaches for assessing the effectiveness of control over labour legislation, determining both the purely scientific - research interest and the methodological urge to seek a modern approach to assess the effectiveness of control, through which to reveal the specificities of control activities.

The proposed economic approach to study the effectiveness of control is from two aspects, namely - according to the level of use and according to the degree of generality, as well as according to the methods considered and the grouping of relevant indicators according to the relevant signs with their respective scientific - practical purpose.

In this sense, the tasks of the economic part of the study are as follows:

- To explore the preconditions that led to the emergence and strong spread of non-standard forms of employment;
- To identify the factors that make it difficult to regulate labour standards and social security protection for persons engaged in non-standard employment;

- Seek and suggest options for regulatory and control measures in non-standard forms of employment, and highlight some good examples of government initiatives;
- Conducting an empirical study of the effectiveness of control over compliance with labor legislation through a proposed system of indicators, which is based on the testing of direct and indirect resources and costs incurred, express the resource - and cost absorption (capacity) of control activity.

The methodological basis of the research includes both established doctrinal methods of legal science - formal-legal, comparative-legal, historical, as well as general scientific methods of knowledge, such as observation, description, induction and deduction, measurement and comparison, analysis and synthesis. The empirical and quantitative approaches are strongly present. In particular, the study of control effectiveness is based on fuzzy set theory, as a modern theory that enables research to be conducted with both quantitative data and qualitative data, and through this theory it is possible to test a number of imprecise or unspecified questions. With the understanding that the purpose of fuzzy set theory in control practice will continue to prove itself in the future, the authors are confident that this will not be the last study in control to address this issue. In this sense, the development presents one part of the principle purpose of theory in science, but another part has not yet been fully explored in the scope of control practice. For this reason, the researchers do not claim that the economic part of the study is scientifically exhaustive from all possible aspects, but only in the area of the effectiveness of control over the implementation of labour legislation.

The laid foundation for interdisciplinarity in the problematics of control for compliance with labour legislation is an innovative approach that is extremely necessary not only for a proper understanding of the theory, systematics and instrumentation of the control mechanism, but also for its theoretical and normative as well as practical establishment as a decisive instrument for the protection of the labour rights of workers.

The material complies with the legislation in force as of 31.08.2022.

The participation of the individual authors in the writing of the monograph is as follows:

Assoc. Prof. Galina Yolova, PhD - Chapter Three and Chapter Four, Introduction

Assoc. Prof. Dr. Andriyana Andreeva, PhD - Chapter One and Chapter Two, Conclusion
Assoc. Prof. Dr. Hristina Blagoycheva, PhD - Chapter Seven
Chief Ass. Prof. Darina Dimitrova, PhD - Chapter Five and Chapter Six
Chief Ass. Prof. Plamena Nedyalkova, PhD - Chapter Nine and Chapter ten, Questionnaire
Principal asst. Dr. Hristosko Bogdanov - Chapter Eight

The book contains the following chapters:

Chapter One: Evolution in the Philosophy of the Regulation and Theoretical Frameworks on the Control of Compliance With Labour Legislation

Chapter One is devoted to the evolution of the philosophy of the legal framework and the theoretical formulations concerning the control of compliance with labour legislation. Labour law is among the branches of law with the most pronounced protective function. The right to work is at the core of the social relations that arise, develop and terminate, respectively are regulated at each social stage by labour law norms. Labor rights - individual and collective need protection and respectively to this control to ensure their observance.

Chapter Two: Classification of Types of Labour Law Compliance Controls in Current Labour Legislation

Control is a normative regulated activity and given the specific focus on compliance with the norms of labour legislation, its dependence on the specificity of the sources of this legal sector is predetermined. The Labour Code occupies a central place in contemporary labour law, which is also the main source of the normative regulation of state control. Chapter nineteen „Control of compliance with labour legislation and administrative liability for its violation“ contains the legal regulation, accordingly, the type diversity of control can be derived from it.

Chapter Three: State Control Over Compliance With Labour Legislation

The development aims to analyze and derive a comprehensive systematics of the existing national regulations in the field of control, giving their respective analysis and interpretation. It defines and analyzes the general and special subject and object of internal and external control, giving them characteristic specifics in view of the way they are formulated under the codified (Labour Code) and special laws (Labour Inspection Act and the Occupational Safety and Health Act). The general characteristics, nature and structure of the centralized control body - the Executive Agency "General Labour Inspectorate", are examined in the aspects of the current legislation and in the light of the draft of the new Regulations.

Chapter Four: Executive Agency "General Labour Inspectorate": General Characteristics and Structure

On the basis of the study, conclusions are drawn about a continuous trend of continuous improvement and upgrading of the national legal framework, fully in line with the new social relations and the related specificity of the labour relations. A strict hierarchy of control functions is established in the overall system of the structure of the general and specialised control administration, and the synchronous forms of joint control activity have been appropriately found, while maintaining the necessary operational independence. The methodology of the research is based on the traditional methods of legal and theoretical research - formal - legal, comparative - legal method, as well as the traditional methods of doctrine - induction, deduction, analysis and synthesis.

Chapter Five: Specifics of Administrative Control for Compliance With Labor Legislation

The scientific objective of this paper is to examine the national legislation on the control of compliance with labour rights, as well as to examine the new moments in the legal regulation on the transposition of European norms in the field of control of compliance with labour legislation in Bulgaria. As a result of the current regulatory analysis, conclusions and generalizations are drawn on the applicable legal framework concerning the control of compliance with labour legislation. The scientific aim of this paper is to examine the national legislation on the control of compliance with labour rights, as well as to consider the new moments in the legal regulation on the transposition of European norms in the field of control of compliance with labour legislation in Bulgaria.

Chapter Six: Current Legislative Trends in the Field of Labour Rights Monitoring

In pursuit of the stated aim, the author set the following tasks: 1) To examine the nature of the control powers of the Executive Agency “General Labour Inspectorate”; 2) To examine the legal means for exercising control over compliance with the labour legislation, analyzing in detail the types of compulsory administrative measures under Art. 1 of the Labour Code; 3) To outline current legislative trends in the field of monitoring compliance with labour rights after Bulgaria’s accession to the European Union.

Chapter Seven: The Challenges of Labor and Insurance Protection in Non-Standard Forms of Employment

Part of the newly appeared, over the last 25 years, non-standard forms of work do not fall within the scope of labor and social security legislation, while the rest are covered to a certain extent. Therefore, the purpose of the present work is to examine the challenges for the national governments in adapting labor legislation to the new conditions of the labor market and to propose possible measures in this direction. In pursuit of the set goal, the author sets himself the following tasks: 1) To investigate the preconditions that led to the appearance and rapid spread of non-standard forms of employment; 2) To point out the factors complicating the regulation of labor standards and the insurance protection of persons engaged in non-standard employment; 3) To look for and propose opportunities for regulatory and control measures in non-standard forms of employment, as well as to present some good examples of government initiatives.

Chapter Eight: Effectiveness and Efficiency of Control for Compliance With Labor Legislation in the New Conditions

In this part of the study, attention is paid to the need to determine the effectiveness and efficiency of the control activity of the labor control agency. The approach that was used is related to the binding of the results of the control activity of the agency and the resources that it uses to carry out its activity. Indicators for the period 2017-2021 have been calculated, which can be used to determine how effective and efficient the agency’s activity is. Of primary importance for exercising control over compliance with labor legislation, according to the legislation in force in the Republic of Bulgaria, is the Executive Agency "Main Labor Inspection" (EA MLI).

Chapter Nine: Empirical Test and Study of the Legal and Economic Aspects of Control on Compliance With Labour Law

In this part of the development, the problem of the effectiveness of control over compliance with labor legislation is investigated. The methodological basis of the study includes general scientific methods, such as: observation, description, induction and deduction, measurement and comparison, analysis and synthesis. Control effectiveness research is based on fuzzy set theory, as a modern theory that enables research to be conducted with both quantitative data and qualitative data, and through this theory it is possible to test a number of imprecise or unspecified questions.

Chapter Ten: Testing and Defining the Effectiveness of the Supervisory Institution Executive Agency "General Labour Inspectorate"

The approach known until now in the organizations of the private / business / sector was applied in order to test the effectiveness of the control in a budgetary organization, such as the Executive Agency "General Labor Inspectorate". The main conclusion reached that the methodology of testing and determining control effectiveness for the non-public sector is also applicable to public sector organizations. The analysis should not be applied solely as a means for follow-up control. It should be applied on an ongoing basis in order to identify the weaknesses and problems during the relevant current period based on the current data and the current status of the factors that have impact on the change of economic effectiveness.

The conducted interdisciplinary study of the state control of compliance with labour legislation is aimed at realizing the goal set by the authors, which is achieved through the complex application of legal and economic methods. Doctrinally and theoretically, the authors have analyzed the control mechanisms for compliance with labor legislation, examining them through the prism of normative systematics and in the aspect of their economic effects on traditional and alternative forms of employment.

The conclusions and recommendations that are drawn in the individual parts of the work are in response to the specific research tasks. Here they are summarized and will be presented in the two main axes of the study, namely legal and economic aspects of the issues.

As a result of the first axis, around which the research was conducted, namely the legal aspects of state control, the set objective for the analysis of the national legislation on the control of compliance with labour rights, as well as for the examination of the new actual moments in the legal regulation on the transposition of European norms in the field of control of compliance with labour legislation in Bulgaria is realized.

The historical part of the study traces the genesis in the development of the legal institut of control in Bulgarian labour law, as the periodization corresponds to the historical stages from the liberation of the country to the present day. This chronological order shows not only the dependence of control on social relations, but also traces its place and role in the protection of labour rights during the different stages.

In addition, on the basis of the analysis of the current legal framework, in the aspect of general and special acts regulating the control activity, it can be summarized that structurally and systematically develops and consolidates in our legislation a coherent approach in the consolidation of the external specialized form of guarantee of fair and decent working conditions and the related various methods of sanctioning in cases of illegality, at the same time - building on the principles of individual freedom in the exercise of the right to work and related subjective labour rights.The systematics of the legal acts regulating the control of compliance with labour legislation establish a broad system of authorities and competences concerning different aspects of the implementation of national legislation. The regulated scope of competences and the diverse nature of the object of control obviously aim at a comprehensiveness of the supervision of correctness and lawfulness which in practice leads to a legally guaranteed, stable and functioning system of labour relations. On the other hand, the dynamics of the development of labour relations and the related need to rethink the functions of supervision and the need to expand their comprehensiveness and detail necessitate a rethinking of the structuring of the activity, in which aspect is also the proposed Draft of the new Regulations of the Executive Agency "General Labour Inspectorate" (23.06.2022). This establishes a lasting tendency to detail the functions of control activity, as well as to strengthen the control effects and means in detailed areas and corresponding competences, allowing for a regular, continuous and, above all, qualitative and preventive control mechanism.

In continuation of this and as a result of the analysis of the control powers of the EA GLI, the following specific conclusions and summaries can be made regarding the applicable legislation concerning the issues under consideration:

First, the provision of labour in the modern context requires the creation of legal guarantees to respect the rights arising from the provision of labour. The existing legal framework must define the limits within which the reciprocal rights and obligations under the employment relationship can be realised in the context of an employee's dependent position on the employer. The regulation of the right to work, including its constitutional recognition as a fundamental right, demonstrates its function and importance for society and for the individual;

Second, the administrative control of the EA GLI performs an important social function in relation to employees and at the same time has a disciplinary function towards the unfair and unscrupulous employers. These two functions of the administrative control of compliance with labour legislation justify the positive assessment of the legal framework under study;

Thirdly, the protection of the right to work requires the continued active influence of the state through the updating of relevant legislation. Contemporary social conditions pose new challenges to the legislator, requiring administrative law protection of fundamental labour rights. In this sense, administrative control and administrative violations liability provided for in labour legislation are of great practical importance. The recent amendments to the Labour Code aim at more effective implementation of control activities and better prevention in relation to the provided administrative sanctions in case of violation of labour legislation. This demonstrates once again the role and importance of administrative law protection in ensuring the necessary level of protection of the right to work.

In summary, it can be concluded that both inspections for compliance with labour legislation and compulsory administrative measures are an effective means of preventing violations of employees' labour rights. The effectiveness of the administrative coercion imposed under the Labour Code is also enhanced by the provision of Article 405(2) of the Labour Code, according to which an appeal does not suspend the enforcement of the compulsory administrative measure. Through the acts of the Labour Inspectorate bodies, an active impact is sought for the protection of the labour rights affected, in order to guarantee the legitimate interests of employees. It is the will of the legislator to introduce promptness in the elimination of violations of labour legislation, given the social importance of the regulated legal relations.

The foregoing shows that the control of compliance with the rights arising from the employment is subject to very dynamic regulation. As a result of the analysis of the new moments in the legal framework and, in particular, the transposition of the European norms in the sphere of control of compliance with the labour legislation in Bulgaria, the following conclusions, summaries and recommendations can be made regarding the applicable legal framework concerning the issues under consideration:

- there is a tendency to expand the powers of the EA GLI both in terms of the types of coercive measures and the intensity of administrative control. This demonstrates the role and importance of administrative legal protection in ensuring the appropriate level of protection of the right to work;
- The current societal conditions of globalisation and digitalisation pose new challenges to the legal framework requiring administrative law protection of fundamental labour rights (e.g. health and safety at work, right to remuneration, right to rest and leave, etc.). The new social relations after the democratic changes in the country are, on the one hand, related to the transition from a planned to a market economy and the development of private economic activity and, on the other hand, stem from Bulgaria's realised EU membership. The national legal framework, which transposes the European norms in the area of control of compliance with the labour rights of employees, is one of the main factors influencing the control procedures for compliance with labour legislation;
- Despite the significant impact of European acts on the development of our national law, the EU does not have exclusive competence in the field of labour law. The exercise of administrative control over compliance with labour law is a matter for national authorities. In this sense, the role of the EA GLI is very important. Unfortunately, the Labour Code adopted in 1986, despite its repeated amendments and additions, is not fully capable of responding to the changes that have taken place in modern social relations. In view of this, a proposal can be made to the legislator for the drafting and adoption of a new Labour Code which would comprehensively regulate all labour law norms and institutes in accordance with the current development of social relations. Of course, it should be taken into account that the adoption of a code in the field of labour law is not an easy task. It is one of the major branches of law regulating not only the legal relations that arise

in the provision of working force and the employment of labour, but also a number of other relations directly related to labour, including the control of compliance with labour legislation.

The second axis of research in the work are the economic aspects of the issues of the effectiveness of control over compliance with labour legislation. Accordingly, the following final conclusions and generalizations can be made:

1. The control exercised by the Executive Agency “General Labour Inspectorate” combines both state control and social and public control. This is mainly expressed in the contribution of the control activities of the Agency, aimed on the one hand at strengthening the legality and legal order regarding compliance with the labour legislation, and on the other hand at strengthening the moral, unwritten norms characterizing the relations between employers and their employees/workers, and the relations between the state authority and the society as a whole, and especially manifested in the implementation of preventive measures to prevent violations of the difficult legislation.
2. There is a need to systematically analyse and seek possible mechanisms, approaches and activities to improve the Agency’s performance in order to achieve its effectiveness.
3. Analysis should not be applied solely as a means of subsequent control. It needs to be applied on an ongoing basis in order to identify weaknesses and problems in the relevant current period, based on current data and the current status of the factors that influence changes in economic efficiency.
4. The proposed system of indicators, which is based on the testing of direct and indirect resources and incurred costs, express the resource- and cost-absorption (capacity) of the control activity. The proposed approach to the study of the effectiveness of control from two aspects, namely according to the level of use and according to the degree of generality, in relation to the methods considered and the grouping of the relevant indicators according to the relevant indicators have their scientific - practical purpose.

It is clear that there are different approaches to determining the effectiveness and efficiency of the control activities of the EA GLI. When assessing the activities of budget support organisations, the approach to determining the results of their activities is different from that applied in enterprises with a business activity.

In the approach adopted in the study, indicators are compiled that link the results of the control activity in a certain respect to the objectives of the agency and the resources with which the control activity is carried out.

Assuming that one of the main objectives of the control activity of the EA GLI is related to the control of compliance with labour legislation and occupational health and safety for employees in organizations, then we can argue that the more employees in the country are covered by the control, the more effective it is. The study calculated such an indicator for the period 2017 - 2019, through which it was found that the effectiveness of control activity was highest in 2017, and subsequently remained at a slightly lower level for the period 2018 - 2021.

The efficiency of the control activity of the EA GLI is defined as the ratio of the results achieved and the resources invested in it.

Several efficiency indicators have been examined as follows:

- efficiency of controls, for the period 2019-2021. Efficiency in terms of the budget required to carry them out is found to be deteriorating in the period 2019-2021;
- efficiency in the use of human resources. This efficiency is found to decrease in the period 2017 - 2020, improving in 2021;
- efficiency of the final stage of control by the EA GLI. The efficiency is found to be at a good level throughout the study period from 2017 to 2021.

Labour law is among the branches of law with a pronounced protective function, respectively called to secure and guarantee the lawful application of the right to work. In all stages of the development of the legal sector, an important role has been assigned to the monitoring of compliance with the legislation. Through this study, the legal and economic aspects of this important state control activity are presented in a different relationship. It is not only a challenge for the legislator, who has to update the norms of control with the most current tendencies, but also for the doctrine, as well as for the parties to the employment relationship, who, given the dynamics in the legal matter, are not infrequently hindered in its application in practice.

Galina Ognqnova Yolova
University of Economics, Varna, Bulgaria

Andriyana Andreeva
University of Economics, Varna, Bulgaria

Darina Nedelcheva Dimitrova
University of Economics, Varna, Bulgaria

Hristina Vilhelm Blagoycheva
University of Economics, Varna, Bulgaria

Plamena Nedyalkova
University of Economics, Varna, Bulgaria

Hristosko Bogdanov
University of Economics, Varna, Bulgaria

Acknowledgment

The authors of this monographic study express their deepest gratitude to:

All contributors for being willing to share different research perspectives;

The manuscript reviewers for their suggestions and comments;

IGI Global for sending a timely invitation to prepare this manuscript and for continued editing support;

We thank all our partners through whom we were able to conduct the empirical study.

Introduction

The realization of the constitutionally guaranteed right to work and related subjective labour rights has been and will always be a serious challenge for legislation and legal doctrine. Finding a balance in the interests and rights of the subjects in employment relations is the subject and task of the legislative endeavour to establish lasting stability on the one hand, and normative certainty in the countervailing and functionally bound rights and obligations of individuals on the other. In this sense, the development of a durable and guaranteed system of methods and means of control is sought and reflected in the establishment of an institutional and centralized mechanism for the assertion of labour rights, such as state control over compliance with labour legislation. Permanently established, but also built upon with timely and relevant mechanisms, it should be a guarantee of the legislative tendency to protect the right to work and its exercise in a dignified, socially acceptable and fair normative order.

At the same time, the contemporary forms of digitalization of labour and the increasingly aggressive use of artificial intelligence in labour relations pose both legislation and doctrine qualitatively different challenges, necessitating the introduction of new, adaptive to the new social realities normative means to protect the interests of workers. Over the last twenty-five years, in response to the economic trends of digitalization and globalization, new non-standard forms of work have emerged, significantly changing concepts and standards in terms of work position, social security, organization, location and working time periods. For some workers they offer desirable flexibility and reconciliation of personal and professional life. For others, however, non-standard employment is increasingly proving to be a source of precarious work, low earnings and lack of social protection. The traditional employment relationship is undergoing major transformations, directly affecting basic labour rights that are proving extremely vulnerable in the qualitatively different labour environment.

The European Foundation for the Improvement of Living and Working Conditions (Eurofound) mapping exercise identifies nine new forms of employment (ICT-based mobile work, platform work, casual work, co-working, job sharing, temporary management, employee sharing, portfolio work and voucher-based work) and documents their increasing prevalence in the EU, Norwegian and UK labour markets. Three of them (platform work, portfolio work and this joint employment organised by self-employed workers) are not covered by labour law, while the others are partially covered. In this sense, the current regulatory frameworks of governments, tax systems and social protection systems cannot be so quickly transformed to respond to all emerging and diverse forms of employment and to provide adequate income and social welfare protection for employees. Initiatives and regulatory measures to curb unfair practices are already being taken in many countries, but they are still sporadic, partial, for individual activities or professions.

At the same time, the classic forms of labour practices implemented through different models of teleworking are proving to seriously affect the rights of workers guaranteed and upheld by the traditions of labour law - including the right to rest, to leave, to privacy and to detachment from the working environment.

The new culture of "permanent connected persons" existing as a permanent state of affairs already leads to latent overtime, violated right to leave and rest, permanent and serious absence of work-life balance. In this sense, the need to build a qualitatively different and adaptive comprehensive labour legislation in the field of control, which would provide adequate protection and support to persons with non-standard employment, is becoming increasingly clear.

The necessity to study all aspects of the control mechanisms and their role or impact in the protection of subjective labour rights provoked the interest of the authors to a complex interdisciplinary study, combining legal and economic parts, studying in their entirety and with the methods of the respective scientific fields the specifics of state control over compliance with labour legislation. Such a study has not been conducted so far and in this sense its **relevance and contribution to the legal and economic doctrine is more than indisputable.** The combination of a legal and an economic approach to the study of the nature and aspects of control provides a comprehensive study, not carried out in the literature and doctrine, which clearly outlines the meaning, nature and, above all, the effectiveness and efficiency of the control mechanism. In this sense, and on the other hand, the authors' aim is to reinforce the understanding of the need to perceive control as a scientific discipline and, related to this, the increased validation of control activity in practice.

In these aspects, the study has not only theoretical, but also important prescriptive and practical - applied significance - by using quantitative indicators based on the theory of fuzzy sets to measure the effectiveness of the control are established, on the one hand, applicable models for future efficiency, combined, on the other - with doctrinal analytical - legal conclusions and proposals de lege ferenda, also outlined in the light of new, alternative forms of employment.

Given the interdisciplinary nature of the research, it is focused around two axes - legal and economic, to which the parts of the work correspond in structural terms. Accordingly, they are presented by the authors in their interrelation in view of the complex and comprehensive study of the subject.

In this sense, **the aim of the study** is to comprehensively - both doctrinally and theoretically - analyze and study the control mechanisms for compliance with labor legislation, viewed through the prism of normative systematics and in the aspect of their economic effects on traditional and alternative forms of employment.

Subordinated to this general objective, the legal study aims at a comprehensive and complex analysis - historical, topical and comparative - of the national legislation on the control of compliance with labour legislation, as well as to examine the new moments in the legal regulation on the transposition of European norms in the field of control. In this sense are also the tasks set by the authors, namely:

- Historical tracing, in systematics and periodicity, of the development of the institutional mechanism for the control of compliance with labour legislation;
- Comprehensive systematization and analysis of the relevant, establishing the tools and mechanisms of control general and special normative acts, as well as in the light of the analysis of the Draft Statutory Regulations of the Executive Agency "General Labour Inspectorate", through the prism of the new trends for updating the mechanisms of impact and capacity of the control bodies;
- Study of the nature of the control powers of the Executive Agency "General Labour Inspectorate" ;
- Analyzing the legal means for exercising control over compliance with labour legislation, through a detailed analysis of the types of compulsory administrative measures under Art. 404, para. Analysis

of the administrative procedures under Article 404(1) of the Labour Code;
- Outlining the current legislative trends in the field of control of compliance with labour rights after Bulgaria's accession to the European Union.

In this sense, a comprehensive systematics of the existing normative acts in the sphere of control is brought out, giving their respective analysis in the directions of the nature, competences and control powers of the Executive Agency General Labour Inspectorate, methods and means of control influence, nature, meaning and essence of the imposed compulsory administrative measures and administrative penalties.

In the economic part of the study, the directions of the analysis are in the aspects of studying, on the one hand, the measures for exercising control in non-standard forms of employment and, on the other hand, conducting an empirical study of the effectiveness of control over compliance with labor legislation through a proposed system of indicators, which is built on the basis of testing the direct and indirect resources and costs incurred, expressing the resource- and cost-absorption (capacity) of the control activity. Here, the relevance of the analysis is based on the dynamic changes in the normative framework of control mechanisms, the possibility of applying different quantitative methods and approaches for assessing the effectiveness of control over labour legislation, determining both the purely scientific - research interest and the methodological urge to seek a modern approach to assess the effectiveness of control, through which to reveal the specificities of control activities.

The proposed economic approach to study the effectiveness of control is from two aspects, namely - according to the level of use and according to the degree of generality, as well as according to the methods considered and the grouping of relevant indicators according to the relevant signs with their respective scientific - practical purpose.

In this sense, the tasks of the economic part of the study are as follows:

- To explore the preconditions that led to the emergence and strong spread of non-standard forms of employment;
- To identify the factors that make it difficult to regulate labour standards and social security protection for persons engaged in non-standard employment;

- Seek and suggest options for regulatory and control measures in non-standard forms of employment, and highlight some good examples of government initiatives;
- Conducting an empirical study of the effectiveness of control over compliance with labor legislation through a proposed system of indicators, which is based on the testing of direct and indirect resources and costs incurred, express the resource - and cost absorption (capacity) of control activity.

The methodological basis of the research includes both established doctrinal methods of legal science - formal-legal, comparative-legal, historical, as well as general scientific methods of knowledge, such as observation, description, induction and deduction, measurement and comparison, analysis and synthesis. The empirical and quantitative approaches are strongly present. In particular, the study of control effectiveness is based on fuzzy set theory, as a modern theory that enables research to be conducted with both quantitative data and qualitative data, and through this theory it is possible to test a number of imprecise or unspecified questions. With the understanding that the purpose of fuzzy set theory in control practice will continue to prove itself in the future, the authors are confident that this will not be the last study in control to address this issue. In this sense, the development presents one part of the principle purpose of theory in science, but another part has not yet been fully explored in the scope of control practice. For this reason, the researchers do not claim that the economic part of the study is scientifically exhaustive from all possible aspects, but only in the area of the effectiveness of control over the implementation of labour legislation.

The laid foundation for interdisciplinarity in the problematics of control for compliance with labour legislation is an innovative approach that is extremely necessary not only for a proper understanding of the theory, systematics and instrumentation of the control mechanism, but also for its theoretical and normative as well as practical establishment as a decisive instrument for the protection of the labour rights of workers.

The material complies with the legislation in force as of 31.08.2022.

The monographic work is aimed only at the study of labor - legal problems in the application of labor legislation and control in Bulgaria. The problems of effectiveness and efficiency of control are investigated.

The participation of the individual authors in the writing of the monograph is as follows:

Assoc. Prof. Galina Yolova, PhD - Chapter Three and Chapter Four, Introduction
Assoc. Prof. Dr. Andriyana Andreeva, PhD - Chapter One and Chapter Two, Conclusion
Assoc. Prof. Dr. Hristina Blagoycheva, PhD - Chapter Seven
Chief Ass. Prof. Darina Dimitrova, PhD - Chapter Five and Chapter Six
Chief Ass. Prof. Plamena Nedyalkova, PhD - Chapter Nine and Chapter ten, Questionnaire
Principal asst. Dr. Hristosko Bogdanov - Chapter Eight

This publication is in fulfillment of a Contract NIR - 241/16.06.2020 with the University of Economics - Varna for scientific research for applied scientific developments, NPI 43/2020

Galina Ognqnova Yolova
University of Economics, Varna, Bulgaria

Andriyana Andreeva
University of Economics, Varna, Bulgaria

Darina Nedelcheva Dimitrova
University of Economics, Varna, Bulgaria

Hristina Vilhelm Blagoycheva
University of Economics, Varna, Bulgaria

Plamena Nedyalkova
University of Economics, Varna, Bulgaria

Hristosko Bogdanov
University of Economics, Varna, Bulgaria

Chapter 1
Evolution in the Philosophy of the Regulation and Theoretical Frameworks on the Control of Compliance With Labour Legislation

Andriyana Andreeva
University of economics, Varna, Bulgaria

ABSTRACT

Chapter one is devoted to the evolution of the philosophy of the legal framework and the theoretical formulations concerning the control of compliance with labour legislation. Labour law is among the branches of law with the most pronounced protective function. The right to work is at the core of the social relations that arise, develop and terminate, respectively are regulated at each social stage by labour law norms. Labor rights - individual and collective need protection and respectively to this control to ensure their observance.

NATURE, CHARACTERISTICS, AND FUNCTIONS OF LABOUR LAW COMPLIANCE MONITORING

Labour law is among the branches of law with the most pronounced protective function. The right to work is at the core of the social relations that arise, develop and terminate, respectively are regulated at each social stage by

DOI: 10.4018/978-1-6684-9067-9.ch001

labour law norms. Labor rights - individual and collective need protection (Andreeva, A. et al, 2020) and respectively to this control to ensure their observance. Bulgarian labour law has a centuries-old history, beginning after the country's liberation, when the foundations of its economic, political and social development were laid. Inevitably, this is connected with the construction and development of law, including labour law, which is called upon to regulate and protect the relations arising in the provision of labour power.

The monitoring of compliance with labour law can be considered in various aspects.

First of all, it is a specific state activity to ensure legality at different stages of the emergence and development of labour relations.

Secondly, control can also be presented in a more specific aspect, as an authoritative activity exercised by the competent bodies of the executive power in the process of implementing labour legislation.

Through it, the executive branch, in the form of specialised state control bodies, aims to ensure the actual implementation of labour legislation. This character is expressed in the rights and means of influence of the control bodies. Sub-controlled organizations and subjects are obliged to bear the implementation of the control and the consequences it entails, including when they are unfavorable for them (Mrachkov, V., 2016).

In this sense, it is characterized by dynamism and consistency of concrete actions.

Thirdly, while the control activity is an administrative activity referable to the executive power, administrative punishment by its nature is a judicial activity (Staynov, P., 1952)(Lazarov, K., 2001).

Fourth, the control is comprehensive and covers all acts relevant to the legal branch of labour law as well as all branches and activities. Moreover, control activity extends not only to employment relations but also to service relations in terms of compliance with the legal requirements of the civil service.

According to data from the annual report on the activities of the Executive Agency "General Labour Inspectorate" in 2020, S., 2021, p. 6 As a result of the inspections carried out in 2020, a total of 153 739 violations of the requirements of labour legislation, labour migration and labour mobility and the civil service were detected. The distribution of violations by main groups is as follows:

- 79 760 violations of occupational health and safety (OHS) legislation;
- breaches of the legal requirements governing employment relationships (LPRs) - 73 389;

- violations of labour migration and labour mobility standards - 532;
- 58 infringements of civil service rules.

Administrative law protection of the right to work is one of the forms of labour protection regulated in Bulgarian legislation. (Dimitrova, D., 2020b) (Aleksandrov, A., 2016) (Aleksandrov, A., 2017) In the present scientific research, speaking about the control of compliance with the labor legislation, only the administrative control is meant, characterized by the executive-regulatory nature of the activities included in it. This control is characterized by its authoritarian nature, a reflection of which are the means of influence granted to the control bodies. Thus, by using the coercive power of the State, the aim is to remedy the unlawful situation resulting from non-compliance with labour legislation. In this sense, administrative control is to be distinguished from the control exercised by the organs of state power (standing committees of the National Assembly, the Council of Ministers, ministers, etc.); from the activity of the courts in dealing with labour disputes and from the supervision of the public prosecutor's office to observe legality.

It is important to note that in Bulgaria the control of compliance with labour legislation emerged and developed simultaneously with the establishment of the foundations of the legal branch. This specificity is extremely indicative of the foresight of the Bulgarian legislator and the responsible role of the state, which has taken its place in the regulation of labour relations not only in terms of their regulation, but also in terms of their compliance.

Like any concept, control has undergone its evolutionary development, both in normative and etymological aspects.

We consider this genesis in the legal institute - control of compliance with labour law - to be natural for several reasons. On the one hand, when the Bulgarian labour law compliance control started, it was built in an extremely difficult environment. The reasons for this can be summarised as follows:

First of all - lack of sources of labour law. At the beginning of the 20th century in Bulgaria there was no separate branch of labour law, and the regulation of the relations on the provision of wage labour was carried out according to the norms of civil law.

Secondly, there was a lack of fully developed structures of state bodies that could perform specific state functions, including those related to control.

Thirdly, a lack of continuity. In the newly-founded Bulgarian state there are no traditions that would provide certainty when building new structures, but foreign experience is used, which is yet to be transposed and adapted to the specifics of local conditions.

Last but not least, there is a lack of comprehensive legislative experience and traditions in normative drafting, including both in the adoption of the sources of such a significant legal branch as labour law and in the regulation of control over its compliance.

Nevertheless, the Bulgarian legislator shows foresight, which is evident in the consistency of the adoption of the acts. The first act which marked the beginning of labour law sources in the country was the Act on Women's and Children's Labour in Industrial Establishments of 1905. Its adoption was dictated by the "harsh working conditions to which women and children were exposed in production, the unlimited and measureless exploitation of their labour". These are some of the reasons that led to the adoption of this normative act, which not only marked the beginning of Bulgarian labour legislation, but also, in the very first years of its application, made the need for state control over compliance with the protective norms realised. In 1907, the Labour Inspectorate Act was adopted, which marked the beginning of the control of compliance with labour legislation.

The specificity of this control lies in several aspects. On the one hand, it is based on a French model, namely the constitution of a state body controlling all sectors and activities. On the other hand, there is still no independent and clearly defined, as a legal branch, labour legislation and in this sense we can say that the State Labour Inspectorate is the first specialized body in charge of control functions and for the creation of an environment for the prestation of labour in accordance with principles that are not actually regulated at that time.

Control can also be seen from another aspect, namely as one of the first labour law institutes which, along with those enshrined in the Industrial Establishments Women's and Children's Labour Act (working hours, rest periods, etc.), outline the main protective function of the industry. The emergence of control and the creation of a labour inspectorate at this early stage of the construction of the labour law sector can point us to the importance of control activities in guaranteeing the right to work, because despite the lack of detailed regulations, the State created a control mechanism to ensure compliance with the norms. This consistency is then observed in the century-long history of labour inspection, which, passing through different historical periods, has maintained its appearance. The labour law norms established by the State in the person of the competent authorities are monitored with a view to their observance again by the State through the State control exercised by the labour inspectorate. This interrelation shows that, from the time of the establishment of the legal sector, the State has already laid down its functions of labour protection and the control of its lawful employment. Prof. Yanulov calls the labour inspectorate "the soul of social legislation" (Yanulov, I., 1948).

It is also important to trace the terminological diversity reflecting the control activity. In the various years of the development of the institute of control, the terms "labour protection control"(e.g. in Article 8, paragraph 1 of P.M. No. 15, 12.05.1973, etc.), "supervision over the implementation" (Art. 132, par. 1 and 2, art. 133 of the Constitution of 1771 (am.); art. 1, 3, 25, 26, etc. of the Public Prosecution Act (am.)) of the Labour Code and the current expression "control over compliance with labour legislation", adopted in the Labour Code - Chapter Nineteen "Control over compliance with labour legislation and administrative and criminal liability for its violation" have been used.

HISTORICAL DEVELOPMENT OF THE INSTITUTE OF CONTROL IN THE NATIONAL LEGAL SYSTEM

Control over compliance with labour legislation is a guarantee of respect for the constitutional right to work. Its importance for the labour law sector is undisputed. On the one hand, it can be seen as accompanying the emergence and differentiation of the independent legal branch, and on the other hand as an activity guaranteeing the observance of rights between the subjects of the labour law relationship (Dimitrova, D., 2020c). The institute of control goes through a genesis of its development, which is invariably associated with the body entrusted with this specialized state activity. Control was born in the years following the liberation of Bulgaria and the laying of the economic foundations of the third Bulgarian state. In the 90s of the 19 century the need for 'the establishment of labour inspection in factories and all other workshops' was recognised - item 9 of the First Programme of the BJP (In 1891 the Bulgarian Workers' Social Democratic Party was founded. And in 1904 the first trade union associations in Bulgaria were established: the General Workers' Trade Union and the Free General Workers' Union). in 1892.

At the same time, one cannot ignore the fact that in the post-liberation years in Bulgaria there was no labour legislation and no normative act with a special focus to regulate relations between workers and employers. They are governed by general civil law and, in particular, by the obligational contract regulated in Chapter III of the Labour Law, Articles 386-402 of the Law on Obligations and Contracts (State Gazette 268 of 5 December 1892). The contract “For hiring work for the use of another” Pursuant to Section 336 of the LPA, “Hire work is a contract by which one party undertakes to do something for another for a contingent price.” (the first of the three types of contracts for hiring work under Article 386 of the LLA), which appears to be the prototype of the employment contract (Mevorah, N., D. I. Lidzhi& L. Farhi, 1926). In spite of the existence of provisions regulating the obligations of both parties and governing the hiring of labour, this contract does not give the necessary protection to the workers because it is in the field of civil law relations (Article 400 of the DPA “The entrepreneur is responsible for the work of the persons he has used”) and the State does not exercise control.

With the development of capitalist relations in Bulgaria, the legislation developed in parallel, with priority being given to the foundations of constitutional, civil and criminal law. Laws regulating and promoting industrial relations were adopted. In the process of building up the national legal system, the question of legal regulation of labour and the adoption of special laws to regulate it was increasingly raised. The process of laying the foundations of labour law in Bulgaria proceeded in a similar way to most European countries, namely through workers’ struggles. The legal regulation of labour by general civil law continued until 1905, when the first act with labour law content was adopted, the Law on Women’s and Children’s Labour in Industrial Establishments (Approved by Decree No. 13, issued on 23 March 1905. Ann. No. 66 of 26 March 1905, entered into force only six months after its promulgation w/o Article 25 of the Act). The enactment of this act was in line with the trends in the creation of labour legislation in a number of European countries as well. (In Great Britain, the protection of labour and women was established in 1803, in Austria in 1885. At the founding congress of the First International, held in Geneva on 26.09.1906, the resolutions adopted referred to the necessity of the cooperation of the international proletariat in its struggle against the exploitation of women’s and children’s labour.). It was this act that marked the beginning of the creation of the Bulgarian labour legislation (Banov, H., 2020) and paved the way for the control of its compliance. The very first provision of the Act prescribes - Article 1 “Industrial establishments where the labour of children and women of any age is used, regardless of their number, shall be subject to labour inspection exercised by the Ministry of Commerce and Agriculture”. We join the opinion of Prof. Sredkova on the importance of this normative act (Sredkova, K., 2007) on the one hand as the first in our labour legislation, and on the other hand as a conceptual path for the need to create a specialized state body charged with control functions on its compliance. In several of its provisions, the law introduces "labour inspection" terminologically, which clearly indicates a conscious legislative intention to create such a body.

The law introduces a number of requirements related to occupational hygiene and technical safety, which are mainly of a recommendatory nature and are not introduced by mandatory norms. This is due to the fact that the lack of controls prevents their strict compliance. As an example of such a norm can be given the provision of Article 12 stipulating a commitment for owners and directors who must take all measures to protect the health, safety and morale of workers, both in the work premises and in places designated for rest and meals (Dimitrova, D., 2020a).

Two years later the Labour Inspectorate Act was adopted (State Gazette 238/1907). In view of the subject of the present study, the historical analysis will focus on tracing the development of the inspection body. The establishment of the foundations and the subsequent development of Bulgarian labour law are closely linked to the regulation and activity of the Labour Inspectorate. On 3 November 1907, the Labour Inspectorate was established by decree of Prince Ferdinand (Labour Inspectorate Act in Bulgaria - approved by Decree No. 182 of Prince Ferdinand I of 3 November 1907 (Journal of Laws No. 238/1907). According to the decree, the inspectorate is entrusted with functions related to the implementation of laws, rules and regulations on instruction, trade, crafts and the protection of workers." After analyzing the norms, we can conclude that in its original form the authority has both executive and control characteristics. At the same time, its role in the protection of workers' rights is clearly and explicitly noted. It is the regulation of this body that appears to be fundamental and underlies the protective function of the emerging branch of labour law in Bulgaria in the period following its liberation. In comparison with the European norms in this period, it can be concluded that Bulgaria adopted the French model of state labour inspection. In this period the main models in Europe of state inspection bodies controlling compliance with labour law norms and labour protection were two - French and English. Accordingly, the French model was associated with the establishment and operation of a single general labour inspectorate for all industries and activities, while the English model relied on various specialised inspectorates profiled according to the specificities of individual economic sectors (Linspecion du travail - sa mission, ses methodes. Geneve: BIT, 1971, pp. 1-2). The Labour Inspectorate Act fills in the gaps left by the Law on Women's and Children's Labour, introduces norms aimed at ensuring efficient measures for its implementation and gives real protection to workers. Several years are needed for the real implementation of the norms of the law and the establishment of the authority. In 1911 the Labour Inspectorate was established with two chief and ten district inspectors.

The next law of the Bulgarian labour legislation, which can also be seen as deriving from the Law on Women's and Children's Labour, was the Law on Sunday and Holiday Rest (Journal of Laws of 17.02.1911), which repealed the Law on Holidays of 31.01.1900.

From the presented historical overview we can conclude that in the period from the liberation to 1907 in Bulgaria there was no control over the legal relations related to the provision of labour force. The newly liberated Bulgarian state at that time left it to the parties themselves to regulate their relations on the hiring of labour within the framework of the civil legislation in force.

In the early years of the 20th century, under the pressure of workers leading struggles for better working conditions, labour legislation was initiated and immediately afterwards the state stepped into its role of controlling the implementation of labour law norms through a specialised state body - the labour inspectorate. We can say that from 1907 the first historical period in the development of control of compliance with labour legislation began. It is no coincidence that the period began precisely with the establishment of the labour inspectorate, because the role it performs is not only that of a control body, but it is also undoubtedly charged with the mission of contributing to the overall appearance of the welfare state and to the construction and application of labour legislation (Dimitrova, D., 2019).

An important step in the development of control and at the same time of labour legislation was the adoption of the first Bulgarian law in the field of safety and hygiene at work in 1917. Law on Hygiene and Safety at Work - approved by Decree No. 25 of Prince Ferdinand I, dated 01.06.1917 (published in State Gazette No. 129/1917), In addition to its significance as a regulation of social relations in the period to which it refers, this law has stability, given that it was repealed only with the adoption of the first codified act in the field of labour law - the Labour Code of 1951 repealed the Law on Hygiene and Safety at Work of 1917. According to Article 4, trade unions were given the right to establish labour safety inspectorates (State Gazette No. 91/1951). The Labour Inspectorate of the Ministry of Agriculture and Trade was entrusted with the supervision of compliance with the law.

Two other laws should be noted which are relevant to the first period, namely:

- The Steam Boiler and Tank Inspection Act of 1917, regulating certain hygiene and occupational safety measures in the handling of steam boilers. It introduced an 11-hour working day. This Act placed under State control all fixed and mobile steam boilers or tanks in which steam was present or escaping under pressure. Only those of small volume and low pressure are exempted from this control, in whole or in part, depending on whether they present a hazard or whether it is small. Restrictions have also been introduced relating to the age of employees, namely that the servicing of steam boilers and tanks may not be carried out by women and children, but only by male persons not younger than 18 years of age who have the necessary technical training for the purpose.

- The Occupational Hygiene and Safety Act of 1917, which regulated measures to sanitize and make safe production in all industries. This Act introduced a minimum age and working day of 8 hours for children up to the age of 16 and 11 hours for all others. The Act completely repeals the Women and Child Labour in Industrial Establishments Act and the Labour Inspectorate Act. New legal institutes, the Assistant Inspectorate and the Supreme Council of Labour and Workmen's Insurance, have been introduced in the Act.

The supervision of the implementation and enforcement of the Occupational Hygiene and Safety Act shall be entrusted to the Ministry of Trade, Industry and Labour, and the necessary chief and district labour inspectors shall be appointed for this purpose. The Supreme Council of Labour and Workmen's Insurance shall constitute an advisory body to the same Ministry.

These acts appear to be basic for the first period, both for the development of control and for the construction of the regulations of the labour law branch. This stage can be described as capitalist in view of the reflection of existing social relations on legislation and the need to adopt acts relating to the protection of labour and to the control of their observance.

In the Bulgarian labour law doctrine a detailed periodization is made by Radoilski, according to whom the legal regulation in the era of capitalism is divided into the following periods:

1. Period of initial capital accumulation /1878-1900/.
2. Period of industrial capitalism /1900 - 1917/.
3. Period of manifestations of financial capital /1918 - 1944/, which is divided into the corresponding sub-periods (Ivanov, I., 2020).

"From a brief review of the history of labor law in Bulgaria during the capitalist era it is evident that the Bulgarian working class has fought long and hard for labor legislation, that in certain historical periods it has achieved considerable results, that the Bulgarian bourgeoisie has always, after making concessions, struggled to take them away or not to enforce the laws issued" (Radoilski, L., 1957).

From its earliest years, the Inspectorate has embodied the power of the state in enforcing and monitoring compliance with the norms of labour law for the protection of wage labour. Arising out of workers' struggles and their demands for improved working and living conditions, the State Labour Inspectorate has accompanied the development of Bulgarian labour legislation for a century and is an integral part of it. It is entrusted with the functions of monitoring compliance with labour legislation and its actual implementation. This far-sighted decision of the Third Bulgarian State at the very beginning of the 20th century was an act of its conscious European orientation. It still has its deep basis in the rule of law and the social state enshrined in the current Constitution.

In conclusion, the first period can be labeled as the development of the control of compliance with labor legislation in the Kingdom of Bulgaria or capitalist period (Andreeva, A. & Yolova, G., 2011). Terminologically, both terms are correct and can be used to refer to, given the historical period that is reflected, as well as the development of economic relations in the country, which is one of the leading factors in the development of labor legislation. The doctrine also uses another term to refer to this historical period of the development of control, namely New Bulgarian Law (Dimitrova, D., 2021).

The period formally began in 1907 with the first act in the field of labour law enforcement, but its foundations were laid after the country's liberation. It was the construction of the national legal system, the accumulation of legislative experience, the development of scientific research in various branches of law, and the transposition of foreign experience that contributed to the formation of the idea, the normative regulation and the construction of the system of control in Bulgaria.

In spite of the objective obstacles, the Bulgarian jurists of this period managed to cope with the difficult task of creating a national legal system, which was based on the achievements of the legal doctrines of the developed European countries of the late 19th century (Tokushev, D., 2008).

This also applies to the acts laying the foundations of labour law, which, despite some imperfections, as noted by some of the authors of labour law of this era (Radoilski, L., 1957) are of fundamental importance for the evolution of legal institutions and the entire legal branch. This is evidenced by the now century-old history of labour inspection.

The second period is associated with the socialist development of the country after 1944 and can be divided into two sub-periods:

- The first sub-period covers the emergence and consolidation of socialist relations in the country (1944-1950).
- The second sub-period is "typical socialist" (from 1950 to 1989) (Andreeva, A. & Yolova, G., 2011).

In the first sub-period our national legislation faced the difficult task of adapting to the new type of social relations entering the country. In the first years after 9 September 1944, the Tarnovo Constitution was still in force, as well as a number of laws adopted in tsarist Bulgaria, which did not correspond to the new social realities. This necessitated a transformation in our national legislation, which began to change along the lines and under the influence of Soviet legislation.

The change also concerns the labour law, respectively it is also reflected in the sphere of control for its compliance. Under the party influence of the Bulgarian Communist Party (BCP), workers' control was introduced. In the period 1944-1947 it was implemented as follows: by the CF committees (1944), 'factory committees' (1945) and trade union committees (after April 1945). This workers' control was legislated for in the Act on the Establishment of Conciliation Committees for the Interpretation and Application of Collective Labour Agreements (State Gazette, No. 102, 1946) and in the Regulations for the Regulation of Relations between Trade Union Committees and Employers in Industrial Enterprises. The introduction of workers' control is intended, on the one hand, to introduce a variety of types of control over compliance with labour legislation, but at the same time it reflects the encroaching socialist relations and the opposition to ownership and the attitude to private property respectively. This can be inferred from the subject matter of workers' control, which includes such matters as: the orderly conduct of production, accounting for business and financial activities, compliance with labour law by private employers, etc. This type of control aims, on the one hand, to decentralise control and counterbalance state control exercised by labour inspectors, and on the other hand, to 'politically' bind control functions.

In the worker-state control ratio, state control of labour law compliance retains its priority role, and this is in accordance with the principles of socialist society. The General Directorate of Labour of the Ministry of Social Policy was established as the central authority for the application of labour legislation.

An important milestone in this period was the adoption of the first Republican Constitution in 1947, which laid the foundations for socialist Bulgarian legislation, including labour legislation. Article 73 of the 1947 Constitution provides for the right to work: 'Citizens have the right to work. The State shall ensure the realization of this right of every citizen by planning the national economy, developing systematically and continuously the productive forces and creating public works. Labour shall be remunerated according to the quantity and quality of the work performed. Labor is a duty and a matter of honor for every able-bodied citizen. Every citizen is obliged to engage in socially useful work and to work according to his strength and ability. A special law shall regulate the labour duty of citizens".

After the adoption of the Constitution, nationalization of private industrial enterprises was carried out (23.12.1947).

In 1949, Bulgaria ratified the International Labour Organisation's Labour Inspection Convention No. 81 of 1947. The aim of this was to bring national regulations into line with international inspection principles and standards.

The second sub-period, conventionally named "typical socialist", is characterized by the following more important points.

In 1951, the first Labour Code was adopted (Labour Code - promulgated in State Gazette 91 of 1951). This act is of great importance for the labour law sector, given the codification that was carried out. At the same time, it has a significant impact on control. The change is also reflected in the affiliation of the control organisation, namely the safety and health control functions are attributed to the Bulgarian trade unions. According to Article 4 of the Labour Code of 1951, the control functions concerning the application of occupational safety and health standards are delegated to a public organisation, the General Workers' Trade Union (GWTU). The Central Council of the GWTU and the Central Committee of Trade Unions are given the right to establish and organise the election and appointment of labour protection committees, labour inspectorates, labour inspectors, and also councils, commissions and delegates of the State Social Security Department, through which they are to supervise the fulfilment of the obligations of enterprises, establishments and organisations in applying the provisions of the Labour Code. This recognizes the role of trade unions in the process of establishing labour law and controlling compliance with its norms, a process influenced by the Soviet experience (Aleksandrov, N, G., 1959). In the same year, the Ministry of Labour and Social Welfare was closed by an Act repealing all laws issued before 9 September 1944, promulgated in the State Gazette of the Republic of Latvia. State Gazette No. 93/1951 г.

Following the amendments to the Labour Code in November 1957, a number of subordinate regulations were issued to implement the legal provisions and to systematize the legal framework of state control over compliance with labour legislation by trade unions. Among them, the Regulations on the labour protection bodies of trade unions exercising state control (State Gazette, No. 72, 1958) occupy an important place.

In 1966, the Law on the Labour Safety Supervision Inspectorate under the Council of Ministers was adopted (State Gazette, No. 52/1966). Correspondingly, in 1973, the Act on Granting the Bulgarian Trade Unions the Control of Labour Protection (State Gazette No. 53/1973).

In 1971, the third Bulgarian Constitution was adopted (State Gazette 39/1971). It also regulated the right to work as one of the fundamental rights of citizens. The norm of Article 40 stipulates that "(1) Citizens have the right to work. (2) Every citizen has the right to freely choose his or her profession. (3) The State ensures the right to work by developing the socialist social and economic system."

In 1973, the Law on Granting the Bulgarian Trade Unions the Control of Labour Protection was adopted (Journal of Laws, No. 53 of 1973). It repealed the Act on the Labour Safety Inspectorate under the Council of Ministers and gave the Bulgarian Trade Unions the overall control of labour safety in the country.

Other acts from this period are: the Law on Public Health of 1973, the Regulations on the Structure, Rights and Duties of the Departmental Labour Protection Bodies of 1974, the Law on Fire Protection of 1979, etc.

Since 1986, with the adoption of a new Labour Code, the laws relevant to the status and structure of the Labour Inspectorate have been repealed. It contains a comprehensive legal framework for monitoring compliance with labour legislation (Chapter XIX, Section I, Articles 399-412 of the Labour Code). This regulation thoroughly regulates the functions of the Labour Inspectorate as a controlling body (Art. 400-404 of the Labour Code); compulsory administrative measures within the meaning of Art. 22-23 of the Labour Code in case of violation of labour legislation, etc. are systematically arranged (Dimitrova, D., 2022).

The Labour Code also regulates in detail the role of trade unions in labour relations and, in particular, in the control of compliance with labour legislation. In Article 399, para. 1 regulates that trade unions, exercise comprehensive control over compliance with labour legislation in all sectors and activities

(State Gazette No. 26 and 27/1986, as amended). The role of trade unions is not limited to the control functions granted to them and this is evidenced by the detailed regulation in Chapter Three "Trade Unions" (Title am., State Gazette No. 26 of 1986), which regulates in detail their organization and activities. They are entrusted with - Enhancing legal knowledge of workers, participation in planning, taking care of work activity deployment, technological improvement and quality improvement.

During the sub-period of control under consideration, a number of specialised state bodies were also established for external control of compliance with certain areas of labour protection - e.g. the State Sanitary Inspectorate, the Inspectorate for the Control of Steam Boilers, Industrial Furnaces and Lifting Appliances and Tanks (State Gazette, No. 2, 1952), etc.

The third period is associated with the democratic changes in the country and began in 1989. In view of the adopted fourth Bulgarian Constitution, respectively the new norms regulating the prestation of labor in the conditions of a market economy is conditioned by the need to rethink the control functions of compliance with labor legislation and especially the organization of the body.

Thus, in 1991, the State Labour Inspectorate under the Ministry of Labour and Social Policy was established by P.M. No. 193 of 02.10.1991 (State Gazette No. 83/1991, amended and supplemented). In 1992, by the Law on Amendments and Supplements to the Labour Code. With an amendment to Article 399, the State restored its control over compliance with labour legislation (promulgated in State Gazette No. 100/1992). the newly established inspection was also assigned the control functions of occupational safety and health.

As prof. Mruchkov "the legal regulation of the control of compliance with the labour legislation, established by the amendments to the Labour Code of November 1992, finally broke with the permissions of the previous legal regulation, which since the beginning of the 1950s entrusted this state activity to the trade unions, and "returned" it again to the state in the face of the state labour inspection, where its place is also (Mrachkov, V., 2016). These legislative changes are in line with the nature of the control activity and along with the update in the norms of control, the provisions regulating the administrative and criminal liability for compliance with labour legislation have been amended (Art. 309 - 406; Art. 413 - 416).

In the same year, the authority was transformed into the General Labour Inspectorate, respectively in 2000 into the Executive Agency "General Labour Inspectorate" under the Minister of Labour and Social Policy, by the Decree

Table 1. Labour inspection main dates chronological order of normative sources

year	Normative source
1907	Law on the Labour Inspectorate in Bulgaria - approved by Decree No. 182 of Prince Ferdinand I, dated 03.11.1907 (State Gazette No. 238/1907).
1917	Law on Hygiene and Safety at Work - approved by Decree No. 25 of Prince Ferdinand I, dated 01.06.1917 (State Gazette No. 129/1917, amended and supplemented).
1951	Labour Code - repeals the 1917 Labour Hygiene and Safety Act. Under Article 4, trade unions are given the right to establish labour safety inspectorates (published in Izvestia, No. 91/1951).
1951	Abolition of the Ministry of Labour and Social Welfare (Act for the Repeal of All Laws Issued before 9.09.1944, prom. State Gazette No. 93/1951)
1966	Law on the Labour Safety Supervision Inspectorate attached to the Council of Ministers (State Gazette 52/1966)
1973	Act on Granting the Bulgarian Trade Unions the Control of Labour Protection (State Gazette 53/1973)
1986	Labour Code (Journal of Laws No. 26 of 1 April 1986 and No. 27 of 4 April 1986). Pursuant to Art. 399. (State Gazette No. 27/1986) (1) Trade unions shall exercise comprehensive control over compliance with the labour legislation in all branches and activities. (2) Trade unions shall exercise control over compliance with the labour legislation through their leadership and specialized control bodies.
1991	Decree No. 193 of 02.10.1991 (State Gazette No. 83/1991, amended and supplemented) establishing the State Labour Inspectorate under the Ministry of Labour and Social Welfare.
1992	Law on Amendments and Supplements to the Labour Code (State Gazette 100/1992) Art. 399. (amended, State Gazette No. 100/1992) Comprehensive control of compliance with labour legislation in all branches and activities shall be exercised by the General Labour Inspectorate under the Ministry of Labour and Social Welfare. This text re-establishes State control of compliance with labour legislation
1992	Transformation of the State Labour Inspectorate into the General Labour In Decree No. 35 of the Council of Ministers amending and supplementing the Statutory Regulations of the General Inspectorate of Labour (promulgated in State Gazette No. 19/2002), by which the Executive Agency "General Labour Inspectorate" was entrusted with the specialised control activity of employment promotion. spectorate by P.M. No. 270 of 30.12.1992 (State Gazette No. 4/1993, amended and supplemented).
2000	Transformation of the General Labour Inspectorate into the Executive Agency "General Labour Inspectorate" by P.M. No. 92 of 26.05.2000 (State Gazette No. 44/2000).
2002	**Decree No. 35 of the Council of Ministers amending and supplementing the Statutory Regulations of the General Inspectorate of Labour (promulgated in State Gazette No. 19/2002), by which the Executive Agency "General Labour Inspectorate" was entrusted with the specialised control activity of employment promotion.**
2003	Decree No. 77 of the Council of Ministers, State Gazette No. 36/2004, which entrusted EA "GLI" with the specialised control activity on the compliance with the legislation related to the civil service (the control is carried out by state inspectors).
2006	Transfer of the specialised control activity on compliance with the legislation related to the civil service from EA "GLI" to the Ministry of State Administration (State Gazette 54/06)
2010	Entrusting the Executive Agency "General Labour Inspectorate" with the specialised control activity on compliance with the legislation related to the performance of the civil service and the obligations of the parties to the employment relationship
2016	**Law on Labour Migration and Labour Mobility (promulgated in** State Gazette **No. 33/2016), which assigns specialised control to the GLI regarding access to the labour market of foreign nationals in Bulgaria.**

No. 92 of 26.05.2000 (promulgated in State Gazette No. 44/2000). In 2002, the Executive Agency "General Labour Inspectorate" was entrusted with the specialised control activity of employment promotion. In the following year, 2003, the specialised control activity was supplemented by the control of compliance with the legislation related to the civil service (control is carried out by state inspectors). This activity was subsequently transferred to the Ministry of Public Administration (State Gazette No 54 of 2006). In 2010, the specialised monitoring of compliance with legislation relating to the performance of the civil service and the obligations of the parties to the employment relationship was entrusted to the Executive Agency 'General Labour Inspectorate'. In accordance with Article 6 of ILO Convention 81, labour inspectors are civil servants.

The basic requirements of the European Union and the International Labour Organisation for the establishment of a single state control are introduced. Comprehensive control of compliance with labour legislation is carried out by the Executive Agency "General Labour Inspectorate" under the Minister of Labour and Social Policy.

The control of compliance with labour legislation is an authoritative activity exercised at different times by the competent authorities. In view of the change in social relations over the various historical periods, there has also been a change in the affiliation of the bodies exercising control and the dynamics of the activity itself. As a type of administrative control, it is characterised by its authoritarian nature and the executive and prescriptive powers of the bodies charged with its exercise.

REFERENCES

Aleksandrov, A. (2016). Prakticheski problemi na trudovoto pravo, svarzani s kontrola za spazvane i administrativnonakazatelnata otgovornost za narushenia na trudovoto zakonodatelstvo. *Trud i pravo*, (11), 10–15.

Aleksandrov, A. (2017). Mitove i fakti v trudovoto pravo – Za inspektsiyata po truda. *Trud i pravo*, (12), 13–17.

Aleksandrov, N. G. (1959). *Sovetskoe trudovoe pravo*. Gosyurizdat.

Andreeva, A. (2020). i dr. Zashtita za individualnite subektivni trudovi prava (na rabotnika ili sluzhitelya). *Varna: Nauka i ikonomika*.

Andreeva, A., Yolova, G. (2011). *Yuridicheska otgovornost i kontrol za spazvane na trudovoto i osiguritelno zakonodatelstvo.* Varna: Nauka i ikonomika.

Dimitrova, D. (2020). Po nyakoi vaprosi na administrativnopravnata zashtita na pravoto na trud. *Pravoto i biznesat v savremennoto obshtestvo*. Sbornik dokladi Varna: Nauka i ikonomika.

Mevorah, N., Lidzhi, D. I., & Farhi, L. (1926). Komentar na Zakona za zadalzheniyata i dogovorite. Chast II. Sofia: Pechatnitsa.

Mrachkov, V. (2016). *Kontrol za spazvane na trudovoto zakonodatelstvo i administrativnonakazatelna otgovornost za negovoto narushavane. // Mrachkov, V., Sredkova, K., Vasilev, A. Komentar na Kodeksa na truda*. Sibi.

Radoilski, L. (1957). *Trudovo pravo, istorichesko razvitie.* Sofia: Nauka i izkustvo,

Sredkova, K. (2007). *Balgarskoto trudovo zakonodatelstvo – 100 godini i sled tova. // Aktualni problemi na trudovoto i osiguritelno pravo. T. II. Sofia: Sv*. Kl. Ohridski.

Staynov, P. (1952). *Administrativnite aktove i pravnata sistema na Narodna republika Bulgaria*. BAN.

Tokushev, D. (2008). *Istoria na novobalgarskata darzhava i pravo 1878–1944*. Sibi.

Yanulov, I. (1948). *Trudovo pravo*.

Chapter 2
Classification of Types of Labour Law Compliance Controls in Current Labour Legislation

Andriyana Andreeva
University of Economics, Varna, Bulgaria

ABSTRACT

Control is a normative regulated activity and given the specific focus on compliance with the norms of labour legislation, its dependence on the specificity of the sources of this legal sector is predetermined. The labour code occupies a central place in contemporary labour law, which is also the main source of the normative regulation of state control. Chapter nineteen "Control of Compliance With Labour Legislation and Administrative Liability for its Violation," contains the legal regulation, accordingly, the type diversity of control can be derived from it.

INTRODUCTION

The historical roots of labour law compliance monitoring are indicative of the importance of this legal institution, both for the labour law sector itself, given that it has accompanied its development since its earliest years, and for the role of the state and its responsibility in protecting labour rights.

DOI: 10.4018/978-1-6684-9067-9.ch002

The control of compliance with labour law is a generalised concept, given its importance for labour law, for the protection of the right to work and, in particular, for individual labour law institutes. This inevitably determines its diversity of types, which aims to give maximum completeness, respectively to meet the needs of different historical periods.

Control is a normative regulated activity and given the specific focus on compliance with the norms of labour legislation, its dependence on the specificity of the sources of this legal sector is predetermined. The Labour Code occupies a central place in contemporary labour law, which is also the main source of the normative regulation of state control. Chapter nineteen „Control of compliance with labour legislation and administrative liability for its violation" contains the legal regulation, accordingly, the type diversity of control can be derived from it.

Systematics in types of control can be derived on the basis of various classification features.

First of all, the distinguishing criterion on the basis of which a classification of controls can be derived is the position occupied by the control bodies in relation to the controlled objects.

According to this criterion, control is divided into external and internal control. The legislator has followed this classification in the logical sequence of the texts in the LC.

First of all, in the logical order of the norms, the legislator places the regulation of the Executive Agency "General Labour Inspectorate", which is contained in Article 399 of the Labour Code (Dimitrova, D., 2020a). This is a correct approach given the fact that this body is entrusted with "the overall control of compliance with labour legislation in all sectors and activities". On the other hand, this also shows the importance of the General Labour Inspectorate in the overall system of bodies carrying out control activities for compliance with labour legislation.

From the norm of Article 399 of the Labour Code two types of control exercised by the Executive Agency "General Labour Inspectorate" can be deduced, namely:

- General (overall control) - laid down in par. 1
- Specialised - set out in paragraph 2 "specialised control activity on compliance with the legislation related to the performance of the civil

service and the rights and obligations of the parties to the employment relationship" (Dimitrova, D., 2020a).

Central among the bodies of external control is the Executive Agency "General Labour Inspectorate" (Article 5, paragraph 2, item 1 of the Labour Inspection Act) (Dimitrova, D., 2019). It stands at the head of the control system of bodies and implements the powers granted to it through its local subdivisions - regional directorates of the Labour Inspectorate.

Secondly, the legislator derives, as a type of external control, which is regulated in Article 400 of the Labour Code. It is granted to other state bodies, beyond the one mentioned in the previous article, carry out general or specialized control of compliance with labour legislation by virtue of a law or an act of the Council of Ministers. This control is derived from the point of view of the "place" on the axis "controlling authority - controlled objects / branches or activities". This control is mainly carried out for compliance with occupational health and safety standards as part of the regulations in the labour legislation. An example of such bodies are the fire protection authorities under Article 58 of the Ministry of the Interior Act.

Thirdly, in the legislative arrangement of the types of control is placed the internal - Article 401 of the Labour Code. The norm assigns to the ministers, heads of other departments, as well as local government bodies the power to exercise control over compliance with labour legislation through their specialized bodies. This type of control is carried out by control bodies of the same organisational system as the subjects of the legal relationship. Examples of such control over compliance with labour legislation are the employer's specialised bodies for the introduction and observance of occupational health and safety (Article 24 of the OSH Act), and occupational health services (Article 25 of the OSH Act).

From the above classification it can be concluded that the control of compliance with labour legislation covers different subtypes, carried out by bodies with different scope of their powers and with different means of control. Their specificity is dictated by the particular characteristics of the object and is accordingly enshrined in law in a source of the relevant rank. The existence of multiple bodies operating in parallel and exercising internal and external control requires good coordination between them in order to avoid duplication of functions and efficiency of work. In this respect, the provision of Article 6(1) of the LIA gives the Minister of Labour and Social Policy the authority to direct and coordinate the activities of:

(a) the overall control of compliance with labour legislation;
(b) the integrated control of occupational health and safety.

Pursuant to clause 12, the Executive Director of the National Revenue Agency shall exercise control over employers with regard to the fulfilment of their obligations related to the submission of notifications to the relevant territorial directorate of the National Revenue Agency (NRA) for the conclusion, amendment or termination of employment relationships. The interaction between the control bodies in carrying out the activities under Article 6 of the LIA is explicitly regulated in the provision of Article 7 of the same normative act and is envisaged to be carried out through joint inspections and exchange of information. Joint inspections are carried out on the basis of an order of the Minister of Labour and Social Policy or an official authorised by him.

These varieties are part of the diversity of types of state control of compliance with labour legislation.

In this sense, we can say that control is an important part of the management function of the state. The Republic of Bulgaria is a welfare state and the protection of the constitutional right to work is among its priorities at every stage of social development. We can state this with certainty, given the historical development of control and the acknowledged role of the state in this process.

Various bodies are involved in the implementation of control activities. The specialised administrative body is the EA „GLI". Accordingly, it exercises administrative control over compliance with all labour legislation and the legality of employment relations.

Although the inspection function of the labour inspectorate is the core of its activities, it is not the only one. On the contrary, the Inspectorate is also entrusted with numerous authorization, registration and coordination functions provided for in various laws, which on the one hand help to guarantee the rights of the parties in the provision of labour, but on the other hand burden the already intensive day-to-day control work of the authority.

Its main function is the overall monitoring of compliance with labour legislation. Taking into account the specificity of the sources of this branch of law, namely their multiplicity, multilevel nature and different subjects issuing them, we can conclude that the labour inspectorate controls an extremely wide range of acts falling under the scope of overall state control. Despite the codification of labour law, the Labour Code is not only not a single normative act, but the regulation is constantly updated and expanded to meet new social relations and the needs of the labour market. We support the view of Prof. Mrachkov "that the scope of labour inspection remains unclosed and open to any subsequent labour law" (Mrachkov, V., 2008).

External control implies that the authorities in charge of this activity have a view outside the structures in which the labour activity takes place. These bodies complement and concretise the control exercised by the EA „GLI". This can include both bodies for which the control activity is not the main activity and specialised state control bodies which exercise control over specific activities which are a source of increased danger (e.g. energy).

It can be concluded that state control occupies a central place among the types of control of compliance with labour legislation.

Labour inspection has accompanied the whole process from the origin and development of the industry to the present day. It is the need for state control over labour relations, the protection of wage labour, that underlies the development of the industry. In this respect, the Bulgarian state has always occupied a dignified position. Already at the beginning of the 20th century, in the period of restoration of statehood and laying the foundations of the state institutions of the third Bulgarian state, the labour inspectorate was among the bodies called upon to show Europe the values behind which our state stands. That is why, two years after the adoption of the first act of our labour law, the Law on Women's and Children's Labour, the control mechanism was created to ensure compliance with it.

Labour is at the heart of labour law, which is built precisely to protect it. The need to monitor compliance has always been and will continue to be at the top of the agenda, because the function of the state in relation to labour is not limited to creating, amending and supplementing legal sources. It is also linked to their actual implementation, to the protection of the rights of the parties to an employment relationship, which in turn is an engine for economic development.

Labour relations are of a private law nature, accordingly the method of legal regulation is dispositive. However, the specificity of the organisation of the labour process and the employer's legal capacity associated with its organisation require that the protection of the weaker party be carried out by the State in the person of its competent authorities. This is precisely the vocation of the labour inspectorate, which, by implementing state control in its more than a century-long history, embodies control itself and, not infrequently, the state in its protective role.

Different types of economic and political views have prevailed during the various historical periods of the third Bulgarian state, but the idea of the protection of wage labour and the need for it to be protected by the state has been a red thread running through all these periods. State control of labour law compliance in Bulgaria originated at the beginning of the 20th century and exists to this day, undergoing transformations, but always following the original idea.

Created on the French model of control, the Inspectorate has created its own image reflecting local needs throughout its century-long history. However, despite being based on a European model, the control of labour law compliance can also be acknowledged as a "prominent insight of the Third Bulgarian State" and its progressive European orientation (Mrachkov, V., 2008).

State control of compliance with labour law is now in its second century; it is part not only of the history of labour law, but also, we can confidently say, of the social and legal state.

The Labour Inspectorate is a body with tradition and continuity, which, by its stability over time, is one of the most important guarantors of legality in the exercise of the right to work.

Apart from the control functions of the state, compliance with the norms in the "employer-employee" relations can be ensured through the activities of trade unions and stimulated through the introduction of professional codes of ethics, company codes of conduct, as well as the implementation of socially responsible practices by employers (Serafimova, D., 2021a). Socially responsible initiatives entered Bulgarian practice in the late twentieth century, are based on voluntary implementation by employers and are not regulated by the state. They are generally promoted in other ways - e.g. through membership in international business peer networks and organisations supporting such initiatives, through certification to occupational health and safety standards (OHSAS) or social responsibility standards (SA 8000, ISO 26000), etc. (Serafimova, D., 2021b).

In view of the timing of the control activity. According to this criterion, control is divided into preliminary, ongoing and subsequent.

Each of these types is characterised by specific methods of action, linked to the outcome they are aimed at.

Preliminary control is that which takes place before the relevant legally regulated act is carried out - for example, before a business activity takes place. The aim is to establish that the conditions under which it is to be carried out comply with the legal ones. Ongoing control is that which takes place in the course of the activity itself or, as the case may be, in the process of enjoying or exercising employment and social security rights. This is the core of control activities, given that this type is the most frequently applied. The methods used by the supervisory authorities in carrying out this type of control are: periodic on-the-spot checks; requests for explanations, documents, materials, papers, etc.

Subsequent is the control exercised after the relevant activity has been carried out. This type is the least frequently applied in practice and is usually perceived as part of the ongoing. This is supported by the lack of methods and means of control envisaged by the legislator, which are specific to it, and it uses the methods and means inherent in the ongoing control. However, this control is important from the point of view of monitoring the effectiveness of control activities. Thus, in 2020, EA „GLI" carried out subsequent controls on the implementation of 54.1% of the mandatory prescriptions issued and entered into force in 2020, and 98.3% of the prescriptions checked were implemented. These data show that the intervention of labour inspectors leads to an improvement of working conditions in enterprises, which in turn is an indicator of the high degree of effectiveness of control activities.

The forms of control introduced in the Bulgarian legislation and the parallel and complementary bodies exercising external and internal control imply their close interaction and coordination. It was the realisation of the need to regulate this interaction between the bodies that led to the adoption of the Labour Inspection Act (State Gazette 102 of 28.11.2008). Pursuant to Article 1 of this organisational law, it regulates: 1. the way the national labour inspection system operates; 2. the types of control activities included in labour inspection; 3. the manner of interaction between the State control bodies carrying out labour inspection.

According to the annual report of EA „GLI", joint inspections with other state control bodies are traditionally carried out to increase the effectiveness and efficiency of inspection activities. In 2020, 1721 such inspections were carried out. The largest number of these inspections were carried out with representatives of the Ministry of the Interior (MoI), the National Social Insurance Institute (NSI), the National Revenue Agency (NRA) and the Regional Health Inspectorates (RHI). The largest number of joint inspections were carried out in the economic activities of "Restaurants", "Trade", "Manufacture of clothing" and "Construction".[1]

REFERENCES

Dimitrova, D. (2020). Bezopasnite i zdravoslovni uslovia na trud – angazhiment na rabotodatelya i kontrol za spazvane. *Ikonomicheskata nauka, obrazovanie i realna ikonomika: razvitie i vzaimodeystvia v digitalnata epoha. Sbornik dokladi.* Varna: Nauka i ikonomika.

Mrachkov, V. (2008). Sto godini inspektsia po truda. *Yuridicheski svyat*, (1), 77–102.

Serafimova, D. (2021). Korporativna sotsialna otgovornost – tendentsii i inovativni praktiki na pazara na truda i v sektora na vissheto obrazovanie. Izvestia. Varna: Nauka i ikonomika.

Serafimova, D. (2021). *Interdisciplinary Educational Models for Creating CSR and Sustainability Culture in European Business Schools. 2021 Sustainable Leadership and Academic Excellence International Conference (SLAE).* IEEE. https://doi.org/doi, doi:10.1109/SLAE54202.2021.9788104

Serafimova, D. (2021). Corporate social responsibility – trends andinnovative practices in the labour market and the higher education sector. *Izvestiya. Journal of the University of Economics.*

Chapter 3
State Control Over Compliance With Labour Legislation

Galina Yolova
University of Economics, Varna, Bulgaria

ABSTRACT

The development aims to analyze and derive a comprehensive systematics of the existing national regulations in the field of control, giving their respective analysis and interpretation. It defines and analyzes the general and special subject and object of internal and external control, giving them characteristic specifics in view of the way they are formulated under the codified (Labour Code) and special laws (Labour Inspection Act and the Occupational Safety and Health Act). The general characteristics, nature, and structure of the centralized control body—the Executive Agency "General Labour Inspectorate"—are examined in the aspects of the current legislation and in the light of the draft of the new regulations.

OVERVIEW OF THE ACTS REGULATING STATE CONTROL IN BULGARIAN LAW

Specialised external control of compliance with labour legislation is regulated in an extensive system of acts of different nature and specificity, outlining the framework of control influence in various aspects of the implementation of the right to work and the development of the individual employment relationship. Structured in the context of the hierarchy of the legal framework, we can identify them at several basic levels, namely:

DOI: 10.4018/978-1-6684-9067-9.ch003

1. Within the general subordination of the principles and philosophy of ILO Convention 81 concerning labour inspection;
2. Systematic definition of the nature and competences of control in the general codified labour law act - the Labour Code, where within the overall legal framework the place of centralised control of compliance with labour legislation is also found and realised;
3. Special normative acts, directly relevant and complementary in specific aspects of labour protection, the general framework of control competences, in particular - the Labour Inspection Act, the Occupational Health and Safety Act (OHSA),
4. Regulations of the Executive Agency "General Labour Inspectorate" as the main administrative and organizational by-laws.

This systematics of acts gives the overall picture of a comprehensive and internally consistent legal regulation, establishing the nature, implementation, as well as the measures and mechanisms of control aimed at efficiency and legality in the establishment and development of labour relations. In the mentioned aspects, a structural and systematic development and consolidation of a coherent approach in the establishment of the non-departmental specialized form of guarantee of fair and decent working conditions and the related diverse methods of sanctioning in cases of illegality, at the same time - and building on the principles of the freedom of the individual in the realization of the right to work and related subjective labor rights (Dimitrova, 2019).

The basic aspects of the regulation of labour inspection, built upon and further developed in the actual provisions of the individual Acts, are to be sought in the general subordination of the principles and philosophy of ILO Convention 81 concerning Labour Inspection, adopted at the XXX Session of the General Conference of the International Labour Organisation in Geneva, Switzerland, on 11 July 1933 and entered into force on 7 April 1950. In accordance with the principle of its binding force in respect of member States whose ratification has been registered with the International Labour Office (art. 33), it was ratified by Bulgaria by Decree No. 745 of the Presidium of the Grand National Assembly of 31 August 1949. (SG 207 of 1949) and entered into force on 29 December 1950. As a fundamental act in labour inspection, the Convention is rightly described as having a positive influence on labour law enforcement activities to this day (Mrachkov, 1978) (Mrachkov, 2008).

In spite of their division into the branches of industry and commerce, the main lines of action of the inspectorate of inspection are laid down in the text of Article 3 of the Convention in the following main aspects, namely, ensuring the enforcement of the legal provisions concerning working conditions and the protection of workers in the exercise of their profession, giving information and technical advice to employers and workers on the most efficient methods of complying with the legal provisions, a signalling function to the competent authorities with regard to any shortcomings or abuses found outside the scope of the existing legal provisions, as well as taking action with regard to the obligation of authorised entities to notify it of accidents at work and occupational diseases in accordance with the circumstances and conditions prescribed by national legislation.

By explicitly providing for the Inspectorate to be under the supervision and control of the executive, the principle that its activities should be compatible with the overall administrative practice of the member state is also imposed (Dimitrova, 2022).

The outlined powers of the inspectors are also fundamental for the exercise of control functions, which should be replicated in the ratifying State, given the specificities of its respective legislation. In particular, they amount to the ability of the authorities involved to: enter freely, without prior warning, at any time of the day or night, any establishment placed under the control of the inspectorate, enter during the day premises which they have reasonable grounds for believing are placed under the control of the inspectorate, to carry out such examinations, inspections and investigations as are deemed necessary with a view to complying with labour law provisions, by questioning the employer or the personnel of the undertaking themselves or in the presence of witnesses, and by inspecting records and documents the maintenance of which is prescribed by legislation on working conditions.

In the exercise of their powers, and in particular where irregularities or general non-compliance with labour legislation is found, inspectors have the power both to take direct action to remedy deficiencies found in the facilities, in the design or in the methods of work which they have reasonable grounds to believe endanger the health or safety of workers, and to issue prescriptions or require that prescriptions be issued for the improvement of working conditions or the taking of urgent measures subject to immediate implementation in cases where there is an imminent danger to the health and safety of workers (Dimitrova, 4, 2020, pp. 219-230).

The binding nature of the Act on the Member States implies (Article 18) that appropriate penalties are provided for in national legislation and effectively enforced for breaches of the legal provisions the enforcement of which is placed under the control of labour inspectors, as well as for obstacles created in the performance of their duties.

As a further development of the principle, it is the duty of labour inspectors or local inspection offices to submit to the central labour inspectorate periodical reports of a general nature on the results of their activities, to be made in such manner as the central authority may prescribe and relating to such matters as it may specify in each case. The reports are to be made as often as the Central Government may prescribe, but in any case at least once a year.

Under Article 20 of the Convention, it is the duty of the Central Inspectorate to publish an annual report of a general nature on the activities of the inspection services under its control, within a reasonable period not exceeding 12 months from the end of the year to which it relates.

Copies of the annual reports shall be sent to the Director-General of the International Labour Office within a reasonable time after their publication, but not later than 3 months.

At the national level, within the framework of the codifying regulations of the Labour Code, the main frameworks of centralised control are established in the texts of Article 400 of the Labour Code, according to which, in addition to the Inspectorate as a centralised and extra-departmental body of exclusive control over compliance with labour legislation, other state bodies are also competent to exercise general or specialised control over compliance with labour legislation by virtue of a law or an act of the Council of Ministers.

At the same time, at the level of internal control is the regulation of direct control functions in their subordinate area of ministers, heads of other departments, as well as local government bodies exercise control over compliance with labor legislation through their specialized bodies (Art. 401 of the Labor Code).

Comprehensive, albeit fragmentary and scarce in terms of texts in relation to the codifying nature of the act of the Executive Agency "General Labour Inspectorate" is given in the Labour Code, Chapter Nineteen Control of compliance with labour legislation and administrative liability for its violation, Section I. Control of compliance with labour legislation, Articles 399-412 of the Labour Code.

Pursuant to Article 399, para. 1 - 3 of the Labour Code, the Agency is a specialised external control body, performing control functions in two directions - general, overall external control, as well as specialised external control in special by its nature and nature service relationships (Dimitrova, 2019).

Thus, it is within the competence of the Agency to carry out:

- Comprehensive monitoring of compliance with labour legislation in all sectors and activities, including the payment of unpaid wages and benefits after termination of employment,
- specialised control of compliance with legislation relating to the performance of the civil service and the rights and obligations of the parties to the employment relationship, subject to the absolute prohibition that such control be exercised by a person having a direct or indirect interest in the activities of the controlled establishments.

Specific forms of control, although not in their typical form, are also those provided for in close reference to other laws and state bodies, in which sense they are complementary and supplementary to the scope of control in aspects closely linked to the implementation of the right to work and the development of the employment relationship. In this sense, on the one hand is the Agency's power to file a written request under Article 625 of the Commercial Law - to initiate insolvency proceedings in the event of wage obligations to at least one third of the trader's employees being due and unpaid for more than two months.

At the same time and according to the text of Art. 3 of the Labour Code, the Executive Agency "General Labour Inspectorate" has the competence to notify the National Revenue Agency for the ex officio deletion of a sent notification of a concluded employment contract, when an employer or an official has not complied in due time with a binding prescription under Art. 1(11) - namely, sending a notice to delete a previously sent notice under Art. 3 of the concluded employment contract, in case it is established that there is no evidence of the existence of an employment relationship, or in the cases of Art. 404, para. 11(1) of the Labour Code shall be deemed to have been served on the day on which it is issued, where the employer, the person representing him or the person designated to receive the employer's correspondence cannot be found at the employer's registered office.

The close linkage of specialised control to the activities and functions of bodies and entities is further developed in the form of mandatory cooperation and coordination of activities. In this sense, in addition to the general principle of carrying out control in cooperation with employers, appointing authorities, employees and their organisations, as well as with civil servants, is the obligation laid down for the National Revenue Agency to provide the control bodies with all the tax and social security information they need for the purposes of controlling compliance with labour law and civil service legislation.

As a **specified form of control is the control under the Labour Inspection Act (LIA)** (In force since 01.01.2009, prom. 102 of 28 November 2008, amend. SG 35 of 12 May 2009, amend. SG 82/16 October 2009, amend. SG 16 of 26 February 2010, amend. SG 88 of 9 November 2010, amend. SG 66 of 26 July 2013, amend. 28 November 2014, amend. 14 of 20 February 2015, amend. SG 95 of 8 December 2015, amend. SG 58 of 18 July 2017, amend. SG 97 of 5 December 2017, amend. No. 105 of 18 December 2018), established pursuant to Article 3 of the Labour Code with the aim of creating conditions for more effective and efficient control over compliance with working conditions by improving coordination and interaction in the work of bodies with control and signalling functions in the field of labour and social security relations.

According to the text of Article 4 of the Labour Inspection Act, labour inspection is a large-scale control activity, including the control of compliance with labour and social security legislation and specialised control under the Employment Promotion Act and the Occupational Health and Safety Act.

In this sense, and paragraph 1 of the RDA defines this activity as carried out by an extensive system of control bodies at various levels, on the establishment and enforcement of compliance between the requirements of the legislation and its implementation in enterprises, establishments and places where labour activity is carried out or training is conducted.

The National Council on Working Conditions is the permanent body for coordination, consultation and cooperation in labour inspection.

It is foreseen that labour inspections will be carried out independently or jointly by the executive authorities or their administrative structures of the specialised administration, including inspectors, civil servants and/or other authorised persons in the relevant fields, including the Executive Agency "General Labour Inspectorate".

Moreover, for the purposes of control, in the aspects of labour and social security legislation, it is introduced in the competence of the Minister of Labour and Social Policy to manage and coordinate the activities of the overall control of compliance with labour legislation, the integrated control of ensuring healthy and safe working conditions, as well as the specialised control under the Employment Promotion Act and the Disability Act. In this regard, its direct functions include the development and coordination of the overall state policy in the field of labour inspection, by annually developing a National Labour Inspection Programme and submitting it to the Council of

Ministers for adoption, as well as annually preparing a report on the status, trends and problems of labour inspection activities and proposing measures for their improvement.

The main form of control under the Labour Inspection Act are joint inspections carried out on the basis of an order of the Minister of Labour and Social Policy or an official authorised by him and carried out in accordance with the National Labour Inspection Programme, at the request of the Council of Ministers, at the request of the public prosecutor's office, at the suggestion of the National Council on Working Conditions, following complaints and reports of violations of the legislation, as well as in the event of accidents in enterprises and in the event of work accidents causing death, disability of more of three workers, or which is reasonably expected to result in disability.

A report shall be prepared on the results of the joint inspection, containing the findings, the prescriptions given and the measures taken to seek administrative liability, which shall be submitted to the Minister of Labour and Social Policy with a copy to the heads of the control bodies involved in the inspection.

On the other hand, specialised extra-agency control is provided for under the OHSA, and is regulated at three main levels. On the one hand, the Ministry of Labour and Social Policy exercises overall control over compliance with the OSH Act. At the same time, control is exercised by the Minister of Labour and Social Policy, who develops, coordinates and implements state policy in the field of ensuring healthy and safe working conditions, exercising integrated control through the Executive Agency "General Labour Inspectorate" on compliance with legislation and on the implementation of obligations to ensure healthy and safe working conditions in all sectors and activities, regardless of the form of ownership.

The third level, the specialized control activity on the implementation of the Law and related normative acts is carried out by the Executive Agency "General Labour Inspectorate" through its structures (Dimitrova, 4, 2020).

In addition to the specialised external control, the Occupational Health and Safety Act also provides for internal control, introduced, quite logically, as significantly limited in its scope, within the relevant field. In this sense, it concerns control bodies which are part of the same organisation as the control, specialised in their activities, which are mainly and primarily aimed at ensuring compliance with the occupational health and safety standards.

Functioning at a different level from intra-departmental control are the occupational health and safety services and technical safety officers and services provided for in Articles 24 and 25 of the Occupational Health and Safety Act. Although some of these, such as occupational health services, do not have direct control powers, they, together with the committees and working conditions, reflect the close systematic link between the control exercised and its supporting functions, including signalling and preventive functions.

Thus, according to Article 24, paragraph 1 of the Occupational Safety and Health Act, in order to organize the implementation of activities related to the protection from occupational risks and the prevention of these risks, the employer, depending on the scope of the activity, the nature of the work and the nature of the occupational risk, appoints or designates one or more officials with appropriate education and qualification or establishes a specialized service, and the employer regulates their functions and tasks in accordance with the specific conditions and in accordance with a regulation of the Minister of Labour and Social Policy.

Occupational health services shall be established by employers independently or jointly with other employers, as well as by legal or natural persons registered under the Commercial Act, the Cooperative Societies Act or the Not-for-Profit Legal Persons Act, as well as by companies under the legislation of a Member State of the European Union or of a State party to the Agreement on the European Economic Area, to provide services to workers.

As units with mainly preventive functions, they advise and assist employers, committees and working conditions groups in planning and organising activities on:

1. ensuring and maintaining safe and healthy working conditions;
2. promoting the health and performance of workers in relation to their work;
3. adapting work to the capabilities of the worker, taking into account his physical and mental health.

The main activities of the occupational health services are:

1. assisting employers in establishing an occupational safety and health organisation;
2. assessing occupational risks and analysing the health status of workers;
3. proposing measures to eliminate and reduce the risks identified;
4. monitoring the health status of workers;
5. training of workers and officials in occupational health and safety rules.

Working conditions committees and groups also have direct control functions over compliance with OHS standards. Although they are outside the specialized institution, the committees, envisaged as internal bodies as early as the Women's and Children's Labour Act (1905), express a basic idea inherent in labour inspection - compliance with labour laws, in which sense they are also the prototype and precursor of specialized control (Mrachkov, 2008, p. 80).

Thus, according to Art. 27, par. 1 of the Occupational Health and Safety at Work Act, in enterprises with more than 50 employees, working conditions committees shall be set up with 4 to 10 members, including representatives of the employer and an equal number of representatives of the employees on occupational safety and health, and also, if necessary, representatives of the supervisory authorities, the occupational health service and external experts.

The chairman of the working conditions committee shall be the employer or his representative and the vice-chairman shall be the workers' representative for occupational safety and health.

In enterprises with five to fifty employees inclusive, as well as in the individual structural units of the enterprises, occupational health and safety groups shall be set up, which shall include the employer or the head of the respective structural unit and one representative of the employees for occupational safety and health.

These bodies are also responsible for inspecting compliance with occupational health and safety requirements, monitoring the state of occupational injuries and occupational morbidity, and participating in the development of programmes to inform and train workers on occupational health and safety issues.

The legal framework examined in a systematic way according to the hierarchy of the acts gives us grounds for drawing certain conclusions. On the one hand, there has been, in continuous compliance with the Convention, a further development of the national legal framework as regards the powers and forms of control. At the same time, there is a continuing trend towards their continuous refinement and upgrading in full accordance with the new social interrelationships and the specificities of employment and labour realisation. Each of the acts at its respective level complements and develops the previous ones, thus establishing a comprehensive, complete and internally consistent legal regulation.

On the other hand, the hierarchy of the control function in the overall system of the structure of the general and specialized national administration has been strictly observed, and the synchronous forms of joint control activity have been appropriately found, while preserving the operational independence and, in this sense, the exceptional importance of the subordinate and special provisions aspects.

OBJECT AND SUBJECT OF THE STATE CONTROL FOR COMPLIANCE WITH THE LABOUR LEGISLATION

Control activity, studied within the social management system theory, is highlighted as its typical property, a functional and significant part of any type of management process, performing regulatory, protective, at the level of maintaining balance in the system, informative, preventive and even compensatory functions (Kandeva, 1998, pp. 290-293). On the other hand, in its aspect at the level of the state and/or administrative apparatus, control is interpreted as a basic, "organizational-legal means of lawful and proper administration" and in this sense - as a type of social, managerial activity, which is in itself a guarantee means of lawfulness in management (Dimitrov, 1994, p. 260).

If approached from the perspective of the general theory of managerial, centralized control, we can summarize that its main, characteristic features can be reduced to the following points, namely:

1. as a manifestation of management, control is a type of executive - order activity, in which sense it differs from all other control - guarantee means of legality, having non-legal, respectively social, personal, etc. character,
2. it is carried out by administrative bodies and officials exercising powers of control in/within or over the administration/in the context of a centralized, hierarchically structured administration,
3. it is legal in type and administrative control in content, which means that it directly creates, modifies or terminates certain rights and obligations, implementing management with control content in the functioning of the dispositional power,
4. in view of its subject content, it is a control of legality and / or correctness of management, which considered in unity and systematics is defined by some authors as "legality",
5. has as object the ruling subjects. (Andreeva, A., Yolova, G., Dimitrova, D., 2004, p. 140).

Insofar as control is a specific authority activity, subject to the general framework of ensuring the legality and correctness of the activity carried out, given its evaluative nature, it has as its purpose and object the establishment of compliance of actual practices with the legal framework in the processes of application of labour legislation. In this sense, its development implies the establishment of a permanent system for the prevention and elimination of offences in the application of labour legislation. Its regulation within the framework of general and special laws aims at a systematisation of both external and internal and general and specialised control, distributed, taking into account the competences of its respective bodies, at separate and different levels. In that sense, the latter is established in several different aspects, differentiated in view of their object, nature and normative basis, but in compliance with the general definition of an executive - executive activity with a centralized and unified subject - legality and correctness in the application of labour legislation.

The systematics of the legal acts regulating the control of compliance with labour legislation establish a broad system of bodies and competences concerning various aspects of the application of national legislation. The regulated scope of powers and the varied nature of the object of control obviously aim at a comprehensiveness of supervision for correctness and lawfulness, which in practice leads to a legally guaranteed, stable and functioning system of labour relations.

Insofar as by its nature and character it is an authoritative activity of a primarily evaluative nature, the idea of structuring it is undoubtedly to build a comprehensive, internally inconsistent and workable mechanism for ensuring legality and legality in the activities of realizing the right to work. In this sense, on the one hand, given the diverse nature of the acts and, on the other hand, the specificities of the related control bodies and competences, a significantly broad scope and subject matter of control activity is established. In view of the latter, the structuring of the object of control following the systematics of the labour law acts provides grounds for deriving a certain structure based on its characteristics, scope and specificities, namely:

- general and comprehensive external control,
- comprehensive specialised external control, and
- specialised internal control.

At the same time, and given its primarily administrative nature, given its subject matter in a narrow sense, the control exercised is primarily structured as control of persons, control of acts and control of actions.

At the level of the codified act, the main control body is the Executive Agency "General Labour Inspectorate", which has been assigned and therefore - as broadly as possible, although not always specified functions for comprehensive control of compliance with labour legislation in all sectors and activities, including the payment of unpaid wages and benefits after termination of employment.

The formulation of the object of the Agency's control as a comprehensive control (Mrachkov, 2010, pp. 901-902) over the compliance with the entire labour legislation creates an exceptional comprehensiveness with regard to the existing and respectively - newly adopted laws and regulations. In this sense, it is rightly pointed out that "its function of comprehensive control over compliance with labour legislation itself turns out to be of a large and constantly expanding scope..., as the scope of application of the EA GIT remains open and open to any subsequent labour law..., including acts in the enterprise to regulate labour relations" (Mrachkov, 2008, pp. 98-99).

As regards the specialised object of external control, it is established in the general and special laws. In this sense, in the first place are the specified, although not very justifiably given the introduction of the general form of comprehensive control objects, within the competence of the EA GIT, respectively - on compliance with the legislation related to the performance of the civil service, respectively - the rights and obligations of the parties to the service relationship.

Defined as special are also the competences of the Agency in cases of violation of the registration regime, where it is provided that it shall notify the National Revenue Agency for an ex officio deletion of a sent notification of a concluded employment contract, when an employer or an official has not complied with a mandatory prescription under Art. 1(11) of the Labour Code or in cases under Article 404(5) of the Labour Code.

The Agency's powers to declare the existence of an employment relationship are also subject to special scrutiny. Thus, in the event of a finding that work has been performed without a concluded employment contract (Art. 405a of the Labour Code), the existence of the employment relationship, established by the admissible and possible means of proof, shall be declared by a decree issued by the control bodies of the Labour Inspectorate, and the decree shall also determine the starting date of the employment relationship. On the basis of the decree, the inspection authorities shall instruct the employer to offer the employee an employment contract, either from the date of the employment relationship as defined in the decree or from the date of the decree.

In cases where no employment contract is concluded between the parties, the decree shall supersede the employment contract and it shall be deemed to have been concluded for an indefinite period with a five-day working week and an eight-hour working day.

In this context, the highly preventive nature of the Agency's control impact on undeclared work could rightly be underlined. Thus, according to a report of the Minister of Labour and Social Policy, "in recent years, the EA GIT has contributed to the reduction and prevention of the informal economy through its active stance. Thanks to its comprehensive control activities, the agency in 2021 checked 33,000 enterprises, with over 1.4 million employees and paid over 2.7 million BGN in wage arrears. According to the data of the control activity of the GIT in 2021, about 2/3 of all 40 788 pcs. of inspections were focused on undeclared work."

As regards the subject of control exercised by the Executive Agency "General Labour Inspectorate", it is generally established as a subject on actions or acts derived from the general form of the employer's supporting obligations, established in particular in the text of Article 403a of the Labour Code. The latter stipulates that in the undertaking, in its divisions, sites and workplaces, as well as in other places where wage labour is performed, the employer must keep the following documents at the disposal of the inspection authorities:

- a copy of the internal regulations,
- a list of employees sent by the undertaking providing temporary work
- documents relating to the allocation of working time and the organisation of work: orders for overtime, on-call time, on-call time, part-time work and named work schedules for the period for which aggregated working time is established.

In furtherance and implementation of the principles of ILO Convention 81, the CT provides for a wide range of measures and control mechanisms. The situations of their application have been extended in scope insofar as they concern not only and only direct and identified violations, but also cases of prevention and cessation of violations of labour legislation, of legislation related to the civil service, as well as the prevention and elimination of their harmful consequences. In this case, the measures are taken not only by the control body, on its own initiative, but also by bodies exercising external and internal control, in particular other state bodies exercising general or specialised control over compliance with labour legislation by virtue of a law or an act of the Council of Ministers, respectively ministers, heads of other departments, as well as local government bodies exercising control over compliance with labour legislation through their specialised bodies.

Specific in terms of competence, although general in terms of object, is the control exercised by trade unions given their signalling function to the direct control bodies. Here, as in the case of the other internal bodies - committees on working conditions under the Occupational Health and Safety Act, the close mediating role of the signaling function is apparent, complementing and supporting the otherwise service-oriented nature of the control activity.

In this sense, and in accordance with Article 406 of the Labour Code, the empowerment of trade unions with the right to report violations of labour legislation to the supervisory authorities, as well as to request administrative punishment for the guilty persons, is directly related to their powers to visit at any time the enterprises and other places where the work is carried out, as well as premises used by employees, to request from the employer explanations and the submission of information and documents required by them, as well as to be informed directly by the employees and services on all employment law compliance matters.

The supervisory authorities are obliged to inform the trade unions of the measures taken within one month.

As a comprehensive specialized external control is also established in the Labour Inspection Act, concerning again comprehensive control of compliance with labour and social security legislation and specialized control under the Employment Promotion Act and the Occupational Health and Safety Act.

At the level of the latter, as already mentioned, the competence of the Minister of Labour and Social Policy includes the general guidance and coordination of activities for the implementation of the overall control of compliance with labour legislation, the integrated control of ensuring healthy and safe working conditions, as well as the specialised control under the Employment Promotion Act and the Disability Act.

A shortcoming of the legal framework is precisely the contradiction in the formulation of the object of control under the general and special laws. In this sense, on the one hand, and by reference to the text of Article 399 of the Labour Code, the overall control of the Agency should undoubtedly include, as has already been specified, the entire labour legislation with the relevant general, special, including - sub-legislative and internal acts for the respective unit. At the same time, the Labour Inspection Act provides in the competences of another systematics of bodies again the same scope of control, extending, rather pointlessly, given the fact of its inclusion by analogy in the object of the Executive Agency of the General Labour Inspectorate and the special laws - the Law on Health and Safety Conditions of Work, the Law on Employment Promotion, the Law on Persons with Disabilities. This concretization of the acts, and the very etymology of the law as a special one, gives grounds to assume that it is a specialized external control, but the formulation of the object in practice and the way it overlaps as a characteristic and essence with the notion of overall control in a certain sense creates inconsistency in the competences and hierarchy of the control structure.

In addition is the fact that control activity under the Labour Inspection Act is legally defined as large-scale and carried out by an extensive system of control bodies at various levels, respectively - in concrete terms and as an object of control - establishing and enforcing compliance between the requirements of the legislation and its application in enterprises, sites and places where labour activity or training is carried out.

In its typical sense, the specialized external control is the one under the Occupational Health and Safety Act, with a specific object, which can also be deduced from its subject scope, namely - compliance with the rights and obligations of the state, employers, employees, representatives of employees in occupational safety and health, persons who work on their own account or in partnership, and other organizations and legal entities to ensure occupational health and safety. In this sense, the sub-objects of control are the rules and principles of prevention and measures to stimulate improvements in the safety and health of workers for the prevention of occupational risks, the protection of safety and health, the elimination of risks and causes of occupational injuries and occupational diseases, information, consultation, training and balanced participation (Article 1, paragraphs 1 and 2 of the Occupational Health and Safety Act).

The immediate subject of control under the Occupational Health and Safety Act is established at two main levels - with regard to the obligations of employers and with regard to the activities of other natural or legal persons responsible for ensuring occupational health and safety, irrespective of the obligations of workers under this Act, and whether this activity is carried out by their bodies or entrusted to other competent services or persons.

In this sense, on the one hand, the main subject of control are the obligations of employers to ensure healthy and safe working conditions of employees by applying the necessary measures, including the prevention of occupational risks, providing information and training, as well as ensuring the necessary organization and means, in compliance with the basic principles of prevention of occupational accidents, namely - avoiding risks, assessing risks that cannot be avoided, limiting risks at their source, adapting work to the worker, especially with regard to the design of workplaces, the choice of work equipment, work and production methods, in order to alleviate or eliminate monotonous work, work with an imposed rhythm, and to reduce their impact on the worker's health, adapting to technical progress, replacing what is dangerous with what is safe or less so, identification of existing hazards and sources of factors harmful to health and safety, implementation of a consistent comprehensive prevention policy covering technology, work organisation, working conditions, social relationships and the impact of elements of the working environment and work process, use of collective protective equipment in preference to personal protective equipment, giving appropriate instructions to workers.

On the other hand, the actions of all legal and natural persons who independently employ workers, legal and natural persons who use workers provided to them by an enterprise that provides temporary work, as well as persons who, on their own account, work alone or in partnership with others, are obliged to ensure occupational health and safety in all work-related cases, both for workers and for all other persons who are on other occasions in or near the work premises, sites and places (Article 14(1) of the Occupational Health and Safety Act).

Comprehensive control over compliance with the Health and Safety at Work Act is exercised by the Ministry of Labour and Social Policy, by reference and structuring of the hierarchy - and by the Minister of Labour and Social Policy, who develops, coordinates and implements state policy in the field of ensuring healthy and safe working conditions, and in this sense - exercising integrated control through the Executive Agency "General Labour Inspectorate" over compliance with the legislation and the implementation of obligations to ensure health and safety at work in all sectors and activities, regardless of ownership.

To the specialized external control with a special object - the activity of the occupational health services is the control of the state health control bodies (Article 54a of the Occupational Health and Safety Act). The subject of the control, carried out on an ongoing basis and in cases of complaints and signals, are the registration and compliance of the data and documents referred to in Art. 25d, para. 1 and Art. 25e par. 25a(1) with the actual situation, the implementation of the activities agreed with the employer under Art. 1 relating to the health of workers, as well as the documents certifying the activities of the service.

In the exercise of their control functions, the state health control bodies shall have the right to free access to the occupational health services, to request information and documents from the occupational health service in connection with its activities, to issue binding prescriptions to the occupational health service for the elimination of established violations, and to draw up acts for established administrative violations.

Specialised internal control under the Occupational Health and Safety Act is exercised by the committees and groups on working conditions, within the competence of which the overall activity of health and safety protection and of workers is set as the subject of control, which corresponds to their right to carry out inspections of compliance with the requirements for occupational health and safety (Article 29, paragraph 1 of the Occupational Health and Safety Act). In order to carry out their control functions, workers' representatives on working conditions committees and groups are entitled to:

1. access to available information on working conditions, analyses of occupational injuries and illnesses, and the findings and prescriptions of inspection bodies;
2. require the employer to take the necessary measures and make proposals to eliminate hazards or to temporarily limit health and safety risks;
3. to refer to the supervisory authorities if they consider that the measures taken by the employer are not sufficient to ensure the health and safety of workers;
4. to participate in inspections carried out by the supervisory authorities.

The Vice-Chair of the Working Conditions Committee and the Occupational Health and Safety representative on the Working Conditions Group are entitled to:

1. access to all workplaces in the enterprise or division;
2. to be informed directly by employees on all health and safety matters;
3. to participate in the investigation of accidents at work and in establishing the causes of occupational diseases;
4. to participate in the drafting of internal rules and regulations in the field of occupational health and safety, for which the employer must invite them;
5. require the employer or the safety and health authority in the undertaking to stop the operation of work equipment or to prohibit the use of dangerous chemical substances and mixtures.

The representatives shall also have signalling functions to the relevant control authorities in cases where, after it has been established that work equipment and/or dangerous chemical substances and mixtures present an imminent danger to the health and life of workers and there is no other way to minimise the risk, they notify the responsible official and/or the employer in writing of the identified danger and appropriate measures are not taken.

The fact is that the National Council on Working Conditions, as a permanent body for coordination, consultation and cooperation in the development and implementation of policy to ensure occupational health and safety, has no direct control functions, insofar as it is provided for in its powers only to coordinate the activities of the bodies entrusted with control in the field of working conditions, as well as to take decisions to carry out joint inspections under the Inspection Act. (Article 40(1)(6)(9) of the Occupational Health and Safety Act).

REFERENCES

Andreeva, A., Yolova, G., Dimitrova, D., (2004). *Osnovi na publichnata administratsiya.* Varna: s.n.

Dimitrov, D. (1994). *Administrativno pravo.* Sofiya.

Dimitrova, D. (2019). Savremenna rolya na Izpalnitelna agentsiya; za zashtita na pravata na stranite po trudovite pravootnosheniya. Pravoto i biznesat v savremennoto obshtestvo: *Sbornik s dokladi ot 2-ra Natsionalna nauchna konferentsiya, 8.* Varna, Nauka i ikonomika.

Dimitrova, D. (2020). Bezopasnite i zdravoslovni usloviya na trud - angazhiment na rabotodatelya i kontrol za spazvane. *Ikonomicheskata nauka, obrazovanie i realna ikonomika: razvitie i vzaimodeystviya v digitalnata epoha: Sbornik s dokladi.* Varna, Nauka i ikonomika .

Dimitrova, D. (2022). Current Trends in the Field of Control over Compliance with Labour Legislation. Economics and Computer Science: Varna. *Knowledge and Business, 8,* 14–20.

Mrachkov, V. (1978). *Balgarskoto trudovo zakonodatelstvo i mezhdunarodnite trudovi konventsii i preporaki.* Sofia: s.n.

Mrachkov, V. (2008). Sto godini Inspektsiya po truda. *Yuridicheski svyat, 1,* 94.

Mrachkov, V. (2010). *Trudovo pravo, Sedmo izdanie.* Sofya: Sibi.

Chapter 4
Executive Agency "General Labour Inspectorate": General Characteristics and Structure

Galina Yolova
University of Economics, Varna, Bulgaria

ABSTRACT

On the basis of the study, conclusions are drawn about a continuous trend of continuous improvement and upgrading of the national legal framework, fully in line with the new social relations and the related specificity of the labour relations. A strict hierarchy of control functions is established in the overall system of the structure of the general and specialised control administration, and the synchronous forms of joint control activity have been appropriately found, while maintaining the necessary operational independence. The methodology of the research is based on the traditional methods of legal and theoretical research - formal - legal, comparative - legal method, as well as the traditional methods of doctrine - induction, deduction, analysis, and synthesis.

INTRODUCTION

Outside the regulation at the level of the codified law, at the sub-legislative level the main act regulating the structure and competences of the Executive Agency "General Labour Inspectorate is its Rules of Procedure, adopted

DOI: 10.4018/978-1-6684-9067-9.ch004

by Decree of the Council of Ministers No. 2 of 13.01.2014, as its main administrative and organizational sub-legislative act.

According to the same, in organisational aspect the Agency is an independent legal entity on budgetary dependence to the Ministry of Labour and Social Policy. The Agency is organised in a general and specialised administration, structured in a Central Directorate and 28 territorial Labour Inspection Directorates, with a total staff of 492 full-time positions.

The headquarters comprises the directorates of the general administration, the Directorate General of Labour Inspection, the directorates of Legal Assurance of Inspection Activities and International Labour Migration and individual posts.

The specialised administration is organised in the Directorate for Legal Support for Inspection Activities, the Directorate for International Labour Migration, the Directorate General for Labour Inspection with 28 territorial units - Labour Inspection Directorates - located in the administrative centres of the districts.

In specificity and further development of the acts of higher legal force, it is provided that the Executive Agency "General Labour Inspectorate" shall carry out its activities by:

1. exercising comprehensive control over compliance with labour legislation in all sectors and activities;
2. exercise specialised control over compliance with the Occupational Health and Safety Act, the Employment Promotion Act, the Labour Migration and Labour Mobility Act, legislation relating to the performance of the civil service and the rights and obligations of the parties to the employment relationship and other regulations where this is mandated by law;
3. provide information and technical advice to employers and employees on the most effective methods of complying with labour legislation, legislation regulating occupational health and safety and other regulations the control of which is entrusted to the Agency by law;
4. exercise the right provided for in the Commerce Act to file a petition for the opening of insolvency proceedings against a trader where wage obligations to at least one-third of the trader's employees are due and unpaid for more than two months.

5. to notify the competent authorities of any incompleteness or deficiencies in the labour legislation in force.

The directorates operating within the general structure are also specified in the general and separate control activities established at a broad and comprehensive level within the general competence.

Thus, according to Article 15 of the Rules of Procedure, the Directorate General of Labour Inspection is established as a specialised intra-departmental body whose functions are to:

1. assist the Executive Director in the implementation of State policy relating to the functions of the Agency;
2. control, coordinate, analyse and summarise the activities of the territorial structures of the Agency - the Labour Inspection Directorates;
3. prepare an annual and long-term plan for the Agency's activities;
4. organize and be responsible for the activities related to the planning, implementation of the annual plan and accountability of the control activities carried out by the Labour Inspection Directorates;
5. provide leadership to the Labour Inspectorate Directorates in monitoring compliance with labour legislation, occupational health and safety, employment promotion, labour migration and labour mobility and legislation related to the performance of the civil service;
6. summarize and analyze information on the status and problems in the control of labor legislation, occupational health and safety, employment promotion, labor migration and labor mobility and legislation related to the implementation of the civil service;
7. prepare the annual report on the Agency's activities;
8. organise the Agency's permitting activities in the field of ensuring occupational health and safety in blasting;
9. give opinions in the development of draft regulations in the field of labour inspection;
10. give opinions in the development of guidelines, procedures and rules for inspection in the field of occupational health and safety;
11. liaise with other state bodies and cooperate with the social partners on matters relating to labour inspection;
12. assist and supervise the activities of the Labour Inspectorate Directorates related to establishing the causes of accidents;
13. liaise with the National Insurance Institute in the analysis of occupational injuries and occupational diseases;

14. carry out controls throughout the country on compliance with the labour legislation, the Law on Health and Safety at Work, the Law on Employment Promotion, the Law on Labour Migration and Labour Mobility, the legislation related to the performance of the civil service, and the rights and obligations of the parties to the employment relationship, and other regulatory acts, when the control is assigned by law;
15. responds to requests and inquiries from natural and legal persons on matters related to compliance with labour legislation, occupational health and safety, civil service and employment promotion;
16. carry out inspections in enterprises and industries at risk according to a list approved by the Executive Director;
17. provide information and technical advice to employers and employees on the most effective methods of complying with labour legislation, occupational health and safety legislation, legislation relating to the performance of public service and the rights and obligations of parties to the employment relationship and on the implementation of the Employment Promotion Act and the Labour Migration and Labour Mobility Act;
18. collect, summarise and provide information on the implementation in the Republic of Bulgaria of the European Union legal acts in the field of compliance with labour legislation, civil service and employment promotion;
19. at the request of the Directorate for Legal Assurance of Inspection Activities, prepare opinions on contested compulsory administrative measures to remedy violations of the regulatory requirements of the labour legislation, the civil service and the legislation on employment promotion;
20. give instructions and supervise the implementation of the programmes and measures specified in the Agency's annual activity plan in the field of compliance with labour legislation, the civil service and employment promotion.

At the same time, the Directorate for International Labour Migration performs direct functions of specialised control within the general framework. According to Article 14 of the Rules of Procedure, the main functions of the Directorate, specialised and detailed in its respective portfolio, are as follows:

1. to develop procedures and rules for the implementation of specialised control over compliance with the Employment Promotion Act, the Labour

Migration and Labour Mobility Act, other normative acts in the field of employment, as well as labour legislation in relation to the posting of employees in the framework of the provision of services in the territory of other countries;

2. to give methodological instructions in connection with the implementation of the programmes and/or measures set out in the Agency's annual activity plan in the field of specialised control of compliance with the Employment Promotion Act, the Labour Migration and Labour Mobility Act, other statutory acts in the field of employment, as well as labour legislation in connection with the posting of employees in the framework of the provision of services in the territory of other countries;
3. to give opinions and resolve requests, inquiries and signals received by the Agency in connection with the implementation of specialised control over compliance with the Employment Promotion Act, the Labour Migration and Labour Mobility Act, other normative acts in the field of employment, as well as labour legislation related to the posting of employees in the framework of the provision of services on the territory of other countries;
4. to exchange information with competent authorities, including those of other countries, on the legislation on the recruitment/employment of foreigners and on established violations of the conditions and procedures for recruitment/employment, including cases of illegal employment of Bulgarian citizens on the territory of the country concerned and of foreign citizens on the territory of the Republic of Bulgaria (Dimitrova, 2020, pp. 270-277).

On the other hand, this structure provides methodological guidance to the Labour Inspectorate Directorates in the exercise of specialised control over compliance with the Employment Promotion Act, the Labour Migration and Labour Mobility Act, other regulations in the field of employment, as well as labour legislation in relation to the posting of employees in the framework of the provision of services in the territory of other countries, and itself, upon assignment by the Executive Director, carries out control over compliance with labour legislation, occupational health and safety, the Employment Promotion Act, the Labour Migration and Labour Mobility Act and legislation relating to the performance of public service.

The Directorate of International Labour Migration also has direct standard-setting competences related to its functions of developing, implementing and monitoring compliance with rules and principles in the exercise of the right to work. In this context, it is envisaged that it will be involved in the drafting of regulations relating to the exercise of specialised control over compliance with the Employment Promotion Act, the Labour Migration and Labour Mobility Act, other employment regulations and labour legislation relating to the posting of employees in the framework of the provision of services in the territory of other countries, and that it will participate with its representatives in the preparation of opinions on draft regulations and other legislation related to the exercise of specialised control over compliance with the Employment Promotion Act, the Labour Migration and Labour Mobility Act, other regulatory acts in the field of employment, as well as labour legislation in relation to the posting of employees in the framework of the provision of services on the territory of other countries.

At the same time, the Directorate collects, summarises and provides information on the implementation in the Republic of Bulgaria of European Union legislation in the field of free movement of persons, as well as on the posting of workers in the framework of the provision of services and temporary work.

Territorial subdivisions of the General Directorate of Labour Inspection are the Labour Inspection Directorates, carrying out their activities on the territory of the respective region, exercising comprehensive control over compliance with labour legislation in all sectors and activities, exercising specialised control over compliance with the Occupational Health and Safety Act, the Employment Promotion Act, legislation related to the performance of civil service, and the rights and obligations of the parties to the employment relationship and otherregulations where mandated by law, provide information and technical advice to employers and employees on the most effective methods of complying with labour laws, of the legislation regulating occupational health and safety, resolve requests, signals and inquiries of individuals and legal entities, prepare and provide analyses on occupational traumatism and compliance with the regulatory acts, the control of which is assigned to the Agency, collect, summarize and provide information on the implementation in the Republic of Bulgaria of the regulatory acts of the European Union in the field of occupational health and safety, labour relations and employment promotion.

The Regulations provide for planned and unplanned inspections as the two main forms of work and control of the Labour Inspection Departments. According to Art. 18, par. 1 and Article 19, planned inspection is carried out in accordance with the annual activity plans of the directorates in the implementation of the programmes and measures set out in the annual activity plan of the Agency.

Unscheduled inspections are carried out both at the initiative of the Executive Director, the directors of the directorates of the specialized administration, and at the discretion of the inspectors, and at the initiative of entities external to the structure - at the order of the Minister of Labour and Social Policy, at the order of the court, of the authorities of the prosecutor's office and of the authorities conducting pre-trial criminal proceedings, at the requests and signals of employees under labour law, of organizations of employees, as well as in connection with information from the mass media, requests and signals from the appointing authorities, heads of inspectorates in administrative structures and trade unions or complaints from civil servants, as well as to establish the causes of accidents occurring in the course of and in connection with work.

In fulfillment of the competences and in case of detected violations, it is envisaged, in further development of the general but specified framework of the Labour Code (Article 21, paragraph 4), that the inspectors apply the coercive administrative measures provided for in the relevant normative acts (Dimitrova, 2022, pp. 59-66), issue a decree under Article 405a of the Labour Code declaring the existence of an employment relationship, draw up an administrative violation act and initiate administrative punishment proceedings, as well as to give verbal orders in cases of established administrative infringements that can be corrected in the course of the inspection.

The dynamics of the development of labour relations and the related need to rethink the functions of control and the need to extend their comprehensiveness and detail make it necessary to rethink the structuring of the activity. In this sense is also the Draft of the new Structural Regulations of the Executive Agency "General Labour Inspectorate" (23.06.2022).

The main objective of the proposed project is to ensure better efficiency in the implementation of the control activities of the Executive Agency "General Labour Inspectorate" and to optimize the work processes by refining the functions of the directorates, improving the coordination between the different structural units and increasing the administrative capacity in the implementation of the control activities of the Agency.

The draft proposes a new structure of directorates both in the general and in the specialized administration of the Labour Inspectorate by creating seven General Directorates of the Labour Inspectorate with fourteen Territorial Directorates of the Labour Inspectorate, which will carry out the control functions of the agency on the ground. By structuring them on a territorial basis, in accordance with the administrative-territorial division of the country, the quality of work, management and coordination of control activities in each region is expected to improve.

The Directorates-General are to coordinate, plan, analyse and report on the results of control activities and will propose measures to improve them.

With the creation of the Directorates-General of Labour Inspection, their respective directors will be given the necessary operational autonomy to better manage the directorates and the possibility for the directors-general of the territorial directorates to take independent decisions within the framework of the powers conferred on them, tailored to the specific characteristics of each area, which is expected to improve the quality of work.

According to the Draft, the envisaged Directorates General are responsible for:

1. exercise overall control over compliance with labour legislation in all sectors and activities;
2. to exercise specialised control over compliance with the Occupational Health and Safety Act, the Employment Promotion Act, the Labour Migration and Labour Mobility Act, legislation relating to the performance of the civil service and the rights and obligations of the parties to the employment relationship, and other regulations the control of which is entrusted to the Agency by law;
3. carry out inspections in enterprises and industries at risk according to a list approved by the Executive Director;
4. provide information, advice and technical advice to employers and employees on compliance with labour legislation, legislation regulating occupational health and safety;
5. resolve requests and signals within their competence and prepare answers to inquiries of natural and legal persons in connection with the control exercised by the Agency;
6. annually examine, summarize and report to the Secretary General of the Agency on the identified gaps, deficiencies or problems in the implementation of the legislation and in relation to the implementation of the control activities, and make a proposal for their elimination;
7. prepare plans, reports, information and an annual report on their activities, on the basis of which they shall submit proposals for programmes and measures to be included in the Agency's annual and long-term plans;
8. prepare and provide analyses on occupational traumatism and compliance with the legal acts regulating occupational health and safety;
9. collect, summarise and provide information on the implementation in the Republic of Bulgaria of the European Union legal acts in the field

of occupational health and safety, labour relations, labour migration and labour mobility and employment promotion;

10. record Collective Bargaining Agreements at the enterprise level in the Register of Collective Bargaining Agreements in the relevant Directorate and in the Agency's automated information system.

As opposed to the current structural regulations, the draft proposes that the directorates of the specialised administration exercise comprehensive control over compliance with labour legislation in all sectors and activities and specialised control over compliance with the Occupational Health and Safety Act, the Employment Promotion Act, the Labour Migration and Labour Mobility Act, legislation related to the performance of the civil service and the rights and obligations of the parties to the employment relationship, and other statutory provisions.

The specialised administration under the project is planned to be organised, in addition to the already established directorates, in a Directorate for Occupational Safety and Health and a Directorate for Labour, Labour Relations and Combating Undeclared Work, with specific functions and competences, easing on the one hand the administrative burden and the performance of functions, and on the other - contributing to specificity in prevention and control.

Thus, the Occupational Safety and Health Directorate to be established is given the competence to:

1. develop methodological guidelines, procedures and rules, and provide methodological guidance to the Directorates-General in their supervision of compliance with legislation regulating occupational health and safety, and, at the direction of the Executive Director, of other legislation the supervision of which is entrusted to the Agency;
2. in cooperation with the Directorate for Control of Inspection Activities, develop methodological guidelines, procedures and rules for the implementation of administrative punishment activities and the enforcement of compulsory administrative measures in the field of legislation regulating occupational health and safety;
3. participate with its representatives in inter-ministerial working groups for the preparation of draft normative acts in the field of legislation regulating occupational health and safety, the control of which is exercised by the Agency;
4. give opinions on amendments and supplements to the legislation regulating occupational health and safety conditions, the control of which

is exercised by the Agency, and on the order of the Executive Director on other legal acts;

5. annually draw up an analytical report on its activities, on the basis of which it shall submit proposals for programmes and measures in the field of control of legislation regulating occupational health and safety to be included in the annual and long-term plans of the Agency. Participate in the preparation of the Agency's annual plan and annual activity report;
6. investigate, summarise and report to the Secretary-General any deficiencies, shortcomings or problems identified in the monitoring of the legislation governing occupational health and safety by the Directorates-General and make a proposal for their remedy;
7. collect, summarise and provide information on the implementation in the Republic of Bulgaria of European Union legislation in the field of occupational health and safety;
8. prepare answers, give opinions, information and consultations on received signals, requests and inquiries, in connection with the control of compliance with health and safety at work, as well as on other legal acts, upon the order of the Executive Director;
9. liaise with other public authorities and cooperate with social partners on matters related to occupational health and safety controls and related regulations;
10. assist the activities of the General Directorates relating to the identification of the causes and circumstances under which accidents at work occurred, in and on the occasion of work;
11. on the basis of the Agency's control activities, prepare an analysis of occupational injuries occurring at and on the occasion of work;
12. liaise with the National Insurance Institute in the analysis of occupational injuries and occupational morbidity.

According to Article 18 of the draft, the planned Directorate of Labour, Labour Relations and Combating Undeclared Work will have its respective, narrow aspects and sectoral functions to:

1. develop methodological guidelines, procedures and rules and provide methodological guidance to the Directorates-General in their supervision of labour relations, specialised supervision and the Disability Act, and, at the direction of the Executive Director, on other regulations the supervision of which is entrusted to the Agency;

2. together with the Directorate for Control of Inspection Activities, make proposals and participate in the development of methodological guidelines, procedures and rules for the implementation of administrative punishment activities and the application of compulsory administrative measures to control labour and employment relations;
3. participates with its representatives in interdepartmental working groups for the preparation of drafts of normative acts in the field of labour and service relations, and, if assigned by the Executive Director, other normative acts, the control of which is exercised by the Agency;
4. issue opinions in the amendment and supplementation of laws and regulations related to the control of employment relations and the control of the performance of the civil service and the rights and obligations of the parties to the employment relationship, and, upon the order of the Executive Director, on other regulations;
5. annually prepare an analytical report on its activities, on the basis of which it shall submit proposals for programmes and measures in the field of control of labour and service relations to be included in the annual and long-term plans of the Agency. Participate in the preparation of the Agency's annual plan and annual activity report;
6. investigate, summarise and report to the Secretary-General any deficiencies, incompleteness or problems identified in the monitoring by the Directorates-General of the employment relationship and the legislation relating to the performance of the civil service and the rights and obligations of the parties to the employment relationship and make a proposal for their remedy;
7. prepare answers, give opinions, information and advice on received signals, requests and inquiries, in connection with the control and on the most effective methods of compliance with the labour legislation and on the legislation related to the performance of the civil service and the rights and obligations of the parties to the service relationship, as well as on other regulations, upon the order of the Executive Director;
8. provide written or oral advice on compliance with labour legislation and legislation relating to the performance of the civil service and the rights and obligations of the parties to the service relationship, and, where assigned, on other legislation within the jurisdiction of the Agency;
9. carry out interaction with other state bodies and cooperation with social partners on issues related to the control in the field of labour relations and legislation related to the performance of the civil service and the rights and obligations of the parties to the employment

relationship, as well as on other legal acts, the control of which is entrusted to the Agency;

10. carry out activities related to the development and implementation of projects financed or co-financed by European Union funds, for which the Agency is a specific beneficiary, concerning the control and inspection activities of the Agency;
11. participate in the programming of Operational Programmes, in the part that is within the competence of the Agency;
12. organise the preparation of the documentation for participation in public procurement procedures for the approved projects concerning the control and inspection activities of the Agency, financed or co-financed by European Union funds;
13. participate, if necessary with a manager, coordinator or experts, in the management teams of the approved projects financed or co-financed by European Union funds, for which the Agency is a specific beneficiary;
14. shall organise the keeping of the documentation relating to public procurement procedures involving the expenditure of funds financed or co-financed by European Union funds;
15. prepare, within the appropriate time limits, all the required reports, turnover sheets and the accounting, within the required time limits, of all irregularities concerning projects financed or co-financed by European Union funds.

According to the Impact Assessment of the Project "such a scheme aims at an effective, impartial and efficient control, being also an anti-corruption measure, as the proposed model will ensure two main levers - a strong central authority on the one hand, and balanced by a strong local authority on the other, which will interact in steering the work processes in the right direction."

The stated expected results following the amendment of the Agency's Rules of Procedure are more effective implementation of control activities and better prevention in relation to the administrative penalties provided for violations of labour legislation, increased collection of fines and financial penalties for violations of labour legislation, improved functioning of the labour market and general protection of workers, including through better prevention of repeated and systematic violations related to undeclared work.

Moreover, the change aims to optimize the administrative capacity by increasing the effectiveness and efficiency in the work of the territorial units, as the allocation of the inspection staff is expected to improve the efficiency of the control of the implementation and compliance with labour legislation.

Stressing that one of the main priorities of the administration, and in particular of the EA GIT, is to increase the control and the imposition of financial penalties or fines when violations related to undeclared work are detected, it is rightly justified that the draft of the new Rules of Procedure proposes measures to increase control, which is aimed at both increasing controls and prevention in this area.

At the same time, by increasing the expertise of the Agency, the implementation of preventive controls is expected to improve. A special provision is foreseen in the 2022 State Budget Act to increase the Agency's staffing by up to 200 staff to perform additional assigned functions as a key mechanism to strengthen the Agency's capacity and minimise the risk of non-performance of assigned functions.

The proposed changes are a sensible and timely legislative approach, aimed on the one hand at detailing the functions of control activities, and on the other - aimed at strengthening the control effects and means in more closely regulated aspects and their respective spheres, allowing for a regular, continuous and above all - qualitative and preventive control mechanism - on a wider range of objects of control and with increased operational and administrative capacity.

REFERENCES

Chastichna predvaritelna otsenka na vazdeystvieto. (n.d.). Public Consultants. https://www.strategy.bg/PublicConsultations/View.aspx?lang=bg-BG&Id=6918

Dimitrova, D. (2020). *Sivata ikonomika – aktualni merki za protivodeystvie v KT. Pravoto i biznesat v savremennoto obshtestvo: Sbornik s dokladi ot 3-ta Natsionalna nauchna konferentsiya*. Varna, Nauka i ikonomika.

Dimitrova, D. (2022). Vidove prinuditelni administrativni merki po chl. 404, al. 1 ot Kodeksa na truda. *Trud i pravo, 31*, 59-66.

Doklad otnosno Proekt na Postanovlenie na Ministerskia savet za priemane na Ustroystven pravilnik na Izpalnitelna agentsia. (n.d.). Public Consultants. https://www.strategy.bg/PublicConsultations/View.aspx?lang=bg-BG&Id=6918

Proekt na Ustroystven pravilnik na izpalnitelna agentsia. (n.d.). Public Consultants. https://www.strategy.bg/PublicConsultations/View.aspx?lang=bg-BG&Id=6918

Chapter 5
Specifics of Administrative Control for Compliance With Labour Legislation

Darina Dimitrova
University of Economics, Varna, Bulgaria

ABSTRACT

The scientific objective of this chapter is to examine the national legislation on the control of compliance with labour rights, as well as to examine the new moments in the legal regulation on the transposition of European norms in the field of control of compliance with labour legislation in Bulgaria. As a result of the current regulatory analysis, conclusions and generalizations are drawn on the applicable legal framework concerning the control of compliance with labour legislation. The scientific aim of this chapter is to examine the national legislation on the control of compliance with labour rights, as well as to consider the new moments in the legal regulation on the transposition of European norms in the field of control of compliance with labour legislation in Bulgaria.

INTRODUCTION

Monitoring compliance with labour legislation is a specific part of the state's management activities, carried out by specialised bodies within the executive power system. The purpose of this control activity is to ensure the

DOI: 10.4018/978-1-6684-9067-9.ch005

lawful development of labour relations, which is only possible if the labour legislation is actually applied and strictly observed.

The scientific aim of this paper is to examine the national legislation on the control of compliance with labour rights, as well as to consider the new moments in the legal regulation on the transposition of European norms in the field of control of compliance with labour legislation in Bulgaria.

The study is structured in three parts. § 3.1 examines the nature of the control powers of the Executive Agency "General Labour Inspectorate". § 3.2 discusses the legal means for exercising control over compliance with labour legislation, analysing in detail the types of compulsory administrative measures under Art. 404 (1) of the Labour Code. § 3.3 highlights current legislative trends in the area of monitoring compliance with labour rights following Bulgaria's accession to the European Union.

As a result of the conducted research, conclusions, summaries and recommendations are made on the applicable legislation concerning the issues under consideration. The practical necessity of the analysis of the control for the observance of the labour rights stems from the main objective of this control activity - namely, ensuring the lawful development of the labour relations, which is possible only with the real application and strict observance of the labour legislation. The topicality of the topic is determined by the importance of the issues concerning the legal framework for the observance of labour rights in accordance with the commitments arising from Bulgaria's membership in the European Union. Inductive, deductive and descriptive-analytical methods of generalization were applied in the course of the study.

This study was developed in the framework of the author's participation in a national scientific project for applied research N°43/2020 on "Legal and economic aspects of state control over compliance with labor legislation". Implementing organization of the research project is University of Economics - Varna.

Control Powers of the Executive Agency "General Labour Inspectorate": Types and Practice

The right to work, understood in the sense of rights arising from the performance of work, is a fundamental human right. Labour is a high constitutional value, therefore its guarantee and protection are included in the basic principles of the current Constitution - Article 16 and Article 48. At the same time, the obligation of States to take appropriate measures to protect this right is enshrined in a number of international instruments (International Covenant on Economic, Social and Cultural Rights, Treaty on European Union, Treaty on the Functioning of the European Union, Charter of Fundamental Rights of the European Union).

The constitutional right to work is a social right. Through them, the legislator creates conditions for satisfying both material and spiritual needs of citizens (Stoychev, 2002, p. 232, p. 263). But social rights are not only public goods of a material or spiritual nature, they are also an expression of the ethical and moral values of society. They are part of the individual's rights, dignity and security (Mrachkov, 2020, p. 40), especially in the current period when globalisation processes give rise to many fears of job losses and social injustice (Blagoycheva, 2019; Blagoycheva, 2020). Therefore, each State is responsible for respecting the labour rights of its citizens both at the national level and within international institutions.

Administrative control of compliance with labour legislation has been studied in a number of publications (Danailov, 1987; Mrachkov, 1985; Andreeva & Yolova, 2009; Andreeva & Yolova, 2011; Andreeva & Dimitrova, 2019; Dimitrova, 2020; Bogomilova, 2016; Aleksandrov, 2016; Andreeva & Yolova, 2018; Koev, 2011). The importance of the right to work as a fundamental constitutional social right and the means of its protection have been relevant in all historical periods of the development of our national legal system. However, at the present moment the issue at hand has a new relevance given the changed social reality of precarious work in the context of digitalization, where employers have expanded their employer power despite the lack of such regulation at the legal level (Andreeva & Yolova, 2020a; Andreeva, 2020; Andreeva & Yolova, 2020b). The pandemic situation and the measures taken to preserve public health have changed the rules of labour law, giving other priorities (Andreeva & Yolova, 2020c; Andreeva, 2019). This implies increased administrative control by the state to ensure that employees' labour rights are respected and that employers do not act arbitrarily.

Our country has its own traditions both in regulating the right to work as a constitutional social right and in monitoring compliance with labour rights. In spite of the many legislative changes during the various historical and socio-political periods since the restoration of the Bulgarian state in 1878 until today, our country has adhered to its international obligations to respect fundamental social rights - such as the right to work (Dimitrova, 2021).

The regulatory framework sets the framework within which public relations develop in every sphere, including in the area of administrative control over compliance with labour legislation. The protection of the right to work requires the active influence of the State with appropriate regulation, given that employees are the weaker party in the employment relationship due to their subordinate position vis-à-vis the employer and the working arrangements established by the employer (Dimitrova, 2020).

Administrative control is one of the main forms of administrative protection of the right to work, regulated in the Bulgarian legislation. The other form of administrative remedy is administrative criminal liability (Andreeva & Yolova, 2008a; Andreeva & Yolova, 2019). In the realization of fundamental constitutional rights, administrative legal relations most often arise, and acts that violate constitutional rights are in most cases administrative violations (Hristoforov, 1966, p. 150).

The specificity of the legal regulation concerning the control of compliance with labour legislation is determined by the sources of labour law as the main branch of our national legal system. In Bulgaria, the sources of labour law are characterized by diversity both in terms of their legal force (given the subordination of legal acts) and in terms of the subjects who have the right to issue acts - sources of this branch of law (Andreeva & Yolova, 2020d, p. 19).

Among the national sources in the field of labour law, the main place is occupied by the laws that regulate in detail the labour relations, the basic labour rights of employees, as well as the control by the state of compliance with the labour legislation. Among the legal acts, the purpose of which is directly aimed at regulating the state control over the observance of the rights arising from employment, the following should be mentioned: the Labour Code, the Occupational Health and Safety Act, the Labour Inspection Act, the Labour Migration and Labour Mobility Act, the Employment Promotion Act.

Of the aforementioned normative acts, the Labour Code can be defined as the most significant source of labour law in Bulgaria because it regulates essentially a wide range of issues. Since its adoption in 1986, it has undergone dozens of amendments and additions, including with regard to the regulations concerning the monitoring of compliance with labour legislation.

Control over compliance with labour legislation is a specific administrative activity of bodies in the executive power system aimed at ensuring the lawful development of labour relations. Administrative control is an important means of ensuring compliance with the legal regulation of labour relations and the rights arising therefrom. It is a legal guarantee for the real realization of the basic rights of employees - to healthy and safe working conditions, to wages, to rest and holidays.

Control over compliance with labour legislation is exercised by the bodies of various state administrations, whose activities are regulated in other legal acts besides the Labour Code. For example, under Article 5(2) of the

Labour Inspection Act: Labor inspections shall be conducted by inspectors, public officials and/or other authorized persons in: 1. The Executive Agency "General Labour Inspectorate"; 2. The State Agency for Metrological and Technical Supervision; 3. The Nuclear Regulatory Agency; 4. The Directorate for National Building Control to the Minister of Regional Development and Public Works; 5. General Directorate "Fire Safety and Population Protection" of the Ministry of Interior; 6. regional directorates "Agriculture", which perform functions under the Law on Registration and Control of Agricultural and Forestry Machinery; 7. Ministry of Energy; 8. Ministry of Transport; 9. Ministry of Environment and Water; 10. Ministry of Defence; 11. Ministry of Health; 12. National Revenue Agency; 13. National Insurance Institute; 14. other administrations entrusted by a normative act to carry out activities under the Labour Inspection, which in turn includes the control of compliance with labour and social security legislation and specialised control under the Employment Promotion Act and the Occupational Health and Safety Act.

A key place among them is occupied by the Executive Agency "General Labour Inspectorate" under the Minister of Labour and Social Policy, which carries out comprehensive control over the implementation of and compliance with labour legislation (Art. 399, para. 1 of the Labour Code). The Agency is a department without the rank of a ministry (but within the system of the executive power), and its Executive Director is an executive authority by virtue of Article 19(4)(3) of the Law on Administration. The structure, composition, functions and activities of the Executive Agency "General Labour Inspectorate" shall be governed by the Rules of Procedure adopted by a decree of the Council of Ministers (State Gazette No.6 of 21 January 2014). The Agency is structured into a Head Office and 28 territorial directorates, and the Executive Director is given the power to delegate to the directors of the relevant directorates, or to Agency staff, individual powers in accordance with the regulations. In this sense, the bodies competent to control compliance with labour legislation are the directors of the territorial directorates or the employees (inspectors) of the Agency who have been granted control powers by order of the Executive Director of the Executive Agency "General Labour Inspectorate". Pursuant to Article 21, paragraph 2 of the Regulations of the Executive Agency "General Labour Inspectorate": The powers of an inspector shall be vested in the heads of administrative units in the specialised administration, employees appointed to the post of inspector, legal advisers, and other employees of the Agency appointed to expert posts who are expressly authorised by the Executive Directo.

The control exercised by the bodies of the Executive Agency "General Labour Inspectorate" is a specialized external control for compliance with labour legislation (Mrachkov, 2018, p. 945, p. 948). The administrative control in question is extra-departmental, given that the controlled entities (employers or appointing authorities) are not hierarchically subordinate to the control authorities (Dermendzhiev, Kostov & Hrusanov, 2010, p. 265). As this activity is exercised on a special basis - the provisions of the Labour Code, it is also defined as specialised external control. It is characterised by the fact that it covers only individual areas of activity of the controlled. Specialised control is always based on explicit statutory empowerment, where a specific statutory instrument must strictly and exhaustively define: by whom control is exercised; over whom; on what activities and directions; by what methods control is exercised; what are the legal means of influence (Lazarov, 2000, pp. 213 – 215).

The General Labour Inspectorate Executive Agency is a specialised inspection body established and functioning in accordance with ILO Convention No. 81 concerning Labour Inspection. This control shall be exercised alone or in conjunction with other public administrations and with the assistance of employees' and employers' organisations. The activities of the Executive Agency "General Labour Inspectorate" are traditionally based on prevention and publicity in labour inspection, cooperation with institutions, social partners and NGOs. The Agency supports the activities of tripartite councils on working conditions at national, regional and branch level and the activities of committees/groups on working conditions in enterprises[1].

Prepared by the author (Source: Annual reports of the Executive Agency "General Labour Inspectorate" for 2017, 2018, 2019, 2020, 2021.; available at: https://www.gli.government.bg/bg)

There are two main reasons for the lack of data from the last two years on inspections carried out with the participation of trade unions and representatives of working conditions committees/groups: first, the challenge of the COVID-19 pandemic, and second, the creation of formal barriers to employer participation in inspections of representatives of working conditions committees/groups [2]. But despite the difficulties and challenges, these data show that the intervention of labour inspectors, as well as the implemented cooperation with institutions, social partners and NGOs, generally lead to an improvement of working conditions, which is an indication of the high degree of effectiveness of the inspection activity.

The powers of the inspectors of the Executive Agency "General Labour Inspectorate", through which the control of compliance with the labour

Table 1. Cooperation in labour inspection

Year	Total number of checks carried out	Joint inspections with representatives of other state bodies - the Ministry of Interior, the National Insurance Institute, the National Revenue Agency and the Regional Health Inspectorates	Checks involving trade unions	Checks with representatives of working conditions committees/ groups	Follow-up - checks on the implementation of mandatory prescriptions
2017	45 645 pcs.	1146 pcs.	189 pcs.	1964 pcs.	85% of the inspected prescriptions have been implemented
2018	43 958 pcs.	875 pcs.	150 pcs.	2625 pcs.	97% of the inspected prescriptions have been implemented
2019	40 216 pcs.	1074 pcs.	112 pcs.	1779 pcs.	98% of the inspected prescriptions have been implemented
2020	37 145 pcs.	1721 pcs.	No data	No data	98.3% of the inspected prescriptions have been implemented
2021	40 788 pcs.	1367 pcs.	No data	No data	98.9% of the inspected prescriptions have been implemented

legislation is implemented, are regulated in Article 402 and Article 403 of the Labour Code. The powers include both the rights and obligations of the competent public authorities (Dimitrova, 2010, p. 103), in this case the control bodies of the Executive Agency "General Labour Inspectorate". The supervisory authorities have a number of rights regulated in Art. 402, para. 1, points 1 to 5of the Labour Code.

- **Right of access** – this includes the right of inspectors at any time to visit places where work is being carried out, premises used by employees and to require persons present to produce identification. This language means that there is no legal impediment to the visit taking place outside working hours. The right to require persons on the premises to produce proof of identity makes it possible to establish whether they are employees and whether they have duly concluded employment contracts;

- **Right to request the necessary information** – the supervisory authorities shall have the right to require from the employer (respectively the appointing authority) explanations, information and the submission of necessary documents, papers and certified copies thereof in connection with the supervision exercised. This allows the rapid gathering of facts and evidence on compliance with employment law;
- **Right to information by employees** – consist of directly informing employees through discussions with them on all matters relating to the exercise of control, and requiring them to declare in writing facts and circumstances relating to the employment activity carried out, including information on wages. This makes it possible to collect data on the correspondence between the payroll charged and the wages actually paid;
- **Right to take samples and specimens for testing** – means that controllers can not only take samples, specimens and consumables (e.g. from manufactured products), but also make them available to licensed laboratories for analysis. This right shall be exercised by the control authorities in the case of the need for high-quality laboratory tests. Technical means and apparatus may also be used and measurements made of various factors (chemical, physical) of the working environment in connection with the exercise of control over the work activity carried out;
- **The right to establish the causes and circumstances of accidents at work** – in this case, the supervisory authorities, within the limits of their competence, have the right to investigate and establish the specific causes and circumstances in which accidents at work occurred (e.g. by carrying out an inspection of stockpiled equipment, collecting written documents on current health and safety rules, requesting written explanations from workers and responsible officials). This right covers clarification of the specific facts and circumstances under which the accident occurred, i.e. not only whether there is an injury, but also whether it is directly related to factors of the work environment (Shirvanyan, 2021, pp. 106 – 107).

Corresponding to the abovementioned powers of the administrative bodies having functions in the field of control over compliance with labour legislation are the obligations laid down in Article 402(2) of the Labour

Code to provide assistance on the part of employers or appointing authorities, officials, workers and employees.

Accordingly, when carrying out checks on compliance with labour legislation, the supervisory authorities also have the following obligations (Art. 403, para. 1, items 1 and 2 of the Labour Code):

- **Obligation of professional secrecy** - the inspection bodies must keep confidential any confidential information about the employer that has come to their knowledge during the inspection in connection with the inspection. Inspectors of the Executive Agency "General Labour Inspectorate" are also obliged not to use this information in their business activities. This prohibition logically applies to the period after the cessation of the control functions of the person concerned, since inspectors should not have and carry on business during the time they exercise such functions;
- **Obligation to keep the source of the signal secret** - supervisory authorities must keep confidential the source from which they have received a report of a breach of labour law. The purpose of this obligation is to build trust in supervisory authorities and to protect employees from possible employer sanctions – for example disciplinary action or even dismissal.

Control bodies shall exercise their powers in cooperation with both employers and employees (Art. 402, para. 5 of the Labour Code). This stems from the principle of cooperation between those involved in the process of monitoring compliance with labour legislation, since labour is a significant social good and its protection is important for the whole of society.

The purpose of the control measures applied is not only to protect the labour rights of employees, but also to ensure free and fair competition between employers. Knowledge and correct application of labour legislation contributes to the protection of workers' rights and the improvement of working conditions in enterprises[3].

In addition to exercising control over compliance with labour legislation and imposing penalties for its violation within the national state, the Executive Agency "General Labour Inspectorate" also has functions to carry out administrative cooperation through the Internal Market Information System with the competent authorities of the Member States of the European Union (Art. 417, para. 1 of the Labour Code). Thus, in 2016, a new Chapter Twenty was created in the Labour Code to implement Chapters Three and Six of

Directive 2014/67/EU "Administrative cooperation through the Internal Market Information System and cross-border enforcement of financial administrative sanctions and fines, including fees and charges".

Pursuant to Article 417, paragraphs 2 and 3 of the Labour Code, as the main body exercising control over compliance with labour legislation, the Executive Agency "General Labour Inspectorate" is competent to receive and send through the Internal Market Information System requests for:

- for collection of public claims under Art. 162, para. 7 of the Tax-insurance Procedure Code;
- for the collection of claims for financial penalties or fines imposed for breaches of labour legislation relating to the posting and dispatching of employees in the framework of the provision of services, the performance of which cannot take place in the territory of Bulgaria.

The types of administrative cooperation, including the sending and receiving of documents through the Internal Market Information System, with the competent authorities of other countries and the time limits within which it shall take place are regulated (Art. 418 of the Labour Code). It also regulates the execution of valid acts sent with a request for collection through the Internal Market Information System, by which the competent authorities of another Member State of the European Union impose financial administrative sanctions or fines on Bulgarian employers for violation of labour legislation concerning the posting or sending of employees (Art. 419, para. 1 of the Labour Code).

The administrative control provided for under the Labour Code has mainly a preventive and deterrent purpose. In this way, on the one hand, employees are protected and, on the other hand, fair competition between undertakings is ensured, which supports the functioning of the labour market. Therefore, although under the Bulgarian legal system labour law is a private law branch, its norms have a protective role and intensive administrative law protection of fundamental labour rights is provided for.

Thus, the Labour Code, as the main normative act in the field of labour legislation, regulates the control activity for compliance with the legal regulation of labour relations. The specialized legal literature emphasizes that if compliance with labour legislation is not monitored and penalties are not imposed for its violation, the addressees of these norms would perceive them as "wishful" (Aleksandrov, 2016). The administrative control provided for in the labour legislation is therefore of great practical importance.

This stems from the particularities of the employment relationship. On the one hand, these are legal relations between equal entities which arise on the occasion of the concluded employment contract. On the other hand, in the employment relationship, the employee has traditionally been perceived as the weaker party. Which is an argument for ensuring respect for labour rights through public law remedies.

The administrative protection of the right to work aims to increase the level of protection of the economic interests and social rights of employees. In this sense, labour legislation must correspond to modern economic conditions and the level of industrial relations in the country, in order to guarantee the rights and interests of the parties to the employment relationship. It is therefore necessary to develop national labour law legislation in line with European Union law and ILO standards.

The reasons for the amendments to the Labour Code of 2020 (State Gazette, No. 109 of 22 December 2020) are that the analysis of the regulatory framework has identified the need to improve and enhance the quality of control and sanction activities in order to ensure the proper implementation of the obligations arising from the labour legislation[4]. In this regard, specific proposals have been adopted to improve the possibilities for effective control activities and provide for sanctions for non-cooperation or non-compliance with obligations arising from coercive administrative measures, which are currently not fully guaranteed.

CONCLUSION

As a result of the analysis of the control powers of the Executive Agency "General Labour Inspectorate" the following conclusions and generalizations can be made regarding the applicable legislation concerning the issues under consideration:

First, the provision of labour in the modern context requires the creation of normative guarantees to respect the rights arising from the provision of labour. The current legal framework must define the limits within which countervailing rights and obligations under the employment relationship can be realised in the context of an employee's dependent position on the employer. The regulation of the right to work, including its constitutional recognition as a fundamental right, demonstrates its function and importance for society and the individual;

Second, the administrative control of the Executive Agency "General Labour Inspectorate" performs an important social function in relation to employees and at the same time has a disciplinary function against unfair and unscrupulous employers (Andreeva & Dimitrova, 2019). These two functions of the administrative control of compliance with the labour legislation justify the positive assessment of the legal framework under study;

Thirdly, the protection of the right to work requires the continued active influence of the state through the updating of relevant legislation. Modern societal conditions pose new challenges to the legislator, requiring administrative law protection of fundamental labour rights. In this sense, the administrative control and administrative criminal liability provided for in the labour legislation are of great practical importance. The amendments to the Labour Code aim at more effective implementation of control activities and better prevention in relation to the provided administrative sanctions for violation of labour legislation. This demonstrates once again the role and importance of administrative law protection in ensuring the appropriate level of protection of the right to work.

Legal Means for Exercising Control Over Compliance With Labour Legislation: Nature and Types

The specifics of the control activities and powers of the Executive Agency "General Labour Inspectorate" have been studied in the legal literature (Andreeva & Dimitrova, 2019). Supervision is an important means of ensuring compliance with labour regulations. It is a legal guarantee for the realisation of the fundamental rights and obligations of the parties to the employment relationship.

Monitoring compliance with labour legislation is a specific part of the state's enforcement activity (Mrachkov, 2018, p. 945, p. 948; Mrachkov, Sredkova & Vasilev, 2016, p. 1148). In this sense, the control powers of the Executive Agency "General Labour Inspectorate" are essentially an administrative activity carried out by specialised state bodies, part of the executive power system. The purpose of this control activity is to ensure the lawful development of labour relations, which is only possible if labour legislation is actually applied.

The administrative control of the Executive Agency "General Labour Inspectorate" shall include the carrying out of inspections and the application of compulsory administrative measures by the control bodies. If, as a result of the control, violations of labour legislation are detected, the Labour Code provides for the imposition of administrative penalties, but administrative liability is not part of the control (Andreeva & Yolova, 2008a; Andreeva & Yolova 2008b). It is a well-established understanding in the legal doctrine that administrative punishment is not included in the control jurisdiction, but is a jurisdictional (judicial) activity (Balabanova, 2004, p. 79). Administrative liability for violations of labour legislation is a separate legal institute, therefore it is not considered in this study.

The specifics of the control of compliance with labour legislation are expressed in its characteristics as an administrative activity, in the powers of the control bodies, as well as in the means of influence on the controlled subjects. In view of the fact that the control exercised by the Executive Agency "General Labour Inspectorate" for compliance with the labour legislation is a specialised external administrative control (see the previous § 3.1), the question arises as to the legal means for influencing the controlled subjects. This means examining by what means this control is exercised. It is characteristic for the specialized administrative control (supervision) that these means are always explicitly defined by a special normative act, which specifies the specific means that may be applied by the controlling authorities (e.g. spot checks, requesting information and explanations, requesting references and other documents, etc.) (Lazarov, 2000, pp. 215 – 216; Dermendzhiev, Kostov & Hrusanov, 2010, p. 268).

The control activity of the Executive Agency "General Labour Inspectorate" includes two main legal means for influencing controlled employers or appointing authorities - carrying out inspections and imposing compulsory administrative measures. These remedies are included in the general term "labour inspection", the legal definition of which is given in § 1 of the Additional Provisions of the Labour Inspection Act. "Labour inspection" is an activity carried out by control bodies, primarily inspectors from the Executive Agency "General Labour Inspectorate", to establish and enforce compliance between the requirements of the legislation and its implementation in enterprises, establishments and places where labour activity is carried out or training is conducted.

According to this definition, inspection is an activity carried out by the control bodies to establish compliance between the requirements of labour legislation and its actual application in enterprises, establishments and places where wage labour is performed or labour activity takes place.

Comprehensive control of compliance with labour legislation is exercised by the Executive Agency "General Labour Inspectorate" and inspection activity is carried out by inspectors through inspections of the places where labour activity is carried out and through inspections of documents (Art. 399 of the Labour Code). Control shall be carried out at all places (enterprises, establishments, organizations, cooperatives, establishments, sites, etc.) where wage labour or labour activity is performed or training is conducted (Art. 2, para. 1 of the Occupational Health and Safety Act). In the field of compliance with health and safety at work, persons working on their own account or in partnership are also subject to control (Art. 1, para. 1 of the Occupational Health and Safety Act). Checks can be carried out both planned and unplanned (Article 17 of the Regulations of the Executive Agency "Main Labour Inspectorate").

The planned inspections shall be carried out in accordance with the annual activity plans of the territorial directorates in implementation of the programmes and measures defined in the annual activity plan of the Executive Agency "General Labour Inspectorate", which shall be approved by the Executive Director in consultation with the Minister of Labour and Social Policy (Art. 18, para. 1 and Art. 6, para. 2, item 1 of the Statutory Regulations of the Executive Agency "Main Labour Inspectorate"). The purpose of the planned inspections is to take into account the importance of a number of factors for compliance with labour legislation - territorial structure of the economy, degree of risk in enterprises, severity and type of labour law violations, level of occupational injuries and diseases (Article 18, paragraph 2 of the Rules of Procedure of the Executive Agency "General Labour Inspectorate").

The entities entitled to initiate unscheduled inspections are listed in Article 19 of the Regulations of the Executive Agency "General Labour Inspectorate" and can be divided into two main groups:

- **First,** by order of the competent state authorities having control functions over compliance with labour legislation, namely, the Minister of Labour and Social Policy; the Executive Director; directors of the directorates of the specialised administration; a court; prosecution authorities; authorities conducting pre-trial criminal proceedings; and other state authorities expressly designated by law;
- **Second,** at the requests and signals of workers in an employment or service relationship, as well as of their professional or trade union organizations - these are those persons in the employment relationship who provide their labor force to the employer in exchange for payment,

as well as the organizations protecting their labor rights (Rachev, Andreeva, Yolova & Vladova, 2008, pp. 26 – 27).

In some cases, where the inspection reveals that the employment relationship is being conducted lawfully, the inspection ends. In case of non-compliance with the requirements of the labour legislation, the control bodies shall apply the compulsory administrative measures specified in Art. 404(1) of the Labour Code. Pursuant to Article 21(4)(1) of the Rules of Procedure of the Main Labour Inspectorate Executive Agency: If a violation of the legislation is detected, the inspector shall apply compulsory administrative measures specified in the regulatory acts under which the Agency carries out control activities.

Coercive administrative measures are the main means of control to prevent and stop violations of labour legislation. The essence of compulsory administrative measures, their main features and types have been studied in our legal doctrine (Lazarov, pp. 15 – 235). This type of administrative coercion is not punitive in nature. Its application does not entail administrative criminal liability and does not impose any administrative penalty, since it does not create adverse legal consequences for its addressee and is not aimed at his correction and re-education.

It should be noted here, however, that insofar as compulsory administrative measures have been studied in legal doctrine, they have been considered too generally as one of the types of administrative coercion and only their general characteristics as an institute of administrative law have been clarified (Dermendzhiev, Kostov, & Hrusanov, pp. 362 – 370). There is a lack of in-depth independent research on coercive administrative measures to prevent and stop labour law violations. Insofar as some authors focus on the control of compliance with labour law, it is within the general issues of labour law (Mrachkov, pp. 955 – 968). In this sense, the study of compulsory administrative measures imposed by the labour inspectorate is unsatisfactory. Administrative coercion in labour law is distinguished by its own specificities, which need an independent analysis.

This administrative coercive measure constitutes an external psychological influence on its addressee. The immediate purpose of this impact is to stop the breach of employment law and to encourage the person concerned to voluntarily comply with his obligations arising from his status as employer or appointing authority.

By their legal nature, compulsory administrative measures constitute a set of actions and means of the competent control authorities. They are aimed, on the one hand, at preventing and stopping administrative infringements and, on the other hand, at preventing and eliminating the harmful consequences of these infringements (Article 22 of the Administrative Offences and Penalties Act). Unlike administrative penalties, which are imposed only for administrative offences, compulsory administrative measures may be applied both for offences committed and as a preventive measure where there is a direct and imminent risk of such offences. For the application of this measure it is sufficient that one of the legal facts referred to in the hypothesis of Art. 404(1) of the Labour Code. It is not necessary that the employer, by its acts or omissions, has culpably violated the provisions of employment law or has culpably failed to perform its obligations. In contrast, in order to impose an administrative penalty under a general rule, it is necessary that the act has been committed culpably, i.e. that there is not only the objective but also the subjective aspect of the relevant offence.

In view of the foregoing, coercive administrative measures for the prevention and cessation of violations of labour legislation are not a means of implementing the administrative responsibility of the employer or the appointing authority. They have a preventive effect. They protect not only the addressee (the employee) but also the object of the infringement (the right to work, i.e. the rights arising from the performance of the work). For these measures to apply, it is sufficient that the act is unlawful, as they apply without regard to fault.

Violations of the regulatory framework of labour relations may manifest themselves in various unlawful acts and affect a wide range of aspects of employees' subjective rights. This makes coercive administrative measures an effective means of preventing labour law violations.

The types of compulsory administrative measures for the prevention and termination of violations of labour legislation, as well as for the prevention and elimination of their harmful consequences, are regulated and exhaustively listed in Art. 404(1) of the Labour Code.

First of all, these are the compulsory instructions (Article 404(1)(1) of the Labour Code) given to employers, user enterprises under Article 107t of the Labour Code, appointing authorities and officials. They indicate the violation found and give a deadline for its elimination, i.e. this type of compulsory administrative measures aims at:

- rectification of labour law violations;
- remedying breaches of legislation relating to the civil service;
- ensuring the fulfilment of social and welfare obligations for employees;

- ensuring compliance with the obligations to inform and consult employees under both the Labour Code and the Act on Information and Consultation of Employees in Multinational Enterprises, Group Enterprises and European Companies;
- remedying deficiencies in the provision of health and safety at work.

Second is the suspension of the commissioning of buildings, machinery and equipment, industries and objects under Art. 404(1)(2) of the Labour Code. This measure may be imposed if the rules on health and safety at work and welfare are not complied with.

Next are the measures under Art. 404(1)(3) and (7) of the Labour Code - suspension of enterprises. The specialized literature states that this is the strongest in terms of its legal intensity compulsory administrative measure (Mrachkov, 2018, p. 958), which is applied in two cases:

- **first**, stopping the operation of enterprises, industries and sites, including their construction and reconstruction, as well as machinery, equipment and workplaces, when the rules for occupational health and safety are violated, endangering the life and health of people. In this case, a special sign shall be erected indicating the imposed compulsory administrative measure, and its unauthorised removal shall be subject to administrative liability;
- **second**, in the event of a repeated breach of the requirement that the employment contract be in writing (Art. 62, para. 1 of the Labour Code). In this case, the operation of the worksite or establishment shall be suspended until the violation is corrected. This coercive administrative measure exerts an authoritative influence on the employer to put an end to the continuing illegal practice of employing employees without concluding written employment contracts with them.

Another coercive administrative measure is the suspension of illegal decisions or orders of employers, appointing authorities and officials (Art. 404, para. 1, item 4 of the Labour Code). These may be orders or instructions from the employer or other officials. These may relate, for example, to the suspension of the employer's or appointing authority's decision concerning a notice of impending redundancy previously received as grounds for dismissal, the suspension of a dismissal order prior to its service and the like.

Removal from work of employees is a measure under Art. 404(1)(5) of the Labour Code, which is applied to individual employees when they are not familiar with the rules on occupational health and safety or do not possess the necessary legal capacity, as well as to employees under the age of 18 for whom the permit to accept work under Article 302(2) of the Labour Code has been withdrawn[5] and Art. 303, para. 3 of the Labour Code[6]. It does not matter whether this is due to the employer's omission or the employee's culpable conduct. With the imposition of this compulsory administrative measure, the employee must cease the performance of his/her work duties. This can be a temporary condition that lasts until the reasons are no longer relevant - for example, until the health and safety rules are known. But it may also be necessary to terminate the employment relationship with the employee - if he or she does not have the necessary legal capacity or professional qualifications. Case law holds that if the violation was committed by entering into an employment contract with an unauthorized person, then upon termination of the contract, the violation is remedied[7].

The next compulsory administrative measure is under Art. 404(1)(6) of the Labour Code. It consists in giving prescriptions for the introduction of a special regime for safe work in the event of a serious and imminent danger to the life and health of workers. This measure shall be resorted to in case of impossibility to apply the provision of Art. 404(1)(3) of the Labour Code, i.e. to suspend the activity of enterprises. This is done when it is technically impossible or difficult to stop the activity of the undertaking, and when it involves serious economic consequences[8]. The application of this measure seeks proportionality between the administrative coercion and the public utility of its introduction (Mrachkov, 2018, p. 961).

Among the compulsory administrative measures regulated in Art. 404 (1) of the Labour Code, the ones referred to in items 8 and 12 have a particularly important place, since they are related to the right to remuneration acquired through the exercise of one of the most important subjective rights - the right to work. Accordingly, the payment of wages in the amount agreed between the parties and within the prescribed time limits, as well as the manner of payment, is one of the most important obligations for the employer (Andreeva, 2018).

The compulsory administrative measures under Art. 404 (1)(8) of the Labour Code for the elimination of violations related to the payment of wages to employees during a valid employment relationship - namely charging on payroll a lesser amount than that paid to the employee for the work he or she has performed (Andreeva & Dimitrova, 2019). In cases where the control bodies of the Executive Agency "General Labour Inspectorate" establish the above-mentioned violation, they have the right to impose two types of compulsory administrative measures - compulsory prescriptions and suspension of the activity of the enterprise.

"Compulsory prescriptions" as a compulsory administrative measure are imposed when it is found that "an amount less than the amount paid by the employer or the appointing authority to the employee for the work performed by the employee has been charged to the payroll". This measure is intended to achieve identity between payroll and actual wages paid, in order to ensure full payment of social security contributions for the foreseen social security risks and cases calculated on actual wages. I.e. this compulsory administrative measure is directed against the so-called "payment in hand". In the hypothesis of Art. 404, par. 1, item 8, of the Labour Code, the control bodies of the Executive Agency "General Labour Inspectorate" may not issue mandatory prescriptions for the actual payment of partially paid or completely unpaid wages, but only for charging to the payroll the amounts due.

"Suspension of the activity of the undertaking until the infringement is eliminated" is the more severe compulsory administrative measure under Art. 404(1)(8) of the Labour Code. It is imposed in two cases - when the mandatory prescription is not complied with within the specified time limit or when the same violation is repeated (charging to the payroll less than the amount actually paid). In these cases, a more severe coercive measure is envisaged due to the greater social danger of the labour law violations committed.

In connection with the payment of wages are also the compulsory administrative measures under Art. 404, para. 1, item 12 of the Labour Code for the elimination of violations related to the payment of the remaining unpaid wages to employees, but where the employment relationship has already been terminated (Andreeva & Dimitrova, 2019). In these cases, the control bodies of the Executive Agency "General Labour Inspectorate" have the right to impose the compulsory administrative measure "compulsory prescriptions for the payment of unpaid wages after the termination of employment". The grounds for applying this measure are that the offences were committed at a time when the employment relationship existed but were established after its termination. Notwithstanding the fact that this legal provision is relatively new (adopted by the amendment of the Labour Code by State Gazette No. 102 of 2017), there is already significant case law on its application, the results of which are an indicator of the correctness and effectiveness of this legislative decision[9]. The compulsory administrative measure under Art. 404, para. 1, item 12 of the Labour Code was introduced and is imposed on employers by the need for priority and enhanced protection of the rights and interests of employees. The legislator has assessed the importance of the protected interest, which is dominant over the private interest[10].

The norm of Art. 404, para. 1, item 12 of the Labour Code, raises the question - is it permissible to resolve civil disputes (such as those under labour law) over payment of wages arising between the parties to the employment relationship by imposing compulsory administrative measures?[11].

After the democratic changes of 1989, our country moved from a planned to a market economy, from full state ownership to predominantly private ownership of the means of production. Socio-economic conditions have given rise to new legal institutions and legislative solutions to ensure that the legal framework meets public expectations (Andreeva, 2010; Andreeva, 2016). The 2017 amendments to the Labour Code are dictated by the public interest. Unthinkable a few decades ago, negative social phenomena and serious violations of labour law, such as non-payment of wages or charging payroll less than the amount actually paid, are now commonplace in society. Exactly the mass of such negative social phenomena are the motive for these legislative changes in the control activity of the Executive Agency "General Labour Inspectorate" and the expansion of the range of powers of its control bodies (Andreeva & Dimitrova, 2019).

According to the well-established practice of the Supreme Administrative Court, it is within the competence of the administrative authority (the Labour Inspection Directorate) to issue binding prescriptions concerning the payment of unpaid wages and benefits in connection with terminated employment relationships, as these are clearly not subject to civil law. In its reasoning, the court stated that this also constituted a breach of employment law[12].

Indeed, employment law is a private law branch and classical legal doctrine defines employment relations as private law relations between equal subjects, yet employees are the "weaker" party and need additional legal protection (Andreeva & Yolova, 2020d; Dimitrova, 2020). Considering the socio-economic conditions, a guarantee for the observance of basic subjective labour rights, such as the right to wages, are the enhanced control powers of the Executive Agency "General Labour Inspectorate" to impose coercive administrative measures in this regard.

In Art. 404, para. 1, item 9 of the Labour Code regulates a compulsory administrative measure consisting in giving compulsory prescriptions to employers, appointing authorities and officials to amend the employment contract concluded for part-time work into an employment contract with normal working hours. In the hypothesis of Article 138, paragraph 4 of the Labour Code[13], the supervisory authorities are bound to issue mandatory prescriptions pursuant to Article 404 (1)(9) of the Labour Code for the amendment of an employment contract concluded for part-time work into an employment contract with normal working hours[14]. The amendment of the employment or service relationship in this case shall be carried out in compliance with the mandatory prescription of the supervisory authority.

Specific administrative measures are compulsory instructions to employers or their authorised persons to send notifications to the competent territorial directorate of the National Revenue Agency. They are imposed in two cases:

- First, under Article 404, para. 1, item 10 of the Labour Code - compulsory instructions to employers or their authorised persons to send notification of an employment contract. This measure shall be imposed when the control authorities establish that the period referred to in Art. 62 (3) of the Labour Code for sending this notification has not been complied with[15]. The powers of the supervisory authorities to issue these mandatory injunctions are specific and their subject matter differs substantially from mandatory injunctions relating to violations of property rights under the employment relationship (e.g. right to wages). The obligation to submit a notification under Art. 62 (3) of the Labour Code covers three situations: (a) upon conclusion of an employment contract; (b) upon its amendment and termination; and (c) for its implementation. Different time limits have also been set - in the first two cases a time limit of 3 days and in the last case 7 days[16];
- Second, under Article 404, para. 1, item 11 of the Labour Code - mandatory instructions to employers or their authorised persons to send a notice of deletion of a notice previously sent under Art. 62 (3) of the Labour Code of an employment contract concluded if it is established that there is no evidence of the existence of an employment relationship. In this case, if upon verification it is established that the employer has registered employment contracts, but no actual employment relationship with the employees, on the basis of Art. 402(3), in conjunction with Art. 404(1)(11) of the Labour Code, the Executive Agency "General Labour Inspectorate" shall exercise its powers to ex officio delete the notifications of concluded employment contracts submitted by the respective employer[17].

Acts implementing compulsory administrative measures under the Labour Code are by their legal nature individual administrative acts, notwithstanding the fact that the legislator uses the term "prescription". In the hypothesis of Art. 404, par. 1 of the Labour Code, the prescription is an individual administrative act, but in some judicial acts it is considered to coincide with the compulsory administrative measure[18]. This is not precise - the act imposing the compulsory administrative measure should not be identified with the measure itself. Mandatory prescriptions have the characteristics of individual administrative acts, and the compulsory administrative measures imposed by them may be of different types depending on their purpose - preventive, remedial, restorative (Lazarov, 2000, p. 231; Dimitrova, Mateeva & Dimitrova, 2020, p. 96). Preventive administrative measures shall be applied to prevent the commission of an administrative offence and its harmful consequences (For example, the measures under Art. 404, paragraph 1, item 5, item 6 of the Labour Code). Preventive administrative measures are those which are applied in order to interrupt, suspend the continuation and completion of the specific administrative infringement (e.g. suspension of the activities of undertakings under Art. 404 para. 1, items 3 and 7 of the Labour Code). Restorative coercive administrative measures shall be applied when the offence has already been committed and there is actual damage caused by it (e.g. Article 404, para. 1, item 12 of the Labour Code).

The imposition of a compulsory administrative measure is always done by a new, independent administrative act, which gives rise to separate, independent obligations for its addressees, which are subject to enforcement through compulsion. The application of these measures is not arbitrary, it must be subject to the principle of legality, and should therefore only be applied in cases expressly and precisely provided for by law or decree. They must be imposed in the manner and procedure provided for in the legal provision and must be tailored to the specific infringement and the specific potential or actual harmful consequences. Coercive administrative measures shall be imposed only by the administrative authorities specified in the legal provision (Dimitrova, Mateeva & Dimitrova, 2020, p. 95).

In this sense, the mandatory prescriptions under Art. 404(1) of the Labour Code must be issued by a competent authority (the Labour Inspection Directorate), following an inspection and clarification of the facts and circumstances, in compliance with Articles 35 to 36 of the Administrative Procedure Code. They must be in the form prescribed by law, stating the specific factual and legal grounds for their issuance. As long as the administrative procedural rules, the substantive provisions of the law have been complied with and the purpose of the law has been respected, it is considered that the issued prescriptions are lawful[19].

Next, the acts imposing the compulsory administrative measures must be reasoned. The case law stresses that the importance of these measures under the Labour Code is twofold - on the one hand, they have a deterrent effect, aimed at putting an end to a specific act constituting an administrative offence, and on the other hand, they have a preventive and deterrent character, aimed at preventing the offender from committing similar offences. Accordingly, the mandatory prescriptions given in the control activities of the Labour Inspection Directorate should be specific, clear and unambiguous. If the prescription given is general and vague, creates ambiguities and does not meet the requirement of Article 59, paragraph 2, item 5 of the Administrative Procedure Code, and this prevents the practical possibility of its implementation. It is therefore imperative to specify the specific activities that the employer should carry out in order to be considered as having established the necessary organisation to ensure effective control, as well as the breaches that have been committed in the organisation of work that should be remedied. This means that the individual administrative acts imposing the compulsory administrative measures under Art. 404 paragraph 1 of the Labour Code must be reasoned[20].

An important practical question related to the control of compliance with labour legislation is at what point compulsory administrative measures can be imposed, i.e. can they be applied to an employment relationship that has already been terminated. The Supreme Administrative Court has held in its case law that the compulsory administrative measures regulated in Art. 404 (1) (2) - (9) of the Labour Code contain the requirement of an existing and not of a terminated (non-existent) employment relationship[21]. An exception in this respect are the compulsory administrative measures under Art. 404 para. 1, item 12 of the Labour Code. The said provision enables the inspection bodies of the Labour Inspectorate to issue binding instructions to the employer and the appointing authority for the payment of unpaid wages and benefits after termination of employment[22].

The foregoing also raises the issue of compliance with the requirements for the legality of compulsory administrative measures. Since the compulsory administrative measures are objectified in the issuance of mandatory prescriptions, which are individual administrative acts under Art. 21 (1) of the Administrative Procedure Code, a legal guarantee to ensure their lawful application is the possibility to challenge them. Pursuant to Article 405 of the Labour Code, the compulsory administrative measures under Art. 404(1) of the Labour Code may be appealed under the Administrative Procedure Code.

It should be clarified here that the procedural issues related to the appeal against the compulsory administrative measures are beyond the scope of this submission, concerning the nature and types of legal means for exercising control over compliance with the labour legislation. In view of this fact, the challenge to the acts of the control bodies (directors of territorial directorates or inspectors who are granted control powers by order of the Executive Director of the Executive Agency "General Labour Inspectorate") is not considered in detail, but only some specific points.

Specific to the procedure for issuing a mandatory prescription under Art. 404 (1) of the Labour Code is that it is developed ex officio. A report submitted by the trade unions or a request for the issuance of such a mandatory prescription submitted by an employee shall not be in the nature of a request under Article 24, para. 1 of the Administrative Procedure Code for the issuance of an individual administrative act. Both trade unions and employees do not have the status of parties in these proceedings, respectively the legislator does not give them the right to challenge the refusal to issue a mandatory prescription by the control bodies of the Executive Agency "General Labour Inspectorate". In this sense, the Supreme Administrative Court has accepted in its practice that Article 405 of the Labour Code regulates the appealability under the Administrative Procedure Code only of the imposed compulsory administrative measures under Article 404, para. 1 of the Labour Code, but not the refusal to impose them. The reasoning of the court is that the statutory regulation in a special law compared to the Administrative Procedure Code, which in this case is the Labour Code, excludes the appealability of the refusal to issue a mandatory prescription under Art. 404 (1) of the Labour Code. This does not contradict Article 120(2) of the Constitution, according to which citizens and legal entities may appeal against all administrative acts affecting them, except those expressly provided for by law. In the present case, in view of the nature of the act relating to the imposition of an administrative coercive measure, the assessment of the lack of legal interest in challenging the refusal to impose such a measure was made by the legislator[23].

In the same sense is the practice of the administrative courts. The refusal to impose the compulsory administrative measures provided for in Art. 404 (1) of the Labour Code cannot be defined as a refusal to issue an individual administrative act within the meaning of Art. 21 (1) of the Administrative Procedure Code. The refusal to issue a mandatory prescription under Art. 404 (1) of the Labour Code is not among the exhaustively listed acts under Art. 128, paragraphs 1 and 2 of the

Administrative Procedure Code, which are subject to the jurisdiction of the administrative courts. The imposition of compulsory administrative measures is an act of state administrative coercion in relation to the protection of a certain type of public relations. The grounds for its application, the authorities applying it and the legal entities to which it applies are established by law. The court is not one of the bodies mentioned in the special law - the Labour Code, which have the competence to impose compulsory administrative measures and, therefore, it does not have the power to give binding instructions to the competent authority to take action to impose a compulsory administrative measure[24].

CONCLUSION

In summary, it can be concluded that both inspections for compliance with labour legislation and compulsory administrative measures are an effective means of preventing violations of employees' labour rights. The provision of Article 405, sentence 2 of the Labour Code, according to which the appeal does not suspend the execution of the compulsory administrative measure, also contributes to the effectiveness of the administrative coercion imposed under the Labour Code. Through the acts of the Labour Inspection bodies, an active impact is sought for the protection of the affected labour rights in order to guarantee the legitimate interests of employees. The will of the legislator is to introduce speed in removing violations of labour legislation, given the social importance of the regulated legal relations. Administrative proceedings of such significance require speed and immediate enforceability of law enforcement measures[25].

The analysis of the cited judicial acts concerning the appeal of compulsory administrative measures regulated by the Labour Code shows that the case law is generally consistent and coherent, despite some imprecise formulations. The large number of court decisions on the application of Art. 404 (1) of the Labour Code is an indicator of the active and systematic control activity of the bodies of the Executive Agency "General Labour Inspectorate", which is a guarantee of compliance with labour legislation.

REFERENCES

Aleksandrov, A. (2016). Prakticheski problemi na trudovoto pravo, svarzani s kontrola za spazvane i administrativnonakazatelnata otgovornost za narushenia na trudovoto zakonodatelstvo. *Trud i pravo*, *11*, 10-15.

Andreeva, A. (2010). Vliyanie na ikonomicheskata kriza varhu prekratyavaneto na trudovoto pravootnoshenie. Svetovnata kriza i ikonomicheskoto razvitie. Varna: Nauka i ikonomika.

Andreeva, A. (2016). Zakonodatelni reshenia v balgarskoto trudovo pravo obusloveni ot vrazkata mu s ikonomikata. Pravnata nauka i biznesat – zaedno za ustoychivo razvitie na ikonomikata. Varna: Nauka i ikonomika.

Andreeva, A. (2018). Normativni merki za garantirane na trudovoto vaznagrazhdenie pri nesastoyatelnost na rabotodatelya. *Izvestia na IU*. Varna.

Andreeva, A. (2020). Digitalization as a Factor for the Development of the Modern Labour Legislation. *Digital Economy: Azerbaijan at the New Stage of Economic Development: Conference Proceedings of the International Scientific-Practical Conference*. Baku Business University.

Andreeva, A. (2019). Neprikosnovenost na lichnia zhivot na rabotnitsite v konteksta na digitalizatsiyata. Izv. na Sayuza na uchenite . *Ser. Humanitarni nauki*. Varna: Sayuz na uchenite.

Andreeva, A. (2020). Otrazhenie na digitalizatsiyata varhu trudovia protses - riskove i perspektivi. Ikonomicheska nauka, obrazovanie i realna ikonomika: razvitie i vzaimodeystvia v digitalnata epoha: Sbornik s dokladi ot Yubileyna mezhdunarodna nauchna konferentsia v chest na 100 god. Varna, Varna: Nauka i ikonomika.

Andreeva, A., & Dimitrova, D. (2019). Spetsifiki na kontrola na Izpalnitelna agentsia Glavna inspektsia po truda, v konteksta na garantsiite za izplashtane na trudovoto vaznagrazhdenie. Godishnik na Burgaskia svoboden universitet, 40, 243 – 258.

Andreeva, A., & Yolova, G. (2008a). Administrativno-nakazatelna otgovornost za narushenia na trudovoto i osiguritelno zakonodatelstvo. Godishnik na Ikonomicheski universitet. Varna.

Andreeva, A.; Yolova, G. (2008b). Nakazatelnopravna zashtita na trudovite i osiguritelni pravootnoshenia. *Izvestia na Ikonomicheski universitet.* Varna.

Andreeva, A.; Yolova, G. (2009). Normativni promeni v kontrola za spazvane na trudovoto i osiguritelno zakonodatelstvo. *Izvestia na Ikonomicheski universitet.* Varna.

Andreeva, A.; Yolova, G. (2011). Yuridicheska otgovornost i kontrol za spazvane na trudovoto i osiguritelno zakonodatelstvo. *Univ. izd. Nauka i ikonomika*. Varna.

Andreeva, A., & Yolova, G. (2018). Harmonizirane na balgarskoto trudovoto i osiguritelno zakonodatelstvo s evropeyskite printsipi. Sabiedrība un kultūra. Rakstu krājums, Liepāja: Liepājas universitāte izglītības zinātņu i nstitūts socioloģisko pētījum u centrs vadības un sociālo z inātņu fakultāte, 20, 334 - 341.

Andreeva, A., & Yolova, G. (2018). Za nyakoi osobenosti na administrativnia kontrol i administrativnonakazatelnata otgovornost za narushavane na zdravoslovnite i bezopasni uslovia na trud. Administrativno pravo – savremenni tendentsii v pravorazdavaneto i doktrinata: Sbornik dokladi, Varna.

Andreeva, A., & Yolova, G. (2019). *Administrative Penal Liability for Violations of the Labour Migration and Labour Mobility Act. Globalization, the State and the Individual: International Scientific Journal* (Conference Edition 2019). Free University of Varna.

Andreeva, A., & Yolova, G. (2019). The Right to Work in a Digital Society: Evolution and Trends. Mezhdunarodni klasterni politiki: Balgaro-kitayski forum: Sbornik s dokladi ot mezhdunarodna konferentsia, Varna: Nauka i ikonomika.

Andreeva, A., & Yolova, G. (2020). Pravni aspekti na balansa mezhdu lichen i profesionalen zhivot. Pravoto i biznesat v savremennoto obshtestvo: Sbornik s dokladi ot 3-ta Natsionalna nauchna konferentsia. Varna: Nauka i ikonomika.

Andreeva, A., & Yolova, G. (2020a). Rabotodatelskiyat kontrol v konteksta na digitalizatsiyata. Upravlenie na choveshkite resursi v erata na digitalnite predizvikatelstva: Sbornik s dokladi ot Mezhdunarodna nauchno-prakticheska konferentsia, organizirana ot IU. Varna.

Andreeva, A., & Yolova, G. (2020b). Transformatsia na pravnata vrazka rabotodatel – rabotnik v rezultat na vliyanieto na digitalizatsiyata. *De Jure (Durban)*, *1*(20), 11–18.

Andreeva, A., & Yolova, G. (2020d). Trudovo i osiguritelno pravo. 2. prerab. i dop. izd. Varna: Nauka i ikonomika.

Balabanova, H. (2004). Administrativen kontrol: kontrolna kompetentnost na izpalnitelnata vlast. Varna: Varnenski svoboden universitet Chernorizets Hrabar.

Blagoycheva, H. (2019). Sotsialnata (ne)sigurnost na raboteshtite prez tsifrovi platformi. Pravoto i biznesat v savremennoto obshtestvo: Aktualni pravni predizvikatelstva v ikonomikata: Sbornik s dokladi ot 1-va Natsionalna nauchna konferentsia. Varna: Nauka i ikonomika.

Blagoycheva, H. (2020). Predizvikatelstvata pred sotsialnata zashtita na litsata s nestandartna zaetost. Ikonomicheska nauka, obrazovanie i realna ikonomika: razvitie i vzaimodeystvia v digitalnata epoha: Sbornik s dokladi ot Yubileyna mezhdunarodna nauchna konferentsia v chest na 100 god. Varna, Varna: Nauka i ikonomika.

Bogomilova, Zh. (2016). Kontrol i administrativnonakazatelna otgovornost vav vrazka s pravilata za trudova zaetost na chuzhdi grazhdani v Republika Bulgaria. Trud i pravo, 7.

Danailov, D. (1987). Kodeksat na truda i kontrolat za spazvane na trudovoto zakonodatelstvo. Kodeksat na truda v deystvie. Materiali ot nauchno-prakticheska konferentsia. Sofia. *Profizdat, 1987*, 210–215.

Dermendzhiev, I., Kostov, D., & Hrusanov, D. (2010). *Administrativno pravo na Republika Bulgaria: obshta chast*. Sibi.

Dimitrova, D. (2010). Oblastniyat upravitel kato organ na izpalnitelnata vlast: Disertatsia za prisazhdane na obrazovatelna i nauchna stepen “doktor”, nauchna spetsialnost Administrativno pravo i administrativen protses, shifar. Sofia: Sofiyski universitet.

Dimitrova, D. (2020). Po nyakoi vaprosi na administrativnopravnata zashtita na pravoto na trud. Pravoto i biznesat v savremennoto obshtestvo: Sbornik s dokladi ot 3-ta Natsionalna nauchna konferentsia. Varna: Nauka i ikonomika.

Dimitrova, D. (2021). Istoricheski traditsii na kontrola za spazvane na trudovoto zakonodatelstvo. *De Jure (Durban)*, *2*(21), 192–202.

Dimitrova, D., Mateeva, Z., & Dimitrova, D. (2020). *Administrativno pravo i protses*. Varna: Nauka i ikonomika.

Hristoforov, V. G. (1966). Darzhavnite uchrezhdenia – pravna sashtnost i administrativno-praven rezhim. Sofia: Nauka i izkustvo.

Lazarov, K. (2000). *Administrativno pravo*. Fenia.

Mrachkov, V. (1985). *Kontrol za spazvane na trudovoto zakonodatelstvo i otgovornost za negovoto narushavane*. Sofia: Izdatelstvo na Balgarska akademia na naukite, 1985.

Mrachkov, V. (2018). *Trudovo pravo (deseto preraboteno i dopalneno izdanie)*. Sibi.

Mrachkov, V. (2020). Sotsialni prava na balgarskite grazhdani. Sofia. *Siela*, *2020*, 40.

Mrachkov, V., Sredkova, K., & Vasilev, A. (2016). Komentar na Kodeksa na truda, 12-to preraboteno i dopalneno izdanie, Sofia. *Sibi*, *2016*, 1148.

Rachev, R., Andreeva, A., Yolova, G., & Vladova, V. (2008). Trudovo i osiguritelno pravo. Varna: Nauka i ikonomika.

Shirvanyan, M. (2021). Spetsifiki v rezhima na trudovata zlopoluka v balgarskoto zakonodatelstvo. Varna. *Steno*, *2021*, 106–107.

Stoychev, S. (2002). *Konstitutsionno pravo*. Siela.

ENDNOTES

1 https://www.gli.government.bg/bg

2 https://www.gli.government.bg/bg/taxonomy/term/370

3 https://www.mlsp.government.bg/trud

4 Draft Act amending and supplementing the Labour Code (002-01-32/03.08.2020); Published: https://www.parliament.bg/bg/bills/ID/163309/

5 Persons under 16 years of age shall be employed after a thorough medical examination and a medical conclusion that they are fit to perform the work concerned and that it will not impair their health or interfere with their proper physical and mental development. Persons under the age of 16 shall be admitted to employment with the permission of the labour inspectorate on a case-by-case basis.

6 (1) Persons aged 16 to 18 shall not be employed in work which is arduous, hazardous or harmful to their health or to their proper physical, mental or moral development. (2) Persons aged 16 to 18 are employed after a thorough preliminary medical examination and a medical report that establishes their fitness to perform the work in question. (3) Persons aged 16 to 18 are admitted to employment with the permission of the labour inspectorate on a case-by-case basis.

7 Decision No. 139 of 28.04.2021 in Administrative Penalty Case No. 100/2021 of the Administrative Court - Shumen.

8 Decision No 4232 of 01.04.2021 in Administrative Case No 367/2021, Division VI of the Supreme Administrative Court.

9 Decision No. 14595 of 25.11.2020 in Administrative Case No. 10630/2020, Division VI of the Supreme Administrative Court; Decision No 13421 of 29.10.2020 in Administrative Case No 8265/2020, Division VI of the Supreme Administrative Court; Decision No 283 of 09.01.2020 in Administrative Case No 1963/2019, Sixth Division of the Supreme Administrative Court; Order No 11465 of 04.09.2020 in Administrative Case No 9165/2020, Division VI of the Supreme Administrative Court.

10 Order No 12522 of 24.09.2019 in Administrative Case No 10999/2019, Division VI of the Supreme Administrative Court.

11 Decision No. 4374 of 29.06.2017 in Administrative Case No. 597/2017 of the Administrative Court - Sofia City.

12 Decision No 58 of 05.01.2021 in Administrative Case No 8019/2020, Division VI of the Supreme Administrative Court; Decision No 16178/28.11.2019 in Administrative Case No 2955/2019, Division VI of the Supreme Administrative Court; Decision No 6569/02.06.2020 in administrative case No 8239/2019, Division VI of the Supreme Administrative Court.

13 A contract of employment concluded for part of the statutory working hours shall be deemed to have been concluded for work during normal working hours in cases where it is established by the supervisory authorities that the employee under that contract performs work outside his or her statutory working hours without any conditions for overtime work in the cases permitted by law.

14 Decision No. 700 of 30.05.2019 in Civil Case No. 668/2019 of Plovdiv District Court.

15 Decision No. 10250 of 30.07.2018 in Administrative Case No. 7425/2017, Division VI of the Supreme Administrative Court.

16 Decision No. of 02.05.2017 in Administrative Case No. 430/2016 of the Administrative Court - Ruse.

17 Decision No 14866 of 02.12.2020 in Administrative Case No 11209/2020, Division VI of the Supreme Administrative Court.

18 Order No. 1542 of 20.07.2021 in Administrative Case No. 1247/2021 of the Administrative Court - Burgas; Decision No. 1114 of 20.06.2017 in Administrative Penalty Case No. 1125/2017 of the Administrative Court - Burgas.

19 Decision No 12381 of 03.12.2021 in Administrative Case No 7758/2021, Division VI of the Supreme Administrative Court.

20 Decision No 1230 of 01.02.2021 in Administrative Case No 11163/2020, Division VI of the Supreme Administrative Court.

21 Decision No. 2355 of 13.02.2020 in Administrative Case No. 14290/2019 of the Sixth Division of the Supreme Administrative Court; Decision No 14436 of 29.10.2019 in Administrative Case No 3846/2018, Division VI of the Supreme Administrative Court; Decision No. 7469 of 20.05.2019 in Administrative Case No. 14184/2017, Division VI of the Supreme Administrative Court; Decision No. 861 of 26.01.2015 in Administrative Case No. 11934/2014, Division VI of the Supreme Administrative Court.

22 Decision No 12770 of 14.12.2021 in Administrative Case No 7465/2021, Division VI of the Supreme Administrative Court.

23 Order No 1669 of 09.02.2021 in Administrative Case No 835/2021, Division VI of the Supreme Administrative Court.

24 Order No. 2293 of 07.04.2017 in Administrative Case No. 10256/2016 of the Administrative Court - Sofia City.

25 Order No 10764 of 04.09.2018 in Administrative Case No 10425/2018, Division VI of the Supreme Administrative Court.

Chapter 6
Current Legislative Trends in the Field of Labour Rights Monitoring

Darina Dimitrova
University of Economics, Varna, Bulgaria

ABSTRACT

In pursuit of the stated aim, the author set the following tasks: 1) To examine the nature of the control powers of the executive agency "general labour inspectorate"; 2) To examine the legal means for exercising control over compliance with the labour legislation, analyzing in detail the types of compulsory administrative measures under Art. 1 of the Labour Code; 3) To outline current legislative trends in the field of monitoring compliance with labour rights after Bulgaria's accession to the European Union.

INTRODUCTION

The formation and development of the legal framework on labour relations in Bulgaria has over a century of history (Dimitrova, 2021; Yolova, 2020, pp. 21 – 47; Banov, 2020, pp. 59 – 72). The Labour Code, adopted in 1986, is still the main normative act in force in the field of labour law, but it has undergone a huge number of amendments and additions, the latest version being the State Gazette No. 62 of 2022. The main legal institutes in the field of labour law were established by the previous legislation and have been further developed and refined by subsequent legislation.

DOI: 10.4018/978-1-6684-9067-9.ch006

The legal regulation of monitoring compliance with labour legislation has evolved, one of the main factors for its development being the recognition of the right to work as a fundamental social right and its regulation at constitutional level. The establishment and development of the right to work as a fundamental constitutional social right is at the heart of the modern legal framework for monitoring compliance with labour legislation (Andreeva, 2009; Andreeva & Yolova, 2011; Andreeva & Yolova, 2018; Dimitrova, 2019a; Aleksandrov, 2020, pp. 161 – 171). Until the democratic changes of 1989, trade unions occupied a central place among the bodies monitoring compliance with labour legislation[1]. Only in 1991, with the establishment of the State Labour Inspectorate under the Ministry of Labour and Social Policy in (later transformed into the General Labour Inspectorate and then into the Executive Agency "General Labour Inspectorate") the state restored its occupational safety and health control functions.

Since the assignment of the control functions to the Labour Inspection bodies, the text of Article 404 of the Labour Code, regulating the compulsory administrative measures as the main means of control for the prevention and termination of violations of labour legislation, has been amended and supplemented many times. In the edition of the State Gazette No. 100 of 1992, Art. 404, par. 1 of the Labour Code contains only five points providing for the application of compulsory administrative measures. With the amendment of Official Gazette No. 25 of 2001, two new provisions have been adopted - item 6 and item 7. The provision of item 8 was supplemented by the amendment of State Gazette No. 108 of 2008, and item 9 - by State Gazette No. 7 of 2012. The provisions of item 10 and item 11 were added by State Gazette No 27 of 2014. The latest compulsory administrative measure is introduced by Art. 404, para. 1, item 12 of the Labour Code by the State Gazette No. 102 of 2017.

The normative analysis of the amendments and additions to Art. 404(1) of the Labour Code shows a tendency towards an expansion of the powers of the Executive Agency "General Labour Inspectorate" both in terms of the types of coercive measures (see previous § 3.2) and in terms of the intensity of the administrative control exercised. The reasons are rooted in the new social relations after the democratic changes in our country related to the transition from a planned to a market economy and the development of private economic activity. This in turn has led to significant changes in the employment relationship between employer and employee.

Contemporary trends in the development of labour legislation, including its monitoring, cannot be assessed unequivocally. Since its adoption in 1986, the Labour Code has undergone several dozen amendments and additions, and in the last three decades, along with the codified act in the field of labour law, a number of other legal acts regulating labour law have been adopted. This led to the decodification of labour law. Thus, in addition to its powers under the Labour Code, the Executive Agency "General Labour Inspectorate" has control powers for compliance with labour legislation under other laws - the Occupational Health and Safety Act, the Labour Inspection Act, the Labour Migration and Labour Mobility Act, etc. As emphasized in the legal literature, the concept of "code" implies completeness of the regulation, completeness of the provided legal institutes and the possibility of independent application without special references (Sivkov, 2021, pp. 37 – 45).

On the one hand, the reason for regulating labour law in other legal acts outside the Labour Code is the dynamics of social relations after the democratic changes in 1989 and the impossibility of including this legal regulation in a normative act adopted under completely different historical and socio-political conditions. Taking this into account, the recommendation for the drafting and adoption of a new Labour Code, which would comprehensively regulate all labour law norms and institutes in accordance with the current development of social relations, can be made as a proposal to the legislator. The codification aims to avoid fragmentation of the norms relating to one legal matter. This avoids contradictions and inconsistencies in the normative regulation of the same legal institutes in several laws, respectively eliminates the need for reference from one law to another. This will ensure the actual implementation of the applicable legal norms by employers as well as control and enforcement authorities (Andreeva & Dimitrova, 2019).

On the other hand, after Bulgaria's accession to the European Union, European acts and judicial decisions increasingly determine the development of our national law (Andreeva & Yolova, 2017; Andreeva & Yolova, 2018; Banov, 2016). От 2007 г. Bulgaria is a Member State of the European Union and in this sense the principles of primacy over the national law of the Member States and direct effect of the rules of European law are applicable in relation to Union law. The transposition of European norms in the field of monitoring compliance with labour legislation in Bulgaria is characterized by certain specificities.

Under the provisions of the Treaty on European Union and the Treaty on the Functioning of the European Union, the Union does not have exclusive competence in the field of labour and social policy. As regards labour law, the European Union complements the initiatives of individual member states by setting minimum standards on working conditions, information and consultation of workers. Membership of the European Union and the ensuing reforms in Member States' legislation, as well as the accompanying processes of globalisation, bring many challenges and give rise to a number of fears of job losses and social injustice. Therefore, each State is responsible for respecting the rights of its citizens and workers at the national level as well as within international institutions. It should be clarified that the subject of the research is the control of compliance with labour legislation, the main subject of which are employers, and the responsibility of the state is not considered.

Given that the European Union has 27 Member States and over 240 million workers, respect for labour rights directly benefits a large number of citizens and has a positive impact on one of the most important and tangible areas of their daily lives. Respect for employees' fundamental labour rights goes hand in hand with the single market. The free movement of goods, services, capital and workers must be accompanied by appropriate rules to ensure that Member States and businesses compete on the basis of the quality of their products and not by lowering labour law standards[2]. Monitoring compliance with labour law in both its legal and economic aspects is therefore of great importance given the impact of globalisation on the labour market (Blagoycheva, 2016; Andreeva & Yolova, 2017; Blagoycheva, Andreeva & Yolova, 2018; Ivanova, 2020).

The significance of the issues concerning the legal framework and the related financial control practice for the observance of labour rights according to the commitments arising from Bulgaria's membership in the European Union has been studied in the literature (Nedyalkova, Dimitrova & Bogdanov, 2022; Nedyalkova, 2019; Nedyalkova, 2020). At the present time, the topic is topical given the changed social reality of precarious work in the context of digitalization, where employers have expanded their employer power despite the lack of such regulation at the legal level. The pandemic situation and the measures taken to preserve public health have changed the rules of labour law, giving other priorities (Andreeva, 2021; Andreeva & Yolova, 2021; Sabev & Doncheva, 2021). This implies increased administrative control by the state to ensure that employees' labour rights are respected and that employers do not act arbitrarily.

At the present stage, the motivation for regulatory changes in the Bulgarian labour legislation largely stems from the obligation of Member States to implement EU law[3]. Thus, the 2016 amendments to the Labour Code (State Gazette No. 105 of 2016) introduced the requirements of two European

Directives (Directive 96/71/EC and Directive 2014/67/EU) providing for mandatory minimum protection rules to be respected by employers in the host country, as well as rules for administrative cooperation and control between the competent authorities of the Member States.

Directive 96/71/EC introduces mandatory minimum protection rules to be respected in the host country by employers posting workers temporarily to carry out work in the territory of the Member State where the services are provided. Accordingly, Directive 2014/67/EU introduces a package of measures ensuring better protection for posted workers in the framework of the provision of services, combating so-called "social dumping" and a more transparent and predictable legal framework for service providers. It aims to improve the process of implementation and enforcement in practice of Directive 96/71/EC by introducing rules on administrative cooperation and control between Member States' competent authorities, administrative requirements for service providers and control measures at national level.

The full functioning of the European Union presupposes that its law is not only established but also applied and respected throughout the Union. Accordingly, Member States are required to adapt their national law to the requirements of European law. In view of the fact that the above-mentioned acts are directives, their implementation in the domestic legal order is by transposition into national law, as they are not directly applicable in principle and have no direct effect.

In the years following Bulgaria's accession to the European Union, in addition to the above-mentioned directives, the provisions of a number of other directives relevant to state control over the observance of employees' rights have been transposed into national labour legislation. Directives are the Union's main legislative tool for building the single internal market and implementing its policies as a whole, and their correct and timely implementation in the Member States must therefore be ensured. The process of transposing European Union legal rules is complex and no measure can be effectively implemented as adopted by the relevant European institution or body without some administrative national measure (Popova, 2011, p. 396; Dimitrova, 2019b).

This intensive process of European influence on Bulgarian law has resulted in important consequences, such as the "Europeanisation" of the national legislation of the Member States and the creation of new common principles of European law (Baltadzhieva & Todorov, 2012). As a result of the direct influence of European law on national law, member states' legislation is enriched through the transposition of directives. But too rapid a transposition of European law into national law has the negative consequence of detaching domestic law from its cultural and historical traditions, and this can damage the national legal order. Among the negative consequences of the hasty assimilation of European law are the deprivation of legal content of classical legal institutes, as well as unsystematicity and contradiction between legal acts.

At the time of the development of this study, one of the latest amendments to the Labour Code is the State Gazette No. 109 of 22 December 2020, and most of the changes concern precisely the control and sanction activity regarding compliance with labour legislation. Through the imposition of administrative sanctions by supervisory authorities for breaches of labour legislation, employees are protected and fair competition between enterprises is ensured, which supports the functioning of the labour market. The above-mentioned amendments to the Labour Code are mainly aimed at improving the adequacy of the labour legislation in relation to the labour market trends, the level of industrial relations, the socio-economic conditions in the country and international acts and standards. In this sense, there is a need to develop labour law legislation in line with EU law, ILO standards and national socio-economic specificities.

Due to changes in the labour market linked to the processes of globalisation and digitalisation, the number of employment relationships that have a cross-border element is increasing (Andreeva & Yolova, 2019; Andreeva, 2020; Andreeva & Yolova, 2020d, p. 19; Blagoycheva, 2021). Job mobility and job hopping is a growing trend in the labour market, especially among young people looking for a fulfilling and suitable job. With the adoption of the proposed bill, the requirements of Directive (EU) 2018/957 of the European Parliament and of the Council of 28 June 2018 amending Directive 96/71/EC concerning the posting of workers in the framework of the provision of services are implemented in our national legislation (OB, L 173/16 from 9 July 2018).

The foregoing demonstrates that Bulgaria's membership in the European Union has had a significant impact on the development of national law in the area of labour law enforcement. European Union labour law covers two main areas:

- Ø working conditions concerning working hours, part-time and fixed-term work, secondment of workers;
- Ø informing and consulting workers on collective redundancies, transfer of undertakings, etc.[4]

As already stated, the Union does not have exclusive competence in the field of labour law, but only complements the initiatives of individual member states by setting minimum standards with regard to working conditions and the information and consultation of employees. However, European Union labour law benefits not only employees but also employers and society as a whole by providing a clear framework of rights and obligations in the workplace, protecting the health of the workforce and promoting sustainable economic growth.

In 2019, the development of EU labour law received a strong boost. European Union social policy issues have been at the forefront of all the Union's institutions. Two European Union acts in the field of social policy adopted in 2019 attract attention due to the fact that they are expected to be structurally decisive for the future development of European labour and social law (Staykov, 2021). These are:

Ø Regulation (EU) 2019/1149 of the European Parliament and of the Council of 20 June 2019 establishing a European Labour Authority[5] and
Ø Directive (EU) 2019/1152 of the European Parliament and of the Council of 20 June 2019 on transparent and predictable working conditions in the European Union[6]

The adoption of European Union law in the social field is the result of many years of efforts to tackle the many problems and challenges facing the labour market in the second decade of the 21st century. But an analysis of the powers of the European Labour Authority leads to the legal conclusion that this specialised agency of the European Union is not an administrative regulatory body of the Union and does not exercise direct supervisory functions within the scope of its activities. This is an administrative body whose main activity is to coordinate the efforts of certain other European Union agencies, as well as the efforts of individual Member States, on various cross-border labour mobility issues within the Union (Staykov, 2021).

The laconic regulation in Regulation (EU) 2019/1149 raises controversial questions in the legal literature. Different forms of control exist in national law with regard to the observance of rights arising out of employment, as well as with regard to legal liability for their violation. Jurisdiction of national authorities exercising administrative control over compliance with labour legislation and administrative liability for breaches thereof have national jurisdiction, i.e. territorial jurisdiction within the borders of the State concerned. The future will show to what extent stakeholders in a cross-border labour conflict will trust the intervention of the European Labour Authority (Staykov, 2021). But now the first joint inspections of Bulgarian and French inspectors in the European Union, organized with the support of the European Labour Authority. And experts of the Labour Inspectorate participate in information meetings on the rights of seasonal agricultural workers in other European countries[7].

CONCLUSION

The foregoing shows that the control of compliance with the rights arising from the employment is subject to very dynamic regulation. As a result of the analysis of the new moments in the legal framework and in particular of the transposition of the European norms in the sphere of control of compliance with the labour legislation in Bulgaria the following conclusions, summaries and recommendations can be made regarding the applicable legal framework concerning the issues under consideration:

First, there is a tendency to expand the powers of the Executive Agency "General Labour Inspectorate" both in terms of the types of coercive measures and the intensity of the administrative control exercised. This demonstrates the role and importance of administrative law protection in ensuring the appropriate level of protection of the right to work.

Second, contemporary societal conditions of globalization and digitalization pose new challenges to the legal framework requiring administrative law protection of fundamental labour rights (e.g. health and safety at work, right to pay, right to rest and holidays, etc.). On the one hand, the new social relations after the democratic changes in Bulgaria are related to the transition from a planned to a market economy and the development of private economic activity, and on the other hand, stem from Bulgaria's membership in the European Union. The national legislation, which transposes the European norms in the field of control of compliance with the labour rights of employees, is one of the main factors influencing the control procedures for compliance with labour legislation.

Third, despite the significant impact of European acts on the development of our national law, the European Union does not have exclusive competence in the field of labour law. Administrative control of compliance with labour law is the responsibility of national authorities. In this sense, the role of the Executive Agency "General Labour Inspectorate" is very important. Unfortunately, the Labour Code adopted in 1986, despite its repeated amendments and additions, has not been able to fully respond to the changes that have occurred in contemporary social relations. In view of this, the legislator may be asked to draft and adopt a new Labour Code that would comprehensively regulate all labour law norms and institutes in accordance with the current development of social relations. Of course, one must take into account the fact that the adoption of a code, in the field of labour law, is not an easy task. It is one of the major branches of law regulating not only the legal relationships that arise in the provision of labour and the employment of labour, but also a number of other relationships directly related to labour, including the control of compliance with labour legislation.

REFERENCES

Aleksandrov, A. (2020). Administrativna i izvansadebna zashtita na individualnite subektivni trudovi prava. Ot: Andreeva, A., Yolova, G., Blagoycheva, H., Aleksandrov, A., Banov, H., Yordanov, Z. Zashtita za individualnite subektivni trudovi prava (na rabotnika ili sluzhitelya). Varna: Nauka i ikonomika.

Andreeva, A. (2020). Digitalization as a Factor for the Development of the Modern Labour Legislation. *Digital Economy: Azerbaijan at the New Stage of Economic Development: Conference Proceedings of the International Scientific-Practical Conference*. Baku Business University

Andreeva, A. (2009). *Normativni promeni v kontrola za spazvane na trudovoto i osiguritelno zakonodatelstvo. Izvestia na Ikonomicheski universitet*. Varna.

Andreeva, A. (2020). Otrazhenie na digitalizatsiyata varhu trudovia protses – riskove i perspektivi. Ikonomicheska nauka, obrazovanie i realna ikonomika: razvitie i vzaimodeystvia v digitalnata epoha: Sbornik s dokladi ot Yubileyna mezhdunarodna nauchna konferentsia v chest na 100 god. ot osnovavaneto na IU. Varna.

Andreeva, A. (2021). Rabota v pandemichna obstanovka i nyakoi predizvikatelstva za stranite po trudovoto pravootnoshenie. Pravoto i biznesat v savremennoto obshtestvo: Sbornik s dokladi ot 4-ta natsionalna nauchna konferentsia. Varna: Nauka i ikonomika.

Andreeva, A., & Dimitrova, D. (2019). Spetsifiki na kontrola na Izpalnitelna agentsia Glavna inspektsia po truda, v konteksta na garantsiite za izplashtane na trudovoto vaznagrazhdenie. Godishnik na Burgaskia svoboden universitet.

Andreeva, A. & Yolova, G. (2011). *Yuridicheska otgovornost i kontrol za spazvane na trudovoto i osiguritelno zakonodatelstvo*. Varna: Univ. izd. Nauka i ikonomika.

Andreeva, A., & Yolova, G. (2018). Harmonizirane na balgarskoto trudovoto i osiguritelno zakonodatelstvo s evropeyskite printsipi. Sabiedrība un kultūra. Rakstu krājums, Liepāja: Liepājas universitāte izglītības zinātņu i nstitūts socioloģisko pētījum u centrs vadības un sociālo z inātņu fakultāte, 20, 334 - 341.

Andreeva, A., & Yolova, G. (2018). Za nyakoi osobenosti na administrativnia kontrol i administrativnonakazatelnata otgovornost za narushavane na zdravoslovnite i bezopasni uslovia na trud. Administrativno pravo – savremenni tendentsii v pravorazdavaneto i doktrinata: Sbornik doklad., Varna: Nauka i ikonomika.

Andreeva, A., & Yolova, G. (2019). *Administrative Penal Liability for Violations of the Labour Migration and Labour Mobility Act. Globalization, the State and the Individual: International Scientific Journal* (Conference Edition 2019). Free University of Varna.

Andreeva, A., & Yolova, G. (2019). The Right to Work in a Digital Society: Evolution and Trends. Mezhdunarodni klasterni politiki: Balgaro-kitayski forum: Sbornik s dokladi ot mezhdunarodna konferentsia. Varna: Nauka i ikonomika.

Andreeva, A., & Yolova, G. (2020d). Trudovo i osiguritelno pravo. 2. prerab. i dop. izd. Varna: Nauka i ikonomika.

Andreeva, A., & Yolova, G. (2021). Za funktsiite na trudovoto i osiguritelnoto pravo v usloviyata na pandemia. Problemi na trudovoto i osiguritelnoto pravo: Sbornik s dokladi ot Natsionalnata nauchna konferentsia v pamet na prof. d-r Atanas Vasilev po povod na 70 g. ot rozhdenieto mu. Sofia: Izd.

Andreeva, A., & Yolova, G. (2017). Tendentsii i predizvikatelstva pred trudovoto i osiguritelnoto zakonodatelstvo - deset godini sled chlenstvoto na R. Bulgaria v ES. *Nauchni trudove na Instituta za darzhavata i pravoto*. Sofia: BAN.

Baltadzhieva, R., & Todorov, I. (2012). *Vzaimodeystvie mezhdu evropeyskoto i balgarskoto administrativno pravo*. Siela.

Banov, H. (2016). Evropa 2020. i trudoviyat dogovor za obuchenie po vreme na rabota. *Pravna misal, 4*, 47 – 64.

Banov, H. (2020). Istorichesko razvitie na individualnite subektivni trudovi prava v balgarskoto pravo. ot: Andreeva, A., Yolova, G., Blagoycheva, H., Aleksandrov, A., Banov, H., Yordanov, Z. Zashtita za individualnite subektivni trudovi prava (na rabotnika ili sluzhitelya). Varna: Nauka i ikonomika.

Blagoycheva, H. (2016). Employment and the Working Poor; Phenomenon in the EU. *International Journal of Economics and Business Administration (IJEBA)*. Piraeus: GNU Public License.

Blagoycheva, H. (2021). Robotizatsia, izkustven intelekt i ochakvani transformatsii na pazara na truda. Pravoto i biznesat v savremennoto obshtestvo: Sbornik s dokladi ot 4-ta natsionalna nauchna konferentsia. Varna: Nauka i ikonomika.

Blagoycheva, H., Andreeva, A., & Yolova, G. (2018). Legal Framework of Occupational Health Servicesin the EU and in Bulgaria. *Izvestiya Journal of Varna University of Economics, 62*, 3 – 4.Dimitrova, D. (2021). Istoricheski traditsii na kontrola za spazvane na trudovoto zakonodatelstvo. *De Jure (Durban), 2*(21), 192–202.

Dimitrova, D. (2019a). Savremenna rolya na Izpalnitelna agentsia "Glavna inspektsia po truda" za zashtita na pravata na stranite po trudovite pravootnoshenia. Pravoto i biznesat v savremennoto obshtestvo: Sbornik s dokladi ot 2-ra Natsionalna nauchna konferentsia. Varna: Nauka i ikonomika

Dimitrova, D. (2019b). Savremenni tendentsii v administrativnoto zakonodatelstvo na Bulgaria. Pravoto i biznesat v savremennoto obshtestvo: Sbornik s dokladi ot 2-ra Natsionalna nauchna konferentsia. Varna: Nauka i ikonomika.

Dimitrova, D. (2020). Po nyakoi vaprosi na administrativnopravnata zashtita na pravoto na trud. Pravoto i biznesat v savremennoto obshtestvo: Sbornik s dokladi ot 3-ta Natsionalna nauchna konferentsia. Nauka i ikonomika.

Ivanova, P. (2020). *Novite tendentsii v trudovite otnoshenia. Izvestia Sp. Ikonomicheski universitet.* Varna.

Nedyalkova, P. (2019). Government Supervision – A Factor for Business Development. Journal of Management Policy and Practice. Atlanta, Georgia, USA: North American Business Press.

Nedyalkova, P. (2020). Quality of Internal Auditing in the Public Sector: Perspectives from the Bulgarian and International Context. Cham: Springer Nature Switzerland.

Nedyalkova, P., Dimitrova, D., & Bogdanov, H. (2022). New Features in the Bulgarian Legal Framework and Financial Control Practice for Compliance with Labour Legislation in the Age of Globalization. IGI Global Publ.

Popova, Zh. (2011). Pravo na Evropeyskia sayuz. Sofia. *Siela*, *2011*, 396.

Sabev, S., & Doncheva, M. (2021). Pandemiyata ot COVID-19 kato yuridicheski fakt. Reformata v administrativnoto nakazvane ot 2020 g., 17 may 2021: Sbornik dokladi, Sofia: Univ. izd. Sv. *Kliment Ohridski*, 93–102.

Sivkov, Ts. (2021). *Izmeneniyata v ZANN ot kraya na 2020 g. – stapka po posoka na priemaneto na Kodeks za administrativni narushenia i nakazania*. Reformata v administrativnoto nakazvane ot. Sbornik dokladi, Sofia: Univ. izd. Sv. Kliment Ohridski.

Staykov, I. (2021). Razvitieto na trudovoto pravo na Evropeyskia sayuz prez 2019 godina – novi iztochnitsi i novi perspektivi za po-nadezhdna pravna uredba na trudovite otnoshenia. Chast parva: Evropeyski organ po truda – sazdavane i pravna harakteristika. Sofia: Izdatelstvo na Nov balgarski universitet.

Yolova, G. (2020). Subektivnite trudovi prava - evolyutsia vav filosofiyata, normativnata uredba i doktrinata. Ot Andreeva, A., Yolova, G., Blagoycheva, H., Aleksandrov, A., Banov, H., Yordanov, Z. Zashtita za individualnite subektivni trudovi prava (na rabotnika ili sluzhitelya). Varna: Nauka i ikonomika, pp. 21 – 47.

ENDNOTES

1 The Labour Code adopted in 1986 (promulgated in State Gazette No. 26 of 1986) in Chapter Three regulates in detail the organisation and activities of trade unions. The central leadership of trade unions has important functions - including the right to initiate legislation and to

participate in the preparation and adoption of legislation on labour, social security and living standards issues.

2 https://ec.europa.eu/social/main.jsp?catId=157&langId=bg

3 Reasons to the Draft Law on Amendments and Additions to the Labour Code (602-01-60/20.10.2016); Published: https://www.parliament.bg/bg/bills/ID/66447/

4 https://ec.europa.eu/social/main.jsp?catId=157&langId=bg, seen on 27th Dec 2020

5 https://www.consilium.europa.eu/bg/policies/labour-mobility/eu-labour-authority/

6 https://eur-lex.europa.eu/legal-content/BG/TXT/?uri=CELEX:32019L1152

7 https://www.gli.government.bg/bg/taxonomy/term/519

Chapter 7
The Challenges of Labour and Insurance Protection in Non-Standard Forms of Employment

Hristina Blagoycheva
University of Economics, Varna, Bulgaria

ABSTRACT

Part of the newly appeared, over the last 25 years, non-standard forms of work do not fall within the scope of labor and social security legislation, while the rest are covered to a certain extent. Therefore, the purpose of the present work is to examine the challenges for the national governments in adapting labor legislation to the new conditions of the labor market and to propose possible measures in this direction. In pursuit of the set goal, the author sets himself the following tasks: 1) To investigate the preconditions that led to the appearance and rapid spread of non-standard forms of employment; 2) To point out the factors complicating the regulation of labor standards and the insurance protection of persons engaged in non-standard employment; 3) To look for and propose opportunities for regulatory and control measures in non-standard forms of employment, as well as to present some good examples of government initiatives.

DOI: 10.4018/978-1-6684-9067-9.ch007

INTRODUCTION

The New Economic Conditions and the Changing Concept of "Employment"

Preconditions for the Spread of Non-Standard Forms of Employment

Labour market regulations and controls play an important role in protecting employees. But recently, a number of new events are beginning to challenge established norms. Over the past 25 years, in response to the economic trends of digitalization and globalization, the labour market has become increasingly flexible and employment relations have undergone dynamic changes.

Along with the traditional forms, newer, non-standard ways of carrying out labour activity are also emerging. These new forms of employment significantly change the concepts and standards in terms of work position, social security, organization, place and periods of working time. Work in the modern economy is becoming increasingly casual, outsourced and fragmented into separate tasks (Fudge, 2006). Workers are managed through algorithms, and even without the platforms, many sectors see the rise of the workforce precisely through temporary and non-standard employment (Cherry, 2016). Furthermore, according to some scholars, this trend will continue to expand to "extreme levels" (Schoukens, 2020, p. 6).

Although standard, permanent full-time employment still predominates in the developed world, various non-standard forms are gradually expanding their scope and beginning to take up an ever-greater share of total employment. In 2016, a quarter of all employment contracts were for "non-standard" forms of employment, and over the past ten years over half of all new jobs were "non-standard" (Ministry of Labour and Social Policy (MLSP), 2020, p. 4).

Indeed, to some extent, the digitization and globalization of value chains can benefit businesses and workers as they provide opportunities for optimized production processes and access to pools of specialized knowledge and skills. Digital platforms and new algorithms may also enhance a business's ability to anticipate demand processes and coordinate the tasks to be completed and the required workforce across time and space. There is also evidence that some companies investing in digital technologies pay higher wages, and digital platforms create opportunities for cross-border employment (Shi, Li, and Fu, 2020). In this regard, a large part of non-standard employment is takes place remotely and this creates work opportunities for persons with limited mobility due to health conditions or caring responsibilities.

Digital technologies contribute to the emergence of new jobs (or low barriers to entry into the labour market) and create possibilities for earning income, including among social groups with unequal standing in the market – young adults, women, the elderly, people with disabilities, as well as people living in remote areas. But while some get the opportunity to develop skills or to better balance work and family life (World Economic Forum, 2020), others face the unpredictability of working hours and income, alternative work patterns, temporary contractual relations, alternative workplaces or irregular working hours (Ahmed, Gore, and Langford, 2020). Some are in a permanent on-call situation, as they are required to be constantly available, even during non-working hours. This lack of detachment merges their personal and professional life and affects negatively their health. Some countries (e.g. France) have adopted labour legislation on the right to detachment, but the vast majority of countries have not yet introduced such solutions (Deganis, Tagashira and Yang, 2021).

At the same time, in 2020 the world faced the global pandemic of COVID-19, which caused one of the worst economic and health crises in a century. According to the OECD (2020), this is one of the worst economic crises since the Great Depression, with impacts on human resources, productivity and the behaviour of employers and the workforce. COVID-19 accelerated the processes of expansion of new forms of employment, forcing many businesses to work remotely and showing that this is possible. At the same time, however, the emergence of new responsibilities led to gaps in employment management and control. And while the global community is looking for ways to economic recovery after the pandemic, the question of how its consequences will affect in the long term not only the quality of employment, but also the way it is organized, becomes important.

It is difficult to cover and describe all variations of non-standard employment, as there is still no uniform, Europe-wide classification of these forms or any generally recognized definition (MLSP, 2020, p. 14). Moreover, there is a lack of harmonization in the designations used by the different countries (terms such as "new", "atypical" or "irregular" employment are used). But in all situations, workers are engaged in the labour market in ways that deviate from the parameters of the standard employment relationship. A mapping by the European Foundation for the Improvement of Living and Working Conditions (Eurofound), started in 2013 (Eurofound, 2015) and systematized in a 2020 report (Eurofound, 2020a), identified nine new forms of employment (ICT-based mobile work, platform work, casual work, collaborative employment, job sharing, interim management, employee sharing, portfolio work and voucher-based work) and documented their increasing prevalence in the labour market in the EU, Norway and the UK.

Based on this mapping and the designations adopted by the MLSP in Bulgaria (MLSP, 2020), the following characteristics of non-standard employment options can be inferred:

1) ICT-based mobile work: employees work remotely, using information and computer technology.
2) Platform work: the platform serves as an intermediary where the interests of employers looking for a certain type of workforce and workers possessing the necessary skills intersect.
3) Casual work: the employer is looking for a worker only when additional workforce is needed – incidentally or for seasonal work. This may also be based on a permanent employment contract, where the employee is on call only.
4) Employee sharing: one employee can be employed simultaneously by several employers, each of whom needs the employee only for a certain time. This, on the one hand, satisfies the needs of the employers, and on the other hand, ensures full employment of the employee. Thus, the employment relationship can be implemented either through a special arrangement between the employers on the distribution of the tasks and working hours of the employee (permanent employee sharing), or through the conclusion of several fixed-term part-time employment contracts with each of the employers (temporary employee sharing).
5) Job sharing: two or more employees are jointly employed by one company, on a part-time basis, for the joint performance of a given job, thus covering the full-time working hours for the relevant position.
6) Voucher-based work: an organization (responsible for the paying of wages and social security and health insurance contributions for the worker) issues a voucher for the worker's labour. It is the company purchasing the voucher that determines when, what and where the worker will work. This form of employment usually applies to low-skilled workers.
7) Collaborative employment: the pooling of skills or resources between freelancers and self-employed individuals in order to offer the employer the performance of activities that they would not be able to perform separately.

8) Interim management: allows for the temporary engagement of external management capacities, by concluding temporary employment contracts (for the implementation of a certain project or the solving of a management problem) with highly qualified professionals.
9) Portfolio work: freelancers or self-employed individuals with certain skills can provide services (usually short-term) to a large number of organisations.

Table 1 shows the prevalence of the different non-standard forms of employment by country in 2020.

The table shows a heterogeneous profile of the individual member states, but it can be noticed that the least common form of non-standard employment in the EU is voucher-based work. Croatia is the only country where all nine forms of non-standard employment are found, and the most "conservative" in this respect are Luxembourg, Spain and Cyprus. Bulgaria is among the countries where these new forms are widespread, the only one missing being voucher-based work. Almost all new forms are envisaged to various degrees in the labour legislation of the different countries. However, platform work, portfolio work and collaborative employment of self-employed remain outside the scope of labour laws.

New technologies bring new patterns of work and a change in the concept of the physical location of the worker. There is no longer a need for a control body to be present at the workplace. It is common practice to work in several compatible workplaces or to work temporarily for different organizations under part-time employment contracts (MLSP, 2020).

Indeed, for some individuals such employment is a voluntary choice, but not for others, who are also faced with the question of the quality of their employment and whether there is an opportunity to increase the number of hours worked by them, if they wish so. For a large part of the part-time employees, the work does not offer opportunities for development and career, it is of low quality, with low pay and sets the employees on the path to falling into the category of "the working poor" (Blagoycheva, 2016).

The increase in the number of persons with non-standard employment may also affect public finances, since employers are not obliged to pay social security contributions and taxes for some categories of such workers. Thus, employers have an incentive to shift more tasks to workers who are less protected and less expensive (OECD, 2018b). However, this would undermine the effectiveness of social protection systems and state budgets.

Table 1. Prevalence of new forms of employment in the EU27, Norway and the UK, 2020

Country	ICT-based mobile work	Platform work	Casual work	Employee sharing	Job sharing	Voucherbased work	Collaborative employment	Interim management	Portfolio work
Austria	X	X		X	X	X	X	X	
Belgium	X	X	X	X	X	X	X		X
Bulgaria	X	X	X	X	X		X	X	X
Croatia	X	X	X	X	X	X	X	X	X
Cyprus	X	X	X						X
Czechia	X	X	X	X	X		X	X	X
Denmark	X	X	X				X	X	X
Estonia	X	X	X				X	X	X
Finland	X	X	X			X	X	X	
France	X	X	X	X	X	X	X	X	
Germany	X	X	X	X	X		X		
Greece	X	X	X		X	X	X	X	
Hungary	X	X	X	X	X		X	X	
Ireland	X	X	X		X		X	X	
Italy	X	X	X	X		X	X	X	
Latvia	X	X	X	X	X		X	X	X
Lithuania	X	X		X	X	X	X		X
Luxembourg	X			X			X		
Malta	X	X	X		X		X		
Netherlands	X	X	X		X		X	X	
Poland	X	X	X	X	X		X	X	X
Portugal	X	X	X	X	X		X		X
Romania	X	X	X	X			X		
Slovakia	X	X	X	X	X				
Slovenia	X	X	X		X	X	X		
Spain	X	X					X		
Sweden	X	X	X				X		X
Norway	X	X	X				X	X	X
United Kingdom	X	X	X		X		X	X	X

Source: Eurofound (2020a, p. 5-6)

The need to compete for jobs with low pay and no guarantees of the future not only place non-standard workers in a continuous state of insecurity, but also erodes opportunities for society's future. The consequences of some workers not being able to set aside funds for a pension or for a possible disability are not yet very noticeable. But in the long term, these will be much more severe, because then the costs of the welfare state will have to be borne by an ever-smaller group of individuals (PvdA, 2017, p. 31) (taking into account the aging of the population).

At the same time, the current regulatory frameworks of governments and the tax and social protection systems cannot be transformed quickly enough to match all emerging, diverse forms of employment and to ensure adequate protection of the incomes and social welfare of the employed.

Digital Platforms

In 2018, the European Commission (EC) and the Organization for Economic Co-operation and Development (OECD) carried out a joint survey among 44 ministries of labour (or the relevant ministry responsible for labour market policy) in the EU, OECD and G20 countries. The survey found that among the new forms of employment, platform work, which occupies an increasingly large share in various business sectors, is the most controversial (OECD, 2019b). Furthermore, as already indicated, such work is one of the three forms of non-standard employment that do not fall under the scope of labour legislation. Platform work can generally be thought of as matching the demand and supply of paid labour through an online web-based platform or application (Deganis, Tagashira and Yang, 2021). Here the relationship is between three parties: 1) the requesting client; 2) the worker performing work or services for remuneration, and 3) the platform as an intermediary. Very often a larger task can be divided into many small parts distributed among individual workers.

Platforms are one of the most widespread and rapidly growing new forms of digitally supported work. According to some estimates, they are growing by more than 25 percent per year globally (Kässi and Lehdonvirta, 2018). In the last two years, the COVID pandemic also played a significant role, by accelerating the digital transformation and causing the further expansion of platform-based business models. In a situation where much of the world was locked down, some platforms played a positive role by facilitating access to multiple services. The acquired experience and the identified benefits will most likely help to preserve much of the remote work even after the world recovers from the COVID crisis, by reorganizing the work processes, and a large proportion of the routine tasks can be now automated. What is more, many individuals, confident in their abilities and professionalism, will prefer to work via platforms, relying on additional income, greater flexibility and a better balance between work and family life.

Currently there are already more than 500 digital platforms operating in the European Union, realizing revenues of more than 20 billion euros. Among them are both small national organizations and large international companies, providing employment to over 28 million people. It is expected that in 2025 the number of such workers will reach 43 million (European Commission, 2021).

Some studies have concluded that platform work benefits all three levels: workers, businesses and society. For the individuals, these benefits consist in increased employment opportunities, promotion of entrepreneurship and reduction of gender gaps (Alonso Soto, 2020; UNECE, 2021). The platform can offer greater employment flexibility and additional income, including to people for whom, for various reasons, standard entry into the labour market is difficult. Businesses benefit from the reduced costs and greater flexibility. The benefits for society are increased employment, greater innovation and growth of the gross domestic product. Platforms facilitate the integration of services in the cash economy into the formal economy, as transactions are recorded by the platform (OECD, 2018a).

At the same time, a large part of the types of work offered on platforms are associated with precarious working conditions, as they lack transparency and predictability of contractual terms, access to appropriate social protection and adequate occupational health and safety. In addition to violating labour standards, there are ample opportunities for employers to shift the burden of business risks onto the workers themselves. Given their usual classification as self-employed or employees but with very short-duration contracts, the workers will be inconvenienced by limited access to social protection. For example, during the COVID pandemic, the lack of social security contributions and paid sick leave forced platform workers to work at risk for their own safety and health (especially those involved in transportation and delivery services) and to bear the financial burdens themselves.

In addition, a greater supply of labour on the platform may lead to lower asking prices of services. In December 2021, a European Commission publication stated that around 55% of people working through platforms earn less than the net hourly minimum wage of the country they are working in.

Moreover, it has been reported that some of the labour provided by platform workers remains outside of the paid hours. On average, they spend 12.6 hours per week doing paid tasks, but also 8.9 hours per week doing unpaid tasks (e.g. searching, researching and waiting for assignments) (European Commission, 2021).

Back in 2017, the European Commission launched COLLEEM, the Collaborative Economy and Employment Research Project focused on the platform economy sector. Its aim is to survey the platforms operating in EU countries and to provide an overview of some of their key indicators – size and reach of the platform, nature of the services on offer and the business models used. Based on these surveys, COLLEEM is to produce data to help better understand the situation in which platform workers are placed – their socio-economic profile, motivation, earnings, frequency of work, as well as the legal, economic and social challenges they face (European Commission, 2016). The report on the first results, published in 2018, indicated that the most important policy issue was precisely the status in employment and offered a definition of the main platform workers, describing them as those who earn more than 50% of their income and/or work more than 20 hours per week via platforms (Pesole et al., 2018). The second round of the survey in 2020 kept this definition, but introduced a task-based approach. Workers were asked "which task took most of their time, how long it usually took to complete the task, how much they earn and which platform they used to carry out the task" (Urzi Brancati, Pesole and Fernandez Macias, 2020). The responses showed that the majority of payments were not based on time worked on the platform, but by task performed.

The terms of employment via digital labour platforms are largely governed by service agreements and are unilaterally determined by the platforms (e.g. wages, working hours, scope of activity, right to use data, etc.). A very small part of the workers is directly employed by employers (most often for construction or maintenance of the platform itself). As regards the rest, it is usually difficult to distinguish between employer and employee (it could be said that they work in a kind of grey zone). Workers are most often categorized as self-employed or independent contractors whose work is mediated via either an online web-based platform (e.g. translations, legal, financial and patent services, freelance software design and development, gamers, YouTubers, etc.) or location-based platforms (such as taxi services, deliveries and home services) (Deganis, Tagashira and Yang, 2021). According to the platforms, being independent contractors, they can control their own income, but are also personally responsible for their social security contributions. This is a serious regulatory gap as it risks deepening the labour market divide between those in standard protected employment and those with limited access to social protection and labour rights. Therefore, a large number of workers dependent on their work via a platform insist on being treated not as independent contractors but as employees.

It is difficult to estimate the proportion of people working in the grey zone, both because of the ambiguity of the legal relationship, which often leads to their misclassification, and because of their false classification. In 2021, a study showed that over 90% of the digital labour platforms in the EU categorize people working via them as self-employed. Of the estimated 28 million people employed via digital labour platforms in the EU, 22.5 million people are correctly categorized as either employees or self-employed, and 5.5 million are likely to have been miscategorized (European Commission, 2021).

Moreover, the protection envisaged in the labour legislation cannot be applied to most of the contracts for mediation or for the provision of services using the platform applications. Very often, the platform itself or the service requester unilaterally determine the scope of the task, the working conditions and the payment to the contractor. Some cases have been identified where microtask requesters refuse to accept completed tasks without giving a valid reason and the worker does not receive payment (Kingsley, Gray and Suri, 2015). There are also situations where the platform unilaterally, without providing an explanation and sometimes even without warning, deactivates a worker's account (Kaltner, 2018; Ross, 2015).

In this regard, although there are already various policies for the social protection of workers in place, governments face serious regulatory challenges in at least two aspects. On the one hand, the rapid development of platforms and the business models they adopt is outpacing governments' attempts to make adequate changes in regulations and controls over such platforms. This compels, to a certain extent, the platform companies themselves to work in an uncertain regulatory environment. Another aspect is the cross-border nature of the platforms. The platform may be located in one country, the worker in another, and the clients in a third and fourth. This complicates the enactment of and compliance with any uniform regulatory requirements. Moreover, the differences in legislative and regulatory approaches in different countries make difficult the possibilities and efforts to rationalize and coordinate approaches to the control and regulation of labour relations in this area.

Factors Complicating the Regulation of Labour Laws and Social Protection in the Digital Environment

The Status of New Types of Employment

Non-standard employment is a vastly popular topic of discussion for at least two reasons. On the one hand, existing regulations are mainly intended for standard employment, where an employee is employed by a single employer on a full-time basis. The emergence of non-standard forms of employment already poses a serious challenge for the implementation of adequate regulations and controls over them. On the other hand, evidence is available (OECD, 2019b) of the prevalence of an imbalance in labour relations between workers and their employers and, in some cases, of a significant concentration of rights and power in employers. This necessitates a new assessment of the capabilities of regulatory mechanisms to deal with the sources and consequences of such an imbalance.

As regards the sources, a critical area to consider is the status of the new types of employment. It is the employment status that acts as a gateway to various worker rights and protections (OECD, 2019b). Therefore, the first step in this direction is the correct classification of workers. This provides them with access to work, income and social protection, opportunities for collective bargaining or lifelong learning.

The regulation of labour relations aims to protect employees from possible abuse by employers in terms of bargaining power or asymmetric control of information. In practice, the self-employed are considered to be separate and autonomous business undertakings, which alone bear the economic risks and enjoy the benefits of their activity. For this reason, they are often excluded from most employee rights, regulations and protections. For example, they do not enjoy unemployment insurance because their employment depends on their own efforts, decisions and the economic risks they are willing to take.

Things are particularly difficult for individuals in the "grey zone" between dependent employment and self-employment (OECD, 2019b). Some employers may erroneously, and others deliberately, classify their employees as self-employed, freeing themselves from social security and tax obligations, and other requirements of the regulated employment. Thus, transferring the risks onto the contractors, they can also gain a competitive advantage over other participants in the industry, through reduced costs. Of course, the workers themselves may also prefer one or the other form of employment, taking advantage of the opportunity to avoid to some extent the tax and social security contribution burdens. All in all, incorrect classification puts employees at risk of weak social and labour protection and places companies that follow the rules at a competitive disadvantage.

Figure 1 presents options for organization and possibilities for regulation of the considered persons with standard and non-standard employment. Diamonds correspond to classification decisions made by the employer or by the workers themselves. The dotted area shows the options of coverage by the labour and social security legislation.

Figure 1. Classification of employment and consequences from the point of view of labour and social protection
Source: OECD (2019b, p. 135)

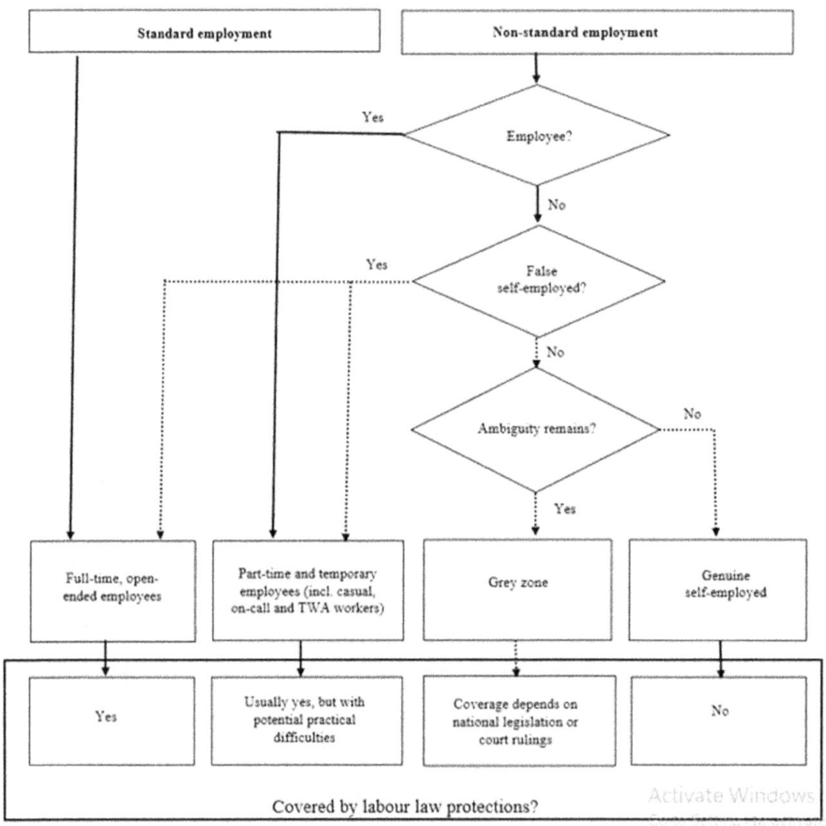

Traditional employment enjoys labour and social protections, but at the same time it is also an important source of income for the state budget and the social and health insurance systems. Misclassification of employment and positioning in the grey zone seriously damage a country's public revenues. Such financial erosion will ultimately affect the entire society.

The employee status itself is in many places not correctly defined and disputes often lead to litigation (Davidov, Freedland and Countouris, 2015). On the one hand, we can adopt the approach that an employee is a person hired by an employer. On the other hand, however, it is not enough to deem relevant only what is written in the employment contract – the actual facts of the employment relationship must be examined in order to conclude whether the person is not actually self-employed. False self-employment may originate from the employer's bargaining power to require that the contract designate the worker as self-employed.

Therefore, law enforcement authorities should strive particularly to minimize the opportunities for and advantages from misclassification of employees. In this regard, in recent years the term "dependent self-employment" has gained traction. Dependent contractors are defined as workers who have contractual arrangements of a commercial nature to provide goods or services for or on behalf of another economic unit, are not employees of that economic unit, but are dependent on that unit for organization and execution of the work or for access to the market (ILO, 2018, p. 10). Consequently, dependent self-employed are own-account workers who in practice rely for a large part of their income on a single employer or client (most often the platform). Many countries lack a working definition of dependent self-employment, and even where there is one, it varies in its characteristics. Therefore, considering the consequences of uncertainty in employment status, the OECD dedicated a whole chapter of its "Employment Outlook 2019: The Future of Work" report to government-oriented recommendations (OECD, 2019b). The main conclusion that can be drawn is that there is a need to identify cases of false self-employment and such where there is real ambiguity and, on this basis, to adopt political measures to regulate the situation.

Gaps in Social Protection

The employment status determines also the next level – social protection. Social protection systems are the main mechanism for income support and for limiting the spread of poverty. Social protection is understood as an established framework of coordinated policies and protective actions to balance social justice through policies for protection against poverty, mainly at the level of the social assistance systems, but also through new measures to strengthen labour markets (Andreeva and Yolova, 2018).

Employment status is at the core of today's social security systems and the benefits workers can count on will depend on whether they are salaried employees, self-employed or in the grey zone. The contemporary social security systems are not sufficiently adapted to the expansion of non-standard employment, as they are designed on the basis of "a stable, open-ended and direct employment relationship between a dependent, full-time employee and their unitary employer" (CEPS, 2018, p. 61). This creates a split labour market consisting of "insiders" who are protected and have access to many benefits and "outsiders" who shoulder the burden of job flexibility (Aussilloux, 2017). Such segmentation can cause suboptimal outcomes for workers and affect long-term sustainability and productivity growth, which in turn will impact countries' innovation and macroeconomic indicators. As already indicated, the growing number of non-standard workers may erode the effectiveness of social protection systems. Since companies are only required to pay taxes and social security contributions for certain categories of contractors, it is less expensive for them to contract with workers from the less protected categories. Thus, in practice, working in a digital environment favours the expansion of the informal economy, due to the emergence of new groups of "invisible" workers who do not contribute to the social security system (Chesalina, 2018).

In many forms of employment, social security cannot adequately cover and protect workers, due to numerous reasons: narrow legislative coverage of activities, biased eligibility criteria, low social security contribution rates, non-compliance by employers, etc. (Blagoycheva, 2020). Income volatility is characteristic for a large part of the self-employed, due to instability of the demand for their services, delayed payment or payment at irregular intervals for their work. Even if the social security contributions are charged on an annual basis, in bad years the workers will again not be able to make the payment. Add to this the fact that some of the self-employed try to avoid paying the full tax and social security contribution, and the assessment of eligibility for means-tested benefits becomes very complicated. Data from the European Commission show that nearly 40% of temporary part-time workers and 32% of temporary full-time workers do not have access to unemployment benefits, and around 10% of temporary part-time workers lack protection through sickness and maternity benefits (Eurofound, 2022).

Here we must also take into account the consequences of the pandemic, which showed (as some paraphrase George Orwell) that "all workers are equal, but some are more equal than others" in terms of their access to social protection (Spasova et al., 2021, p. 5). Although governments introduced a variety of measures to protect employment, they failed to provide protection for all. Among the most disadvantaged were non-standard workers and the self-employed (Eurofound, 2020b; Causa and Cavalleri, 2020), due to low (or even non-existent) entitlements to unemployment and sickness benefits.

Persons in non-standard employment also face other adverse social consequences: distorted consumption patterns (due to job insecurity and low wages) and a changed lifestyle (characterized by reduced socialization). Research shows that it is harder for temporary workers to access loans and housing, as banks and landlords tend to prefer workers with stable jobs and regular income (ILO, 2016). Insecure work and low income can affect also family planning. For example, studies in Italy and Spain prove that unstable employment combined with low levels of welfare leads to reduced birth rates (Barbieri et al., 2015; De La Rica and Iza, 2005).

A large proportion of non-standard workers have limited access to on-the-job training, as employers have no incentive or need to invest in upskilling workers who are not hired under permanent contracts. The same assumption applies to investments in safe and healthy working conditions. ICT technologies contribute to the increase in sedentary work, where workers face ergonomic risks, visual impairment and reduced physical activity.

All these issues necessitate the adoption of measures to enhance the protection of workers in the changed labour market and of their well-being. Among the measures already available to governments, investment in lifelong learning to enable workers to take advantage of new job opportunities remains a priority. At the same time, new, gradual practical measures to improve work life should be sought, building on good initiatives implemented in response to the consequences of the COVID-19 pandemic.

All workers in the labour market should have access to an adequate set of rights and social protection. One of the ways to achieve this is awareness – both employers and workers must be familiar with and understand the labour legislation existing in the country. Another one is to limit the incentives for both companies and employees to use false self-employment as means to avoid taxes and social security contributions. Moreover, introducing more severe sanctions against such misclassification and strengthening the capacity and powers of national labour inspectorates to monitor and detect violations is needed.

Where possible, countries should try to harmonize social security in standard and non-standard forms of employment. In order to cover people who are at risk of poverty and social disadvantage, some countries are already implementing measures to make their social protection systems inclusive of people in the grey zone between dependent and independent employment. However, these are "piecemeal" measures that are inconsistent across countries. For example, in Germany, persons who are not personally subordinated, but are economically dependent on a client, are subject to mandatory pension insurance. The social security legislation in Austria treats freelance workers as employees requiring contributions for old-age pension, unemployment benefits, health insurance, and the right to parental leave. In Denmark, certain provisions enacted specifically for the economically dependent self-employed, along with the universal nature of certain schemes (including disability), lead to a situation where the overall social protection for this category of workers reaches levels similar to the social protection of employees (MLSP, 2021, pp. 25-26).

In Portugal, the "dependent self-employed" have access to certain social benefits (pension, unemployment, sickness and disability). In Germany, these individuals enjoy freedom of association and the right to collective bargaining, and a minimum leave of four weeks (Däubler, 2016), in Spain – minimum wage, annual leave, entitlements in case of wrongful termination, leave for family or health reasons, and the right to collective bargaining (Cherry and Aloisi, 2017).

One fundamental change is coming to the fore and getting seriously considered by many countries – shifting the focus from the employer to the worker and tying social protection to individuals rather than to their jobs. Surveys and interviews conducted with 12,000 workers in 100 countries, and with 70 businesses, 16 platform companies and 14 platform worker associations operating in multiple sectors and countries indicate that workers in the digital age may work for multiple clients/employers and change jobs frequently facilitated by digital platforms (ILO, 2022). Therefore, in order to ensure social protection, it must be tied to the worker, by transferring individual benefits between workplaces, even across national borders. In this regard, France and Germany are considering the introduction of portable "individual activity accounts" that can be used flexibly by workers according to their needs

(OECD, 2019c). The portability of accrued benefit rights between different jobs facilitates workers. They can change jobs or shift from self-employment to dependent employment, keeping the already accumulated rights and using them flexibly, according to their needs. However, the difficulty comes from the fact that the portability of rights is intended to be within the framework of the public redistributive social security system, and some of these workers are actually well-paid. Therefore, it is necessary to figure out how to frame the regulations so as to preserve an appropriate degree of redistribution and risk sharing between disadvantaged and well-off workers.

In any case, the digital transformation is changing the labour market at an accelerated pace and requires increased flexibility of labour regulations. Furthermore, the new realities urgently impose the need for regulatory and administrative reform in order to achieve universal social protection for all members of society.

Possibilities for Regulatory and Control Measures for Non-Standard Forms of Employment

Employment Protection

The new labour market trends pose new questions to policy makers. Are the existing systems of labour law, lifelong learning, social protection, taxation and collective bargaining still relevant in the new conditions of labour markets? And isn't a major shift in political thinking now required to seek safeguards to protect vulnerable workers from abuse and to ensure that compliant employers are not disadvantaged? In fact, already in 2018, a joint study of the European Commission and the OECD showed that many countries have already realized this and have begun to take respective countermeasures (OECD, 2019a), and regulatory authorities in many countries are now paying attention to issues related to working conditions in digital platforms and other non-standard forms of employment. For example, changes in the labour laws of Italy and France provide platform workers with minimum social rights (ILO, 2022). Joint initiatives are being launched between governments, social partners, local organizations and the platforms themselves. However, these initiatives are still unable to achieve full reach due to a number of reasons: limited scope of legislative measures, insufficient power and resources of organizations representing the interests of workers, and in many places also the absence of trade unions.

In December 2021, the Commission proposed a new directive aimed at regulating the work of the platforms, seeking to create a list of control criteria to determine in which cases a platform will be treated as an employer (ILO, 2022, p. 90). This would provide persons working through digital labour platforms with an increased opportunity to enjoy their labour rights and social benefits. However, work on the directive is still hampered by the existing ambiguity of employment status.

On the other hand, the cross-border nature of the platforms' operation caused the Global Commission on the Future of Work, put together by the ILO, to recommend the establishment of a common international system for regulation of digital labour platforms that should require from platforms and their clients to comply with certain minimum rights and protections for their workers (ILO, 2019).

A key point for workers' security is adequate employment protection legislation. Clear rules for hiring and dismissal affect job security, careers and employee well-being. In the case of standard employment contracts, the legislation protects employees against wrongful breach of contract by employers, and authorities control the possibility for unfair dismissal or unpaid wages. In addition to guaranteeing the security of workers, such forms of protection and control also support their career development and well-being. In this regard, the existing labour regulations must undergo a serious update to reflect the new conditions of the digital age. Legislators must try to strike a balance between the necessary flexibility in employment on the one hand and, on the other, to adopt labour standards that protect employment, fair working conditions and workers' income. This is a complex task, requiring a transition from the existing universal frameworks to new, individual solutions, corresponding to the conditions and challenges of new forms of employment and taking into account the impact of digitalization on work, the economy and society as a whole.

The first task of policy makers is to define the status of workers: who will be considered an employee and who will not, and who will be recognized as an employer. However, such clarifications become difficult in a situation of an employment relationship between more than two persons – for example, temporary work through an agency or when working via a platform. Such situations raise the question of who is responsible for complying with labour regulations. When work is undertaken through an agency, it is commonly assumed that the employment relationship is between that agency and the worker and therefore it is the agency that should ensure compliance with labour laws (Countouris et al., 2016). Still, the government could introduce regulations requiring such guarantees from the user company as well – in terms of a safe and healthy working environment, as well as joint and several liability with the intermediary agency (OECD, 2014).

The situation becomes even more complicated when we look at the operation of a platform, as it involves many more interested parties and regulation is more difficult. Although some platforms around the world have already taken the initiative to treat their workers as employees (Cherry and Aloisi, 2017), in most cases they claim that they are not employers, but only provide a space for workers to find clients. The clients themselves are also sometimes difficult to identify as employers, as working via a platform often involves short-duration assignments from multiple clients. Therefore, where there is no possibility to allocate responsibility, it may be determined that platforms and clients must jointly take responsibility for workers' rights. Some authors point out that who bears the responsibility will depend on who undertakes the main functions – from concluding the contract to determining the amount of pay or hourly rate (Adams-Prassl and Risak, 2016). In this case, the labour and social protection obligations will obviously not be tied to only one assumed employer, but will be distributed among many actors with vested interest in the contractor's work. The regulatory authorities of governments may oblige the entire chain (the intermediary platform and the clients) to be jointly and severally liable to the contractor in accordance with the labour regulations. Such a solution can be adopted not only for platform workers, but also for others forms of non-standard employment, where applicable. It is therefore imperative that governments revise and harmonize the regulations and criteria for determining employment status and assuming the relevant responsibility.

There are already examples of implementations in this direction. In France, the following occupations are regarded as having an employment relationship, provided they meet the introduced criteria: performing artists (this also applies to Spain), models, professional journalists and sales representatives (Pedersini, 2002; ILO, 2006). In the Netherlands, it is automatically deemed that an employment contract exists if the worker has worked regularly for an employer for a period of three months (or at least 20 hours per month) (Davidov, Freedland and Countouris, 2015).

As regards workers in the grey zone, who are largely excluded from the scope of the existing legislation, governments must decide which of their employment rights should be extended and how. Explanatory campaigns about the provisions and the scope of the law are not enough to eliminate the grey zone and the uncertainty it brings to both workers and compliant employers. It is precisely the reduction of the grey zone between genuine self-employment and dependent self-employment that is the second key prerequisite for the labour and social security of workers.

In this regard, some countries have identified specific groups of workers to which certain parts of the labour law are to be applied with priority, using different approaches. Some put the emphasis on specific occupations, while others focus on the economically dependent self-employed. For example, some European countries attempt to determine the status of "dependent" self-employed persons by applying the income criterion. In Spain, such status is recognized for those receiving 75% of their income from a single client, while in Portugal the threshold is 50% of the yearly income. Germany treats as dependent self-employed those who: i) work on the basis of a contract for service or a contract for work and services for other persons; ii) do so personally; and iii) receive 50% of their income from a single client (33% for artists, writers and journalists) (OECD, 2019b). Other countries have attempted to bring the status of the self-employed closer to that of employees. For example, in 2004 the Czech Republic organized a tax reform aimed at curbing false self-employment. Although the reform was canceled in 2007, observations show that during this period, self-employment grew less than in the Slovak Republic (OECD, 2008). Since 2008, the Austrian government has integrated independent contractors into the social protection system to limit employers' incentives to avoid taxes and regulations. Thus, these individuals now pay the same social security contributions as standard employees (OECD, 2018b).

Strengthening the sanctions against companies that do not comply with the legislation can also help to address false self-employment. In addition to the imposition of fines, the payment of backdated tax and social security obligations and the imposition of the obligation to change the status of the false self-employed person, with all the ensuing legal and financial obligations, can be applied.

In order to achieve an adequate response to all these legal challenges, additional actions are needed to strengthen the stability and powers of labour inspectorates to control and sanction violations. If these are to cope with the increased responsibilities and scale of work, they will need increased resources and additional training for inspectors. For example, Ireland, Spain and Greece have seen increased targeting of inspections to certain areas or sectors considered to have a higher prevalence of false self-employment (OECD, 2019a).

Given the emergence of new forms of work (largely remote), labour inspectorates will also need new technological tools and devices. All this will surely entail expenditure of financial resources, but it can be expected that the costs will be compensated by the effective work of inspectors in collecting taxes and social security contributions for the wrongly classified workers.

Finally, labour regulations must be adapted in a way that allows workers in the grey zone to at least partially benefit from certain employment protection, regulated working time, fair pay and occupational health and safety.

Safe Working Conditions and Fair Pay

In standard employment contracts, the employer is responsible for ensuring healthy and safe working conditions (Blagoycheva, Andreeva and Yolova, 2019). In many forms of non-standard employment there is a transfer of responsibility for occupational safety and health (OSH) from the employer to the workers. This is based on the lack of training and knowledge of the rights and resources available to workers, which prevents them from taking appropriate measures to ensure safe working conditions and working environment. In some cases, they may even take additional risks to keep up with stiff competition. In addition, labour inspectorates are often not adequately prepared to deal with the new conditions, as some jobs in non-standard employment are often harder to reach and may remain out of sight. Add to this the insufficient support from trade unions, the multi-party nature of labour relations and the short nature of some of the tasks, and it can be expected that there are serious preconditions for uncertainty as to the extent to which the existing legislation is applied.

At the same time, some of the new forms of work are associated with increased (or entirely new) risks. For example, platform work in the transport sector is associated with increased transport accidents, due to insufficient driver experience, haste to overtake a competitor, eagerness to make more trips or overconfidence. Existing data show that in recent years ridesharing has seen a 2%-3% increase in the number of motor vehicle fatalities and fatal accidents as a result of increased congestion and road utilisation (Barrios, Hochberg and Yi, 2018). Working online also may take place in an unhealthy working environment, which can cause visual fatigue, musculoskeletal problems or work-related stress.

Again, the issue comes to the employment status. Compliance with measures and regulation of a healthy and safe working environment usually applies to employees under a permanent employment relationship, but not to others. In order to extend the scope of protection, special provisions could be enacted to regulate working conditions for certain additional occupations as well as for dependent self-employed persons.

The employment status is also a condition for payment of remuneration for the work performed and for guaranteeing a certain minimum income. Collectively negotiated minimum wages are a social tool to prevent exploitation and poverty among workers. Although it is a constant subject of heated discussion (Blagoycheva, 2018), there are studies arguing that small incremental increases in the minimum wage will not have negative employment effects (Card and Krueger, 2015). Thus, in the case of employees under a standard full-time employment contract, the minimum wage can be used as a tool to protect against poverty and an incentive to increase the employees' attachment to their company.

But for a large number of people in non-standard employment (especially those in the grey zone and the self-employed) this incentive cannot be used, because their pay is not based on working time, as it is in the case of regular employees. Their activity (especially of those working via platforms) is not covered by the minimum wage systems. They cannot rely on support through social dialogue or trade unions to negotiate for them.

In most cases, the income from platform work is fluctuating and unstable. It is particularly low where the key conditions of the arrangement are dictated by the platform (combining and distribution of tasks, pricing and terms), as well as when performing microtasks. Some of the reasons for the low pay are that it is not based on time worked, but on tasks performed. Earlier we pointed out that in addition to the time spent to perform the tasks, the workers spend time on searching and waiting for assignments, but this time is not accounted for. Furthermore, the client may refuse to accept the completed task or even to pay for it after accepting it. The option to get paid is to litigate, but since these are usually small tasks, their worth will not cover the lawsuit. Thus, the clients remain unpunished, and the workers face the threat of income insecurity.

Clearly, the absence of minimum wage mechanisms leaves a significant portion of the workforce facing structural challenges related to income inequality. Therefore, it is desirable to consider how to expand the mechanisms for achieving fair pay, so that such workers can avoid the trap of poverty and mistreatment by employers.

One option to expand the legislation in the area of income support is to gradually identify certain groups of workers in the grey zone (these can be contractors with certain occupations or dependent self-employed persons) and to introduce minimum wage criteria for them. For persons receiving payment per completed tasks, a proportional part of the minimum wage to be paid for each completed task can be envisaged. On this basis, the introduction of minimum payment rates for different groups of self-employed persons is already being discussed in several countries. In 2017, the Dutch Labour Party put in its pre-election program the introduction of a minimum wage for the self-employed, to be implemented through collective bargaining of rates (PvdA, 2017, p. 34). In 2016, a proposal was put forward in Germany's federal parliament to introduce minimum rates of pay for the work of freelancers and the self-employed, stating that digital work should not be a legal vacuum where only the client sets the rules (Deutscher Bundestag, 2016, p. 5). In 2017, the minimum wage legislation in Poland was expanded to cover work "performed under service agreements" (OECD, 2019a).

Good practices are already being adopted by platforms. The Czech website Topdesigner.cz and the Spanish adtriboo.com have adopted a minimum and in some cases a fixed price for certain tasks, depending on the average number of hours spent by workers on them (European Parliament, 2016).

Despite what has been done so far and the good intentions for the future, there are still many challenges and difficulties facing the regulatory authorities. This is why they must look for alternative ways of providing social and income support to persons in non-standard employment. One solution is the regulation of collective bargaining rights of persons operating in the grey zone between dependent employment and self-employment. However, the key challenge remains the same: to ensure that the labour market and the competition policy are aligned on this issue. Therefore, the governments face the need for quick orientation in this situation and for finding methods of regulation and control in order to facilitate the enforcement of the existing European acts and national legislations.

REFERENCES

Adams-Prassl, J., & Risak, M. (2016) Uber, Taskrabbit, & Co: Platforms as Employers? Rethinking the Legal Analysis of Crowdwork. *Comparative Labor Law Policy Journal, Oxford Legal Studies Research Paper, 8*. https://ssrn.com/abstract=2733003.

Ahmed, N., Gore, E., & Langford, N. (2020). *Pandemic and Precarity: rethinking what it means to be precarious under COVID 19*. Sheffield Political Economy Research Institute. http://speri.dept.shef.ac.uk/2020/04/30/pandemic-and-precarity-rethinking-what-it-means-to-be-precarious-under-covid-19/ [Accessed 30.01.2022].

Alonso Soto, D. (2020). *Technology and the future of work in emerging economies: What is different*. OECD Working Papers No. 236.

Andreeva, A. & Yolova, G. (2018). *Predizvikatelstva i tendentsii pred sotsialnata zashtita v usloviyata na digitalnoto obshtestvo. Izvestiya Sp. Ikonomicheski universitet*. Varna: Nauka i ikonomika.

Aussilloux, V. (2017). Testing novel approaches: Two takes on individual activity accounts. *A lever for more inclusive social protection*. European Political Strategy Centre (EPSC). https://medium.com/reaffirming-social-values-in-uncertain-times/testing-novel-approaches-two-takes-on-individual-activity-accounts-beab1281fc78

Barbieri, P., Bozzon, R., Schere, S., Grotti, R., & Lugo, M. (2015). The rise of a Latin model? Family and fertility consequences of employment instability in Italy and Spain. *European Societies*, *17*(4), 423–446. doi:10.1080/14616696.2015.1064147

BarriosJ.HochbergY.YiH. (2018) The Cost of Convenience: Ridesharing and Traffic Fatalities. . doi:10.2139/ssrn.3259965

Blagoycheva, H. (2016). Employment and the 'Working Poor' Phenomenon in the EU. International Journal of Economics &amp [IJEBA]. *Business Administration (London)*, *4*(3), 3–18.

Blagoycheva, H. (2018). Employers and Employees – on Both Sides of the 'Minimum Wages' Barricade. *International Scientific Journal Fundamental and Applied Researches in Practice of Leading Scientific Schools, Hamilton, Canada: Accent Graphics Communications, 28*(4), 9 – 15. https://doi.org/https://doi.org/10.33531/farplss.2018.4.02

Blagoycheva, H. (2020). Predizvikatelstvata pred sotsialnata zashtita na litsata s nestandartna zaetost. Ikonomicheska nauka, obrazovanie i realna ikonomika: razvitie i vzaimodeystviya v digitalnata epoha. *Sbornik s dokladi ot Yubileyna mezhdunarodna nauchna konferentsiya v chest na 100 god. ot osnovavaneto na IU*. Varna: Nauka i ikonomika.

Blagoycheva, H., Andreeva, A., & Yolova, G. (2019). Obligation and Responsibility of Employers to Provide Health and Safety at Work – Principles, Current Regulation and Prospects. *Economic Studies*, *28*(2), 115–137.

Card, D., & Krueger, A. (2015). *Myth and measurement: the new economics of the minimum wage*. Princeton University Press. doi:10.2307/j.ctv7h0s52

Causa, O., & Cavalleri, M. C. (2020). How non-standard workers are affected and protected during the Covid-19 crisis: stylised facts and policy considerations. CEPR, VOXeu. https://voxeu.org/article/how-non-standard-workers-are-affected-and-protected-during-covid-19-crisis.

CEPS. (Centre for European Policy studies). (2018). Online Talent Platforms, Labour Market Intermediaries and the Changing World of Work. CEPS. https://www.ceps.eu/ceps-publications/online-talent-platforms-labour-market-intermediaries-and-changing-world-work/.

Cherry, M., & Aloisi, A. (2017). 'Dependent Contractors' in the Gig Economy: A Comparative Approach. American University Law Review, 66(3), 365–689. doi:10.2139srn.2847869

CherryM. A. (2016) Beyond Misclassification: The Digital Transformation of Work. *Comparative Labor Law Policy Journal.* https://ssrn.com/abstract=2734288.

Chesalina, O. (2018) Access to social security for digital platform workers in Germany and in Russia: a comparative study. *Spanish Labour Law and Employment Relations Journal*, 1(7) pp. 17-28. doi:10.20318/sllerj.2018.4433

Countouris, N., Deakin, S., Freedland, M., Koukiadaki, A., & Prassl, J. (2016). *Report on temporary employment agencies and temporary agency work.* International Labour Office.

Däubler, W. (2016). Challenges to Labour Law. *Pravo. Zhurnal Vysshey shkoly ekonomiki 1*, pp. 189-203. . doi:10.17323/2072-8166.2016.1.201.215

Davidov, G., Freedland, M., & Countouris, N. (2015) The Subjects of Labor Law: 'Employees' and Other Workers, in Finkin, M. & Mundlak, G. (eds.), *Research Handbook in Comparative Labor Law,* Edward Elgar. https://papers.ssrn.com/sol3/papers.cfm?abstract_id=2561752.

De La Rica, S., & Iza, A. (2005). Career planning in Spain: Do fixed-term contracts delay marriage and parenthood? *Review of Economics of the Household, 3*(1), 49–73. doi:10.100711150-004-0979-8

Deganis, I., Tagashira, M., & Yang, W. (2021). *Digitally enabled new forms of work and policy implications for labour regulation frameworks and social protection systems.* United Nations Department of Economic and Social Affairs. https://www.un.org/development/desa/dspd/2021/09/digitally-enabled-new-forms-of-work-and-policy-implications-for-labour-regulation-frameworks-and-social-protection-systems/.

Deutscher Bundestag. (2016). *Arbeit 4.0 – Arbeitswelt von morgen gestalten*. Deutscher Bundestag Drucksache 18/10254. https://dipbt.bundestag.de/dip21/btd/18/102/1810254.pdf.

Eurofound. (2015). *New forms of employment*. Publications Office of the European Union, Luxembourg.

Eurofound. (2020a). New forms of employment: 2020 update, New forms of employment series, Publications Office of the European Union, Luxembourg.

Eurofound (2020b). COVID-19: Policy responses across Europe, Publications Office of the European Union, Luxembourg.

Eurofound. (2022). Living and working in Europe 2021, Publications Office of the European Union, Luxembourg.

European Commission. (2016). A European Agenda for the Collaborative Economy. Communication from the Commission to the European Parliament, the Council, the European Economic and Social Committee and the Committee of the Regions. European Commission, Brussels. Available at: https://eur-lex.europa.eu/legal-content/EN/TXT/PDF/?uri=CELEX:52016DC0356& from=EN [Accessed 18.03.2022].

European Commission. (2021). Questions and answers: Improving working conditions in platform work. Brussels, 9 December 2021. Available at: https://ec.europa.eu/commission/presscorner/detail/en/qanda_21_6606 [Accessed 18.03.2022].

European Commission. Digital labour platforms: The COLLEEM research project. Available at: https://joint-research-centre.ec.europa.eu/digital-labour-platforms-colleem-research-project_en

European Parliament. (2016). The Situation of Workers in the Collaborative Economy. Directorate General for Internal Policies, Policy Department A: Economic and Scientific Policy October 2016. Available at: https://www.europarl.europa.eu/RegData/etudes/IDAN/2016/587316/IPOL_IDA(2016)587316_EN.pdf [Accessed 21.03.2022].

FudgeJ. (2006). Fragmenting Work and Fragmenting Organizations: The Contract of Employment and the Scope of Labour Regulation. Osgoode Hall Law Journal, Vol. 44, No. 4. Available at SSRN: https://ssrn.com/abstract=974916

ILO. (2006). The employment relationship. International Labour Conference, 95th Session, Report V (1). Available at: https://www.ilo.org/global/publications/ilo-bookstore/order-online/books/WCMS_PUBL_9221166112_EN/lang--en/index.htm. [Accessed 11.02.2022].

ILO. (2016). Non-standard employment around the world: Understanding challenges, shaping prospects. International Labour Office – Geneva. Available at: https://www.ilo.org/global/publications/books/WCMS_534326/lang--en/index.htm. [Accessed 11.12.2021].

ILO. (2018). Report II: Statistics on Work Relationships. 20th International Conference of Labour Statisticians, 10-19 October 2018, International Labour Office, Geneva. Available at: https://www.ilo.org/wcmsp5/groups/public/---dgreports/---stat/documents/publication/wcms_644596.pdf. [Accessed 11.12.2021].

ILO. (2019). Work for a brighter future. Report of the Global Commission on the Future of Work. https://www.ilo.org/global/publications/books/WCMS_662410/lang--en/index.htm.

ILO. (2022) World Employment and Social Outlook. *Trends 2021.* https://www.ilo.org/global/research/global- reports/weso/trends2021/WCMS_795453/lang--en/index.htm[Accessed 04.10.2022].

Kaltner, J. (2018). Employment Status of Uber and Lyft Drivers: Unsettlingly Settled. *Hastings Women's Law Journal*, *29*(1), 29–54. https://repository.uchastings.edu/cgi/viewcontent.cgi?article=1403&context=hwlj

Kässi, O., & Lehdonvirta, V. (2018). Online labour index: Measuring the online gig economy for policy and research. *Technological Forecasting and Social Change*, *137*, 241–248. doi:10.1016/j.techfore.2018.07.056

Kingsley, S., Gray, M., & Suri, S. (2015). Accounting for Market Frictions and Power Asymmetries in Online Labor Markets, Policy &amp. *Policy and Internet*, *7*(4), 383–400. doi:10.1002/poi3.111

MLSP. (2020) Doklad: Analiz na ochakvanite promeni v organizatsiyata na truda i zaetostta v Balgariya, porodeni ot novovaznikvashtite „novi formi na trud". Available at: https://www.mlsp.government.bg/uploads/1/lm-report-v3.pdf

OECD. (2008). *OECD Employment Outlook 2008*. OECD Publishing. doi:10.1787/empl_outlook-2008-

OECD. (2014). *OECD Employment Outlook 2014*. OECD Publishing. doi:10.1787/empl_outlook-2014-

OECD. (2018a). *Tax Challenges Arising from Digitalisation – Interim Report 2018: Inclusive Framework on BEPS*. OECD Publishing. doi:10.1787/9789264293083-

OECD. (2018b). *The Future of Social Protection: What works for non-standard workers?* OECD Publishing. doi:10.1787/9789264306943-

OECD. (2019a). *Policy Responses to New Forms of Work*. OECD Publishing. doi:10.1787/0763f1b7-

OECD. (2019b). *OECD Employment Outlook 2019: The Future of Work*. OECD Publishing. doi:10.1787/9ee00155-

OECD. (2019c). *Preparing for the Changing Nature of Work in the Digital Era, March 2019*. OECD. https://dokumen.tips/documents/preparing-for-the-changing-nature-of-work-in-the-digital-preparing-for-thechanging.html?page=1.

OECD. (2020). *OECD Employment Outlook 2020: Worker Security and the COVID-19 Crisis*. OECD Publishing. doi:10.1787/1686c758-

Pedersini, R. (2002). Economically dependent workers', employment law and industrial relations. *Eurofound*. https://www.eurofound.europa.eu/publications/report/2002/economically-dependent-workers-employment-law-and-industrial-relations.

Pesole, A., M., Urzí Brancati, C., Fernández-Macías, E., Biagi, F., & González Vázquez, I. (2018). Platform Workers in Europe. *Publications Office of the European Union, Luxembourg., JRC112157*. Advance online publication. doi:10.2760/742789

Pvd, A. (2017) Een Verbonden Samenleving - Verkiezingsprogramma 2017. *Partij van de Arbeid*. https://www.pvda.nl/wp-content/uploads/2017/02/PvdAVerkiezingsprogramma2017EenVerbondenSamenleving.pdf

Ross, H. (2015). Ridesharing's House of Cards: O'Connor v. Uber Technologies, Inc. and the Viability of Uber's Labor Model in Washington, Washington. *Law Review*, *90*, 1431–1469. https://digital.law.washington.edu/dspace-law/bitstream/handle/1773.1/1489/90WLR1431.pdf

Schoukens P. (2020) Digitalisation and social security in the EU. The case of platform work: from work protection to income protection? *European Journal of Social Security*, 1–18. . doi:10.1177/1388262720971300

Shi, L., Li, S., & Fu, X. (2020). The Fourth Industrial Revolution, Technological Innovation and Firm Wages: Firm-level Evidence from OECD Economies. *Revue d'Economie Industrielle*, *1*(69), 89–125. https://journals.openedition.org/rei/8798?lang=en. doi:10.4000/rei.8798

Spasova, S., Ghailani, D., Sabato, S., Coster, S., Fronteddu, B., & Vanhercke, B. (2021). *Non-standard workers and the self-employed in the EU: social protection during the Covid-19 pandemic*. ETUI. https://etui.org/publications/non-standard-workers-and-self-employed-eu.

UNECE. (2021) New forms of employment and quality of employment: Implications for official statistics. *Working Paper Series on Statistics, 8.*

Urzi Brancati, M. C., Pesole, A., & Fernandez Macias, E. (2020). New evidence on platform workers in Europe. Results from the second COLLEEM survey Luxembourg. *Publications Office of the European Union, JRC118570.* doi:10.2760/459278

World Economic Forum. (2020). *The Promise of Platform Work: Understanding the Ecosystem*. WEF. https://www.weforum.org/whitepapers/the-promise-of-platform-work-understanding-the-ecosystem/

Chapter 8
Effectiveness and Efficiency of Control for Compliance With Labour Legislation in the New Conditions

Hristosko Bogdanov
University of Economics, Varna, Bulgaria

ABSTRACT

In this part of the study, attention is paid to the need to determine the effectiveness and efficiency of the control activity of the labor control agency. The approach that was used is related to the binding of the results of the control activity of the agency and the resources that it uses to carry out its activity. Indicators for the period 2017-2021 have been calculated, which can be used to determine how effective and efficient the agency's activity is. Of primary importance for exercising control over compliance with labor legislation, according to the legislation in force in the Republic of Bulgaria, is the Executive Agency "Main Labor Inspection" (EA MLI).

DOI: 10.4018/978-1-6684-9067-9.ch008

INTRODUCTION

Control, its Effectiveness, as an Economic Category on Compliance With Labor Legislation

Of primary importance for exercising control over compliance with labor legislation, according to the legislation in force in the Republic of Bulgaria, is the Executive Agency "Main Labor Inspection" (EA MLI). The Agency carries out comprehensive control related to the application and compliance with labor legislation. The legal aspects of the specific features, of the powers of EA MLI bodies in the implementation of the control activity of the agency, have been studied in the legal books. For the purposes of the exposition in this chapter, we will only note that the control carried out by the EA MLI includes two main methods of control and influence on the control objects, namely: carrying out inspections and imposing coercive administrative measures. The mentioned two control methods are regulated in § 1 of the additional provisions of the Labor Inspection Act.

Historically speaking, the role of the state has increased significantly from the beginning of the 20th century to the present. This increase in the role of the state is accompanied by an increase in budget revenues and budget expenditures. Based on the data of numerous studies in the field of the economy of individual countries, the constant increase in the share of government expenditures as a part of the gross domestic product of the countries can be seen. Therefore, given the growing public expenditure and its importance for society, the efficient use of public funds is of particular interest. In this connection, the question of the effectiveness of the spent budget funds for the various state institutions is also raised. The effectiveness of the control exercised by the EA MLI can be considered as part of this problem. The agency is a secondary allocator of budget funds and its budget is part of the budget of the Ministry of Labor and Social Policy, according to the Law on Public Finances and the relevant Resolution No. 2 of the Council of Ministers of 13.01.2014. As a result of the provisions of the mentioned legal regulation, the EA MLI is fully supported by the budget. Thus, the means through which the control activity of the agency is carried out are public and requirements regarding their effective use may be applied to them.

Efficiency is one of the main economic categories for measuring economic development. Its research and analysis are used to determine the qualitative characteristics of a given system (economic, social, political, cultural). In reasonable and conscious development, people and the organizations they created have a natural drive to perform effective activity. The pursuit of efficiency has always been part of the goal orientation of people and organizations. It can be seen that the desire for effective activity accompanies everyone, the individual, organization, institutions, regions, countries, etc.

As is well-known, the concept of efficiency is too broad and is applied in many areas. In the literature related to the companies carrying out economic activity, there is no dispute that efficiency, expressed as an indicator, is a relation of the beneficial effect (result) to the costs of obtaining it. As for public organizations, budget support organizations, their efficiency is not always expressed as a relation of result to resources for its obtaining. Obviously, the problem of efficiency can be considered from different points of view, depending on the quantities we compare and their relationship with objective facts and phenomena of human reality.

The concept of effectiveness in the Dictionary of the Bulgarian Language (published by the Institute of the Bulgarian Language at the Bulgarian Academy of Sciences) is presented as originating from effective, and effective means - giving a good result, having a positive effect. There is no universally accepted definition of efficiency. In general, efficiency occurs whenever results are matched against the costs required to obtain them. Its quantitative assessment is carried out by forming relations between the achieved result (effect of the activity) and the resources used to ensure this effect. One of the main reasons for assuming that this relation most clearly expresses the determination of effectiveness is that it involves the result of an activity, which is synthesized and expressed through its effect. The effect of performing the activity determines the result of the operation of the activity.

The problem arising is how to approach the determination of the effectiveness of organizations that are supported by the budget and the purpose of their creation and existence is not to achieve an economic result. As in many cases, the approach that we can adopt as a basis is related to our well-known concepts - the determination of efficiency in business organizations.

The concept of efficiency, regardless of the wide variety of nuances in its usage, can be defined as:

а) a correlation between the magnitude of the effect (the final result achieved) and the number of expenses incurred for it and

б) a degree of correspondence between the actually achieved state of the managed object and the state that is set (described) with the set goal.

Accordingly, the closer the actual and target states of the controlled system are, the higher the efficiency is considered to be. To make this comparison possible, it is necessary to answer the following questions:

- What does the effect (end result) mean and can it be measured and under what conditions?
- What are the parameters of the state (target or actual) of the managed object and what are the possibilities for its determination?
- What is the content of the costs to achieve the effect and do they have a single measure?
- Is it feasible (in a purely operational aspect) to compare effect and costs or actual and target state?

Therefore, in budget-supported organizations, we can approach, first of all, by defining the parameters of the goals we want to be achieved and the ones already reached, as a result of the organization's activity.

As Minchev points out, if there are no serious methodological obstacles to establishing the costs of obtaining the effect, the main problem of evaluating the effectiveness of economic management will be the characterization of the state of the managed system and the sensitivity of this state to the impact of the subject of management. That is to say, it is important:

a) that we know what essential parts of the system (farm, complex, branch, sub-branch, production, etc.) are necessary and sufficient to be characterized in order for the assessment of the state in which the system is located to be correct and

б) in what way the state as a whole and its individual characteristics change as a result of the exerted management influences.

Regardless of the fact that Minchev's research is about efficiency in economic organizations, the approach proposed by him can be used as an approach to determine efficiency in budgetary support organizations as well.

On the other hand, if we analyze what has been stated so far, we can assume that efficiency can also be considered as the degree to which you achieve the set goal. When we talk about a private company, the goal can be, for example, maximum profit. Then the one who maximizes the profit is the person who manages effectively. If the goal is an increase in market share, then performance in a private company can be measured by determining the increase in market share.

For the purposes of this work, however, more interesting is the following question - what is the efficiency when the organization is not economic and does not aim for the achievement of an economic goal. In any case, every organization, regardless of whether it is economic or not, sets a goal that is related to the goals of its creation and existence. Therefore, in organizations that do not have set business goals, the effectiveness of the activity can be defined as the degree to which the goals of the organization are reached. This should also be the approach regarding the activities of the Executive Agency "Main Labor Inspection".

When evaluating the activity of budgetary support organizations, such as EA MLI, the approach to determining the results of their activity is different, compared to that applied in companies with an economic subject of activity. A result, which is sometimes difficult to quantify, is also created in organizations of public importance. The reason for this is that these organizations create effects and results of their activity, which, generally speaking, have social significance. These effects are impossible to quantify with the standard approach to business performance assessment.

Historically, there have been various stages in determining the effectiveness of public organizations. Initially (at the beginning of the 20th century) it was assumed that the evaluation of the effectiveness of public organizations should cover only the results of the activity. Later, especially after the Great Depression (1929 - 1934), attention was paid to the fact that, in addition to results, the costs (expenses) incurred to achieve these results are also important. Of course, Ridley and Simon's research is focused on the public services that the municipality provides to citizens, but in any case it is about public (budgetary) organizations that are not created to achieve economic goals. Looking back in time, this is an undoubted development in evaluating the effectiveness of the activities of public organizations. Given the economic difficulties caused by the depression, Ridley and Simon justify the need to determine the effectiveness of these organizations, and for this purpose the costs incurred should be taken into account, not only the results achieved. In other words, it was concluded that efficiency should be considered as a correlation of result to the price (costs) of obtaining it. It is this developed approach to evaluating the effectiveness of public organizations that complements the effectiveness as an economic category.

Another popular approach to evaluating the performance of public sector organizations is the use of "cost-benefit" analysis. From a certain point of view, this analysis is more suitable for evaluating policies in the field of budget-supported organizations.

In the Bulgarian theoretical practice, there are noteworthy studies that shed light on the modern consideration of the content of the effectiveness of public organizations, as an economic category. In his study on measuring the effectiveness of public organizations, Hristov makes generalizations that are extremely useful for measuring the effectiveness of budget-supported organizations. He divides efficiency into economic and technical, concluding that metrics can be derived to measure them. In this regard, as Hristov points out, each of these types of efficiency needs further clarification, as follows:

- Technical efficiency characterizes the achievement of the organization's goals. This makes it possible to formulate efficiency criteria from the goals of the public organization.
- Economic efficiency characterizes the economy and can be defined as a correlation between certain results of the organization's activity, related to the costs of obtaining them.

Therefore, in order to quantitatively assess the effectiveness of public organizations, indicators can be used to determine its effectiveness. Through these indicators, the activity is evaluated, which allows to determine the quality of work in public organizations. The present study deals only with the quantitative evaluation of the effectiveness of the control activity of the EA MLI. Qualitative effects as a result of the agency's control activity are not the subject of this study.

We accept that this approach is relatively appropriate and useful in determining the effectiveness of the control activity of the EA MLI. Thus, we come to the conclusion that to determine the effectiveness of the control activity of the EA ML, one can start from the goals of the executive agency. The goals of the agency can be related to the results of the organization's activity, and the results of the activity can be related to the costs incurred to obtain them. Thus, we can summarize that the effectiveness of the control implemented by the EA MLI is a complex economic category, which is characterized by certain criteria and indicators.

The Place of Effectiveness and Efficiency in the Control of Compliance With Labor Legislation

The concepts of "effectiveness" and "efficiency" are of significant application in economic theory and practice related to financial control. From the point of view of control, another concept is also important, directly related to the two mentioned, and it is "economy". Of course, all three concepts have content and purpose outside the economic theory and practice of financial control, but they are not relevant for the present study.

Historically, in parallel with the expansion of public spending, countries created public organizations to control the legitimate spending of public funds. This function is performed by the audit chambers of individual countries.

As a result of the development of ideas for determining the effectiveness of the results of the activities of public organizations, in 1977, at the IX Congress of INTOSAI, the so-called Declaration of Lima was accepted. This INTOSAI Congress was held in Lima, Peru in 1977, which gave the name of the document - the Lima Declaration. Decisions were made at this Congress, which were dictated by the economic conditions of that period. The Lima Declaration is considered to be one of the significant documents that INTOSAI adopts. The importance of the declaration is related to the fact that it assumes that, in addition to the legality of the budget funds spent (financial audit - legality audit), the audit chambers should also carry out audits aimed at inspecting the economy, efficiency and effectiveness of public organizations. In other words, the declaration, as a result of the final documents of the INTOSAI congress, marks the beginning of the so-called audit of the implementation by the supreme audit institutions (audit chambers) in the individual countries. In Bulgaria, the performance audit is regulated in the Law on the Audit Chamber, where it is stated that: a "Performance audit" is the verification of planning, implementation and control activities at all levels of management in the audited entity with a view to their effectiveness, efficiency and economy, as follows:

а) "effectiveness" is the degree of achievement of the objectives of the audited object when comparing the actual and expected results of its activity;
б) "efficiency" is the achievement of maximum results from the resources used in carrying out the activity of the audited object;
в) "economy" is the acquisition with the smallest costs of the necessary resources for the implementation of the activity of the audited object in compliance with the requirements for the quality of the resources."

In essence, the Audit of the performance carried out by the Audit Office is a mechanism through which the legislative bodies and the public can obtain information about the way in which public funds are spent. Whether budget funds are spent effectively, efficiently and economically.

Thus, if we present these three main criteria, in compliance with which the EA MLI should carry out its control activity, we can summarize the following main characteristics for each of them:

- effective performance of the control activity of the EA MLI should mean: the degree to which the control activity of the EA MLI achieves the set goals. Here it is possible to distinguish at least two approaches.

The first one, in which the extent of the previously set goals achieved by the IA GIT, in relation to the control activity, is assessed. In this approach, to evaluate the performance, we can compare the results achieved with the goals set. Of course, the goals set and the results achieved should be measurable.

In the second approach, if we assume that the main goals of the agency's control activity are compliance with labor legislation and health and safety working conditions for employees in the organizations, then we can assume that the more employed persons in the country have fallen within the scope of the control, the more effective it is.

- the efficiency of the control activity of the EA MLI should be determined by the realization of the control activity with the least possible resources. This could mean achieving maximum results with available resources. Efficiency can also be considered as an assessment of the optimal use of the resources available to the agency, including for the control activity performed by it. As for the efficiency of the control activity of the EA MLI, it can be evaluated as a correlation of the resources used by the organization to the achieved results of the control activity. Efficiency is directly related to the economy of the agency's control activities.
- economy of the control activity of the EA MLI is carrying out the activity with minimum costs. In other words, how economically the agency's human, material and financial resources were used to carry out its control activities.

When determining the indicators for evaluating the efficiency and economy of the control activity of the EA MLI, in certain cases, it is difficult to distinguish their importance for the efficiency, respectively, the economy of the control activity.

Approaches to Determining the Effectiveness and Efficiency of Control Over Compliance With Labor Legislation

Approaches to determining the effectiveness and efficiency of the control implemented by the EA MLI can be derived based on the characteristics of the effectiveness, efficiency and economy of the activity.

As stated above, effective execution of the control activity of the EA MLI should mean the extent to which the control activity of the agency achieves the set objectives. For the present study, we assume that we can apply the approach in which the main objectives of the agency's control activity are compliance with labor legislation and health and safety working conditions for those working in the organizations. Thus, we can measure the effectiveness of the agency's control activity, assuming that the more employed persons in the country it covers more effective it is. From here we can derive an indicator in which the effectiveness of the control activity will be measured as a ratio between the employed persons in the companies inspected by the EA MLI and the employed persons in the relevant year in the Republic of Bulgaria, as follows:

$$ECA = ANEPIC / ANEP \times 100$$

ECA – effectiveness of the control activity, in per cent

ANEPIC – the average number of employed persons in the companies inspected by the EA MLI

ANEP – the average number of persons employed by work and legal service contracts in economic activities and sectors in the country

The data on the average number of employees in the companies inspected by the EA MLI are available on the agency's website. The data on the average number of employed persons by work and service legal contracts in economic activities and sectors in the country are available on the website of the National Statistical Institute (NSI).

The specified indicator can be calculated as a coefficient and as a percentage. Thus, for the period 2017-2021, we have:

Table 1 Performance evaluation indicator in the period 2017-2021

Indicator	2017	2018	2019	2020	2021
ANEP	2 308 129	2 319 762	2 322 561	2 211 773	2 187 716
ANEPIC	1 661 654	1 484 092	1 466 412	1 439 029	1 416 948
Efficiency, coefficient	0,72	0,64	0,63	0,65	0,65
Efficiency, per cent	72%	64%	63%	65%	65%

If we accept this approach, the EA MLI was the most effective in its control activity in 2017, during which 72% of the employed persons in the country were covered by the agency. When analyzing this indicator, in the next four years (2018-2021) the level of effectiveness of the control activity maintains a relatively high level.

Thus, if we assume that the EA MLI succeeds in checking all companies and organizations in which employed persons work during the relevant year, the indicator of the effectiveness of the control activity will be 100%. This, of course, is impossible. On the other hand, the more companies are inspected by the inspectorate, the more effective its control activity is, since, in this way, it extends to more employed persons. Therefore, in order to increase its effectiveness, the agency should seek to exercise control over companies and organizations with more employees. Thus, the results of its control activity and its effects will spread to more employed persons.

As for the efficiency of the control activity of the EA MLI, as stated above, it should be performed by using the least possible resources. Various indicators can be applied to evaluate efficiency. The first of them can be defined as the efficiency of inspections and represents the ratio of allocated budget funds to the number of inspections carried out by the agency. The budget of the EA MLI essentially determines the expenses that the agency makes during the year, and they can also be accepted for the following:

EI = Budget / Number od inspections
EI – effectiveness of inspections, in BGN
Budget – budget of the EA MLI for the relevant year, in BGN
Number of inspections - total inspections carried out by the EA MLI for the year

Data on the budget of the EA MLI is public only for the period 2019-2021, for this reason the indicator is calculated for the same period.

Table 2 Indicator for evaluating the effectiveness of inspections during the period 2019-2021

Indicator	2019	2020	2021
Budget	9 320 000	10 367 000	14 497 000
Number of inspections	40 216	37 145	40 788
Efficiency of inspections in BGN	231,75	279,10	355,42

It can be seen from the data that in 2019, budget costs of BGN 231.75 were made for carrying out one inspection, in 2020 the same indicator worsened, as one inspection already required BGN 279.10 of budget funds. In 2021, the effectiveness of inspections also decreases, then one inspection required BGN 355.42 of budget funds. If we take as a base the first year for which we have data on the agency's budget (2019), the efficiency of the control activity expressed by this indicator deteriorates as follows: in 2020, 20% more budget funds are needed compared to those spent in 2019 and in 2021 compared to 2019 by 53%. This deterioration in the effectiveness of the control activity expressed by this indicator cannot be fully explained by the available public data. As can be seen from the EA MLI budget data, there is a significant increase in capital expenditure in 2021 compared to 2019 and 2020, but it does not justify the deterioration of the effectiveness of inspections to such an extent.

Another indicator that can be used to evaluate the efficiency of the control activity in the EA MLI is the efficiency of human resources. This indicator can be defined as an indicator of human resource efficiency. The human resources efficiency indicator can be presented as a ratio of the number of inspections carried out to the average list of staff in the agency as follows:

EHR = Number of inspections / ANS

EHR – efficiency of human resources, presented as the number of inspections per person

Number of inspections – total inspections carried out by the EA MLI for the year

ANS – the average number of staff for the year. For the purpose of calculating the indicator, the staffing schedule of the agency for each of the years is taken. For the purposes of the research, the number according to the staffing list for the EA MLI was taken, since only this information about the persons employed in the agency is public.

Table 3 Indicator for evaluating the efficiency of human resources for the period 2017-2021

Indicator	2017	2018	2019	2020	2021
Number of inspections	45644	43 958	40 216	37 145	40 788
ANS	495	495	495	495	495
Efficiency of human resources	92	89	81	75	82

The calculated data for the indicator show a deterioration in the efficiency of human resources. In 2017, an average of 92 inspections were carried out for the year with one employee of the EA MLI. The number of inspections per employee decreased to 75 in 2020, illustrating the deterioration of the HR efficiency indicator. The downward trend of the indicator reverses in 2021, with an average of 82 inspections per employee.

Another possibility for evaluating the effectiveness of the control exercised by the EA MLI is the calculation of an indicator that binds the amount of penal decrees entered into force and the average number of the agency's personnel. This efficiency indicator characterizes the completion of the control activity of the EA MLI, expressed in the value of the amounts of fines that the agency has imposed and will collect, as a result of its control activity. In essence, the amount of penal decrees entered into force is also a result of the control activity of the agency and related to the average number of persons working in the agency can be used as an assessment of the efficiency of its control activity. The indicator can also be used as a sign to evaluate the efficiency of the agency to successfully complete its control activity. The indicator can be represented as follows:

ECA = NPD / ANS

ECA – efficiency of the control activity in BGN

NPD - the number of penal decrees that entered into force for the year, in BGN;

ANS – the average number of staff for the year

Thus, for the studied period 2017 - 2021, we can obtain the following data:

Table 4 Indicator for evaluating the efficiency of the control activity for the period 2017-2021

Indicator	2017	2018	2019	2020	2021
NPD	13 518 343	15 799 560	12 938 160	11 622 325	10 531 810
ANS	495	495	495	495	495
Efficiency of the control activity	27 309,78	31 918,30	26 137,70	23 479,44	21 276,38

The efficiency of the control activity calculated with this indicator reached its peak in 2018, when one employee of the agency received BGN 31,918.30 per year from the penal decrees that had entered into force. During the period 2019 – 2021, this efficiency decreased, but should not be treated as an unfavorable trend without further analysis. The reason for the decrease may also be due to the educational effect created again as a result of the control activity of the EA MLI.

Chapter 9
Empirical Test and Study of the Legal and Economic Aspects of Control on Compliance With Labour Law

Plamena Nedyalkova
University of Economics, Varna, Bulgaria

ABSTRACT

In this part of the development, the problem of the effectiveness of control over compliance with labor legislation is investigated. The methodological basis of the study includes general scientific methods, such as: observation, description, induction and deduction, measurement and comparison, analysis, and synthesis. Control effectiveness research is based on fuzzy set theory, as a modern theory that enables research to be conducted with both quantitative data and qualitative data, and through this theory it is possible to test a number of imprecise or unspecified questions.

INTRODUCTION

Control on compliance with and the application of labour law is a complex process implemented by different supervisory institutions responsible for the lawful observation of labour law. Legal provisions are essential for the functioning of the rule of law. The lack of specific legal regulations or the presence of systematic infringements of the legal provisions lead to serious

DOI: 10.4018/978-1-6684-9067-9.ch009

consequences for the operations of organisations and interfere with the concepts for comprehensive general governance by the state.

Whether it comes to internal or external control, the main problem of any type and any form of control is to maximise the achievement of the objectives, tasks and priorities of the controlling operations by using their effectiveness and efficiency and also, in the current context, their economy. The problems associated with the effectiveness of control have been studied and tested by using various methods and approaches, however, the manifestation of the different results from the individual controlling operations and their significant deviation from the permissible norms for economy and effectiveness still remain unknown. These differences, on the one hand, are caused by the resulting control data defined by the organisational and methodological factors of the supervisory institution itself and, on the other hand, are defined by the condition, specifics and characteristics of the object under control. Therefore, we believe it is very difficult to test and study how the individual controlling activities will lead to a change in the overall effectiveness, efficiency and economy of the entire supervisory institution (Nedyalkova, 2020).

The effective functioning of supervisory institutions may be an essential asset for improving public trust in the financial and controlling activities within society. Furthermore, it is this functioning that can achieve added value for the object under control and added value for the supervisory institution itself (Adato, 2022). Ensuring effective control on compliance with labour law and with the legislation in the field of employment, public service and administrative service is a prerequisite for increasing and improving performance. The other factor – economy – can be considered as a consequence of the primary factor, that is, effectiveness. Efficiency needs to be discussed separately, because a certain process may have achieved the relevant norms for effectiveness and economy, but it might be inefficient, i.e., on the one hand it might have failed to fully impact the object under control, and, on the other hand, the intended results might not have been fully achieved. This is why the methodology for testing and identification of the effectiveness and efficiency of the controlling activity differs not only between supervisory institutions, but also between the different types of supervisory proceedings and the specifics of the object under control. This is another proof for the presence of a problem in defining the effectiveness and efficiency of a certain supervisory institution.

Under these new conditions for work, employers had to rapidly adapt to the new external factors. Larger enterprises with a well-developed and established internal control system assigned this task to their internal control units, because they were able to cover all structural units and divisions within the enterprise. Another reason for that is that the internal control unit can act immediately and offer possible solutions for improving the organisation's operations, so that the provisions of the law can be complied with, if it identifies any deviation or infringement of the anti-epidemic measures by the workers and employees.

Internal control is outside the scope of this work and the main focus here will be to present the methodology for testing and defining the effectiveness and efficiency of the controlling operations of Executive Agency "General Labour Inspectorate" in Bulgaria as an external supervisory institution. The type of control exercised in this case is ***specialised control***. This type of control can be both independent and exercised in interaction with other supervisory institutions, it focuses on defending the workers' and employees' employment, insurance and social rights and on "improving the working environment in enterprises". For the purpose of exercising effective and efficient control, the agency has signed cooperation agreements with a number of institutions and organisations of employers and trade unions, such as:

- The National Revenue Agency;
- The State Agency for Child Protection;
- The Social Assistance Agency;
- The National Centre for Hygiene, Medical Ecology and Nutrition;
- Directorate General "Technical Inspection";
- The Employment Agency;
- The Supervisory and Technical Inspection of the Ministry of Agriculture and Food;
- The Confederation of Independent Trade Unions in the Republic of Bulgaria;
- "Podkrepa" Labour Confederation;
- The National Association of Municipalities.

The type of control exercised by Executive Agency "General Labour Inspectorate" is inspection and it focuses on the prevention of any infringement of the labour protection legislation. The principles and methods of the "modern strategies for prevention can be applied in all areas of action within the responsibilities of the labour inspectorate for the application of legislation, such as: occupational health and safety; legal relations in employment; general work conditions; illegal employment; unfair labour practices; resolution of complaints and disputes; investigation of work accidents, conflicts, etc.".

The Executive Agency "General Labour Inspectorate" applies two approaches in its operations. ***The prevention and integration approach***. The two approaches are combined in the practice of control and they are the basis for the development of the overall system for labour inspection. Above all, prevention means to put decisive efforts to decrease the number of accidents at work and occupational diseases. However, in the context of the current labour inspection, prevention means a lot more than simply avoiding hazards and accidents. The prevention approach focuses on the avoidance of any infringement or, if this cannot be completely prevented, mitigating the intensity of the infringement. The purpose of prevention is to ensure compliance with the legal requirements at the onset of the legal employment relations between employers and workers/employees.

The integration approach is applied during the periodic and routine inspection by the Executive Agency "General Labour Inspectorate". This approach assumes that "the majority of inspectors are well-trained "multidisciplinary experts", that is, employees that are generally familiar with all the relevant fields, who are supported by "specialised experts", i.e. specialists with in-depth knowledge in a specific field that usually interfere at the request of the multidisciplinary specialists in the case of more complicated situations requiring their special expertise. The specialised expertise should be concentrated in the specific district labour inspectorates where the need of this type of expertise is the highest, i.e. based on the structure and distribution of the economic activities and crafts, whereas those specialised experts, even if they are based in a certain area, should have competence for intervention both at regional and national level. To achieve and maintain high-quality specialised level of expertise, Executive Agency "General Labour Inspectorate" regularly organises staff trainings and hires external contractors to provide their expert opinion on occupational medicine or occupational health and safety as necessary.

These two approaches are designed for achieving effective and efficient functioning of Executive Agency "General Labour Inspectorate" and also for improving the quality of the Agency's activity. To achieve this objective and vision, the Strategic Plan for the Agency's operation has defined the following tasks:

1. Exercising effective control on compliance with the legislation in the field of employment, public service and labour mobility.
2. Prevention for the purpose of compliance with labour law.

3. Increasing the agency's administrative capacity and the labour inspectors' professional capacity.
4. Enhancing and strengthening of the institutional image of the Labour Inspectorate.
5. Active international activities;

According to the strategic plan of Executive Agency "General Labour Inspectorate", the implementation of effective control on compliance with the legislation in the field of employment, public service and labour mobility can be achieved through the following activities:

1. Development and updating of procedures and methodologies for inspection in the main fields of inspection activity for enforcement of the legislation, where control is exercised by the Executive Agency "General Labour Inspectorate" in accordance with the quality management system of the controlling operations based on the ISO 9001-2008 standard.
2. Focusing the controlling operations on the protection of the workers from new risks resulting from the ongoing socio-economic and technological changes.
3. Priority inspection of sectors with high numbers of employees from vulnerable groups, such as people with disabilities, workers on temporary (fixed-period) contracts and migrant workers, as well as inspection of the lawfulness of the employment relations and of undeclared employment.
4. Exercising subsequent control on the implementation of the administrative measures enforced.
5. Improving the cooperation, coordination and exchange of information between the state supervisory bodies from other institutions, such as the National Revenue Agency, the National Social Security Institute and the Ministry of Interior.
6. Developing procedures to enable the activity of committees/groups for occupational environment in the enterprises.

Executive Agency "General Labour Inspectorate" makes a distinction between the following concepts: a check (verification); control; entry control; inspection and review. In this way, it makes a distinction between the types of controlling activities exercised by the agency in fulfilment of its objectives and tasks. "***A check (verification)***" means a methodological procedure carried out at certain intervals of time for the purpose of confirming, by presenting objective evidence therefor, that the requirements for the specific intended use or application have been fulfilled or for the purpose of application and identification of compliance with certain requirements. The check may include review of documents, checking the workplaces, measurements, interviews with employers and/or employees, etc.. The term "***control***" means "evaluation of compliance by monitoring and assessment accompanied, if necessary, by measurement". The Executive Agency "General Labour Inspectorate" exercises entry control", particularly "inspection activities verifying the compliance of the purchased product with the defined requirements thereto. The main controlling activity exercised by the agency is "inspection", which means an operation exercised by the supervisory bodies of EA "GLI" related to the establishment and enforcement of compliance between the requirements of the law and its application in the enterprises, sites and places where work is performed or trainings are held, whereas the review conducted by the agency focuses on the identification of the administration's suitability, adequacy, efficiency and effectiveness for achieving the quality objectives.

Significance of the Approaches and Methods for Defining the Effectiveness of Control

The types of approaches and methods for defining the effectiveness of control on the application of labour law are studied by applying deduction (by making inferences from the general to the specific premises) and induction (by making inferences from the specific to the general premises). We believe that the application of the two approaches will lead to results that will complement each other and will present the problems studied from different perspectives. The difference between the two approaches is the focus of the flow of information used for the particular analysis. Applying both approaches will result in the proper testing and proving of the study hypotheses. The deductive approach applies the general deductive principles, procedures, stages, methods, techniques, etc. It helps analyse the entire scope of the research. The specifics of the inductive approach, on the other hand, are the result of studying and analysing the specific object of the study (the relevant enterprise, unit, division, structure, etc.). The inference of specific individual solutions is based on the induction approach. The application of both approaches for studying the effectiveness of control requires consideration of all three mutually related axes presented in fig.1:

Thus, the three axes are the controlling activities, the specific supervisory institution and, based on the first and second axis, the effectiveness of the

Figure 1.

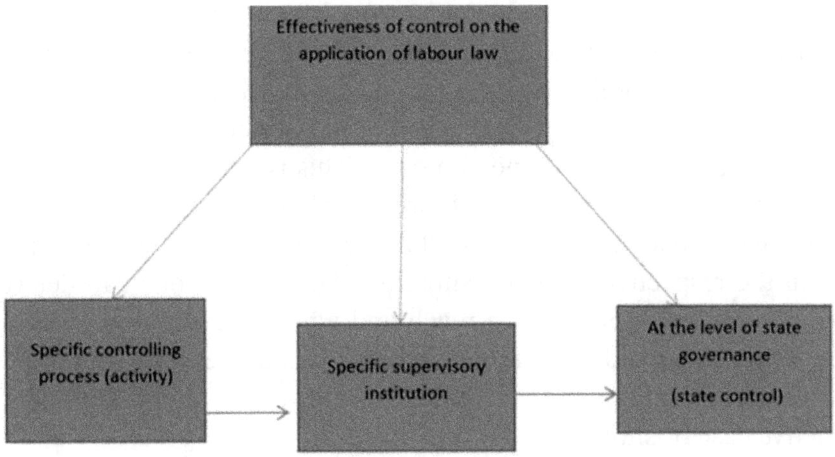

overall state supervision is determined. The first basis is the specific process of control. If the process is not effective and thus inefficient, this result would directly or indirectly affect the supervisory institution and, respectively, this institution, as part of the state supervisory apparatus, will have an effect on state control as a whole. We suggest to conduct the study of the effectiveness and efficiency based on these axes by using different approaches and methods, where the study will depend on:

1. The objective of the study.
2. The empirical information available.
3. Proving the main hypothesis of the study, particularly, that each model for studying the effectiveness has its purpose and provides an accurate, specific and result-oriented information that differs from the one provided by a different model.
4. The essence of effectiveness as an indicator for defining the quality of control on labour law application.
5. Measuring the efforts of the controlling persons to obtain a result that presents the actual situation and events that have affected the change in the object under control.

The concepts of “approach” and “method” have not been fully studied yet and their inaccurate interchangeable use gives rise to certain problems in deriving the final results from the studies and inaccuracies in proving specific hypotheses. The approach shall be defined as the way a certain task or problem will be solved or the way in which one would act in a problematic situation. Several approaches might be applied for resolving a certain practical problem and in this case we will not apply just one universal approach. So, it can be assumed that the relevant problem is of complicated nature and could not be influenced by using just one approach. This is admissible in the case of complex situations and problems, however, when acting with a compilation of approaches, one should analyse the strengths and weaknesses of using them in the respective complex situation. This is how one can determine how far a certain approach can reach and where the manifestation of the other approach should start. Each complex situation entails some relevant risks which are minimised or eliminated with the given approach for the respective case or situation.

The method is the way in which something will be done, or "a way to influence the object for the purpose of achieving a higher level of perfection in that object, disclosing the patterns and trends, analysing the statistics and dynamics of the processes and phenomena, the links within them, between them and outside of them, i.e. the entire range of complex connection within and outside the object and between the object and the environment it exists in" (Dinev, 1989).

The practice of controlling does not apply just a single method. The specifics of the object under control predetermines that the methods should be of different nature of performance. What is common between all method for control is that they are determinate, targeted, result-oriented and reliable. The purpose of each method is to achieve the overall objectives of control – effectiveness, efficiency and economy. According to Manvi Sharma, the best methods of control are:

1. Non-quantitative methods of control: Non-quantitative methods are used by the senior management of the organisation in performing their managerial objectives and tasks, such as planning, organisation, management and controlling the workers/employees (Sharma, 2020).
2. Quantitative control methods – these methods are based on specific data. Mathematics and statistical approaches and analysis as a means for control are applied and those are focused on the specification of the final results.
3. Budgetary control methods – the primary object of financial control is the budget of the respective organisation and, from the perspective of state control, this is the public budget. According to *Manvi Sharma*, some

managers refer to budgetary control as profit plans. The budget should be considered to be "an estimate of income or expenses for a specific time period (say, a year, a quarter, or a month); and the particular estimates it contains become the standards against which future performances will be measured and evaluated" (Sharma, 2020). From the perspective of state control, the budgetary control methods should be examined as a combination of techniques, technologies, rules and instruments used to exercise control on the implementation of the budget.

According to other researchers, the methods for control can be local or general. Local methods are "determined by the characteristic features of the object and subject of control. Depending on the characteristics of the subject, the methods can be: methods for state control, public control, general and specialised control, internal managerial company methods for control, etc." (Dinev, 1989). Furthermore, depending on the nature of the object, the methods can be categorised as methods for control on the employment relations, methods for control on the systems and structural units and methods for control on the effectiveness, efficiency and economy.

The general methods are relevant to uniform or similar objects and they are also applied in each situation of control because by using them, the general techniques of control relevant to each controlling process are applied. The general techniques of control are the techniques of documentary and factual control, whereas the respective types of documentary checks and types of factual checks belong to the local methods for control.

The two main groups of methods (local and general) are applied together, i.e. in a combined manner in the practice of control. In the case of complex objects of control, the combined application of both groups of methods is mandatory. The different alternatives based on which the controlling process can be implemented require a combination of methods for testing, analysing and defining the final conditions of the controlled object. Therefore, it is essential for controlling persons to have the necessary professional competence in order to be able to respond in the most appropriate, accurate and timely manner in the case of complex situations of control, by applying the relevant means and techniques for control.

In the current context of technological industrialisation of the work, employers apply different internal methods for control that help them apply adequate and up-to-date management techniques in order to keep their workers and employees safe and ensure compliance with the quality standards for the manufacturing of the final product. Therefore, the approaches and methods for control described above, which are applied by the supervisory institutions, focus on the achievement of specific objectives, whereas employers apply approaches and methods for internal control aimed at achieving the managerial objectives of the relevant enterprise. Despite using the same terms for the "approaches" and "methods" of control, these are of different character which is predetermined by their purpose.

Similarly, much as the methods for external control can be applied either before, during or after the relevant activity, the methods for internal control also have this functional possibility. The problem of control, whether internal control or external control, is not in the methods and approaches themselves; we believe those are a well-organised system of principles used to obtain certain results and objective presentation of the studied object; the problem lies with the way they are applied in and the moment they are applied at (Nedyalkova, 2019), i.e. it is a matter of time, place and the object they are applied to. Another important problem is that the general conceptual purpose of the respective method is not sufficiently known. It is often the case that a certain method is applied, specific results are derived, however, they do not reflect the specifics and characteristics of the studied object to the necessary extent. Therefore, we assume that it is good to first be aware of the general principle of the scope and purpose of the respective method and approach and then proceed with its application.

Characteristics of the Process Stages for Defining the Effectiveness of Compliance With Labour Law

The process of control by the inspectors of Executive Agency "General Labour Inspectorate" is complex because of the objects under control and also due to the complexity of the controlling procedures for exercising direct control on the relevant objects under control. The two main types of controls exercised by Executive Agency "General Labour Inspectorate" can be generally divided into general and specialised control. General control is the control on compliance with labour law, whereas specialised control is control on compliance with the Occupational Health and Safety Act, the Employment Promotion Act, the legislation related to the fulfilment of public service and the rights and obligations of the parties to contractual relations, as well as other legislation where this has been envisaged by the law. Other activities performed by the agency which are within the scope of its operations, but outside the scope of the controlling procedures, are provision of information and technical advice to employers, workers and employees about the most effective methods for compliance with labour law and on the application of the Employment Promotion Act.

The complexity of the inspection activity exercised by Executive Agency "General Labour Inspectorate" is shown in the stages of the entire process, particularly:

Figure 2.

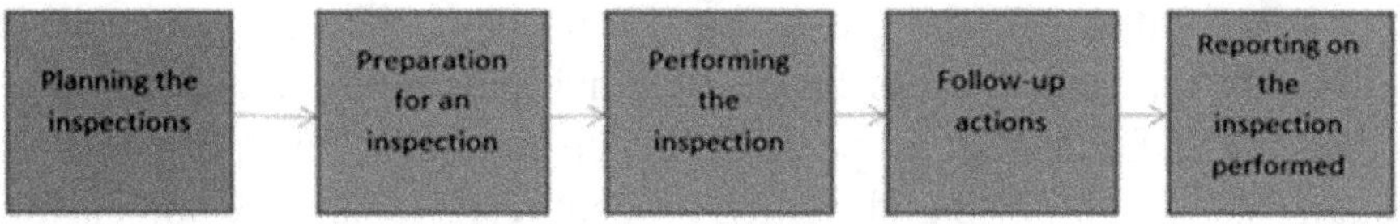

Each stage of the inspection activity shall be tested and analysed to conclude whether the effectiveness requirements have been met or will be met.

During the stage of ***planning the inspection activity***, the problems related to the methods and approaches for achieving long-term effectiveness in the annual plans and short-term effectiveness in the individual plans of the inspection activities are analysed. The planning of the inspection activity is related to the review of priorities both for the relevant year and for the respective inspection activity related to a certain enterprise. In this way, the resources are properly concentrated on the specific inspections planned and the time and involvement of the inspectors in the relevant controlling procedures are properly distributed. During the planning of the controlling operations, special attention is paid to higher risk enterprises where the occupational health and safety does not meet the norms or where the recruitment conditions are not lawful or where both phenomena are present. There is one more problem associated with the planning of the inspection activity, particularly – compliance with the risk identification methodology, where inspectors need to consider the characteristics and specifics of the relevant type of enterprise and business.

For the identification of the effectiveness of the inspection activity at the stage of planning, one should take into account that the operations performed by Executive Agency "General Labour Inspectorate" are a manageable process that influences both the institution itself and society as a whole. This manageable process has influence through the agency inspectors' final decisions associated with control. This is so, because the process itself functions both on the basis of the inspection activities planned and during the implementation of unplanned controlling activities (i.e. in response to whistleblowing, complaints, etc.). Each stage of the controlling operations or each moment of the activity of Executive Agency "General Labour Inspectorate" is characterised by an element ***p*** from the set ***P (p (-P).*** The element ***p*** is called condition of the system where the respective process takes place. "The set P can be of varied nature, e.g. P could be a set of real numbers, in which case the condition of the system", i.e. the system where the controlling process takes place, "is defined by a number. P can be a vector space with a random dimension. In this case, the status of each stage is defined by a vector, the coordinates of which are called status components" (Bonev, 1989). Each stage is specific for each enterprise, even though it goes through fixed established and written procedures, because the objects under control have specific organisational structures and operations which results in changes to the controlling process. Depending on the current status and the decision taken, the controlling process may end in a different way and, respectively, should be analysed by using different approaches.

Another problem that needs to be resolved when planning the inspection activity is the proper distribution of resources both for the fulfilment of the objectives and tasks defined for the relevant year and for achieving the respective strategic objectives and tasks. The resources, especially long-term resources, which include the human factor, building stock and operation of fixed assets, can be used over more than one period. The remaining resources, which are the so-called short-term resources, are the work tools, which may be inputs, materials and other resources necessary for achieving the objectives and tasks of *Executive Agency "General Labour Inspectorate"* during that short period when they are used for the inspection activity or for the provision of administrative services.

The main problem with planning is uncertainty, because in order to achieve economic effectiveness, one needs to cope with the planned optimisation of resources in the context of uncertainty. Furthermore, decision-making in the context of uncertain conditions, under which the relevant controlling process may take place, is also a common problem in practice. Uncertainty may be the result of changes in legislation, changes in the socio-economic environment, demographic changes, etc. During the planning, it is recommended to apply a methodology that has been developed based on the "optimisation activities, so as to achieve stable planning and avoid any unwanted results and events" (Baiyang, 2021). During the planning, the multi-stage process of distribution of resources can be applied, which is also known as Bellman's principle.

The application of Bellman's principle is appropriate for the solution of extrema problems where it is necessary to take decisions during the relevant stages of the process. As a result of the specific decisions taken, the object under control, considered as an organisational structural unit and system, is changed. Another specific feature of Bellman's principle is that it can be adapted and applied during the main strategical planning on the relevant systems the entire organisation is made up of. When the strategy has been developed based on Bellman's principle, it is considered optimal and each initial decision that follows the implementation of the strategic planning is considered significant, whereas any subsequent decision taken during the other stages of the controlling process "shall be taken so that it complies with the optimal strategy about the status obtained as a result of the first decision" (Bonev, 1989).

According to a number of researchers, Bellman's principle of optimality allows to achieve the desired effect in the case of proper distribution of resources, even if this effect is manifested in some minimum values. Much better results can be achieved when working with a sufficient number of resources that would allow more actions and achievement of more objectives, rather than using the existential minimum. Institutions in the public sector, particularly in the executive, have limited resources available to them. We believe that the application of Bellman's principle in the strategic planning of the *Executive Agency "General Labour Inspectorate"* will improve the operations of the supervisory institution in several aspects:

1. Proper and accurate distribution of resources during the strategic periods.
2. Achieving effectiveness in: ongoing controlling proceedings; in the fulfilment of the pre-defined controlling objectives and tasks for the respective year based on the annual control plans.
3. The impact of the dynamic environment where the agency is developing is reduced and despite the changes, the agency manages to achieve its objectives and tasks by applying the pre-defined optimal strategy.
4. When applying Bellman's principle in the practice of control, based on the current condition of the subject and the controlling decision taken with respect to the object under control, the overall system considered as a system for *Executive Agency "General Labour Inspectorate"* can generate revenue, which is not just planned revenue based on the planned inspections, but also additional revenue from the unplanned inspections. In this case, a more in-depth study on obtaining this unplanned revenue should be carried out, particularly with respect to all stages the overall

controlling process goes through. The effective work of the supervisory institutions needs to be studied in detail not only from the perspective of planned revenue, but also from the perspective of unplanned revenue, particularly by estimating the share of unplanned revenue in total revenue.

During the planning stage it is very difficult to give a firm answer to the question about the level of effectiveness of Executive Agency "General Labour Inspectorate" and, particularly, about the activity of its directorates. To make such an evaluation, it is necessary to track, analyse and compare the planned results with the results obtained from the subsequent stages of the controlling practice of the agency and its directorates in order to determine whether there are any deviations (positive or negative) from the predefined norms or everything is only performed based on the planned activities. Sometimes the strict observation of the plans is not the best metric for defining the quality of the activity, especially with respect to the possibility for generating additional revenues. Just like the case with any manufacturing enterprise, everything obtained by the controlling institutions outside the plans, such as resources, funds, materials, etc., is considered a positive deviation from the general plans defined.

The second stage is ***preparation for an inspection***. This stage includes:

1. *Collection of preliminary information* – the preliminary study of the object under control, the specific situation and the examination of the preliminary facts from previous inspection activities helps review the object during the current inspection activity. The preliminary information can be used in a flexible manner and it does not have the same importance and significance as the information obtained from the current inspection. In most cases it is possible to make a comparison between the preliminary information and the information derived from the current inspection and use it for identification of the change in the object during the respective period.
2. *Preparation of materials* – the inspectors need to compile all materials and documents available at the inspected site. They also need to familiarise themselves in advance with the legislation based on which the respective type of inspection will take place. This also includes preliminary reading of the collective bargaining agreement (for the relevant trade or internal for the company) between the management and the respective trade union, which is necessary, so that the inspector can prepare specific

questionnaires related to the specifics of the general collective bargaining provisions that the employer needs to comply with and apply.

3. *Confirmation for performing the inspection* – the confirmation for performing the inspection takes place through an order by the relevant territorial director of the executive director of the agency. It is also recommended to decide in advance whether the inspection will be pre-announced or not, i.e. whether the object under control will receive prior information about the performance of the relevant inspection activities or not.

The third stage is ***the performance of the inspection***. This is probably the most complex stage, because it depends on everything that has been performed during the previous two stages (planning and preparation for the inspection activity) and because all inspection procedures that have been approved are implemented. Depending on the status of the object under control, any infringements and non-conformities that may be identified during the process of control can be either minor or major. In the case of minor infringements, the controlling persons provide the employer with a recommendation to improve the working environment of the enterprise. In the case of major infringements, the controlling persons have the power to refer the matter to the prosecutor. The case is submitted to the prosecutor after performing a second inspection and confirming that the initial recommendations have not been taken into account and the identified weaknesses have not been rectified. The case may also be referred to the prosecutor where multiple severe infringements of the labour law are identified in the enterprise itself, as well as in other cases. The manual for labour inspectors states that for employers who generally comply with the legal requirements and have provided evidence for their readiness to do so, which shall be documented in the inspectors' reports, it is possible to refrain from performing a new inspection for a period of at least twelve months, unless a complaint is submitted against them or unless there is an accident at work.

The main documents each employer must have and which are checked by the inspectors are as follows:

1. Contract with an occupational health service.
2. Instruction books for initial, periodical, daily and special safety instruction to the staff.
3. The employees' files.

4. Internal work regulations.
5. Register of newly issued service books and service books handed upon termination of employment.
6. Register of overtime work.
7. Form 76 (schedule and attendance forms for the employees' working hours and shifts).
8. Internal regulations of the wage rates.
9. Payroll sheets.
10. Contract for servicing the electrical equipment – only in the cases where the company has signed a contract with an external servicing company.

The requirements with respect to these documents are documented in the following legislation: the Labour Code, the Occupational Health and Safety Act, the Regulation on the working hours, rests and leaves, the Regulation on the structure and organisation of the wages, the Regulation for defining the types of occupations entitled to additional annual paid time off, Regulation No. 5 of 29 December 2002 on the contents of and procedure for sending the notice under Art. 62, para. 5 of the Labour Code, Regulation No. 6 of 24.07.2006 on the terms and conditions for granting work permissions to persons under the age of 18, Regulation No. RD-06-3 of 23 February 2022 for the provision of occupational health and safety in the iron and steel industry and non-ferrous metals industry, etc.

4. *The fourth stage is **follow-up actions***. The follow-up actions depends on the results from the previous stage, where the relevant administrative actions need to be undertaken for the rectification of each infringement. According to the official information provided by Executive Agency "General Labour Inspectorate", "traditionally, about 2/3 of the orders for closure of work places, machines, facilities, etc. that present direct hazard for the life and health of workers, are in construction. During the first eleven months of year 2020, 130 orders for closure out of a total of 203 have been issued to construction sites. This sector also has the highest number of official statements for administrative infringement issued - 1567 statements out of a total of 7012 (22% of all official statements). Regarding the official statements for infringements related to occupational safety, almost of of them have been issued to construction sites – 532 official statements out of a total of 1140.

5. *The fifth stage is **reporting.*** This stage can be divided into two substages – the process of reporting the inspection activity performed for a specific object under control and the process of reporting the overall activity of the agency. During the joint inspection, a report is drafted, which contains the conclusions, the instructions given and the measures undertaken for seeking administrative and criminal liability. Within 7 days of the finalisation of the inspection, the report under Art. 5 of the Labour Inspection Act shall be presented to the minister for labour and social policy with a copy to the managers of the supervisory bodies that took part in the inspection. The process of annual reporting is prepared and carried out based on the activity of the entire agency, i.e. the report accounts for the activities of the specific directorates. According to the rules of procedure of Executive Agency "General Labour Inspectorate", the executive director shall report to the minister for labour and social policy on the entire activity of the Agency. The minister for labour and social policy, on the other hand, shall draft an annual report on labour inspection summarising the information received in accordance with Art. 8, para. 1 and shall submit it to the Council of Ministers by 31 May.

REFERENCES

Adato, A. (2022). Factors Affecting Internal Audit Effectiveness: Evidence from Microfinance Institutions Operating in Hawassa, Sidama Region, Ethiopia. *American Journal of Theoretical and Applied Business*, *8*(2), 19–29.

Administrativni uslugi na Izpalnitelna agentsia Glavna inspektsia po Truda. (n.d.). Gli.cov. https://www.gli.government.bg/bg/node/6367

Bonev, K., Lalova, N., & Ivanov, A. (1989). Matematichesko modelirane. G. *Bakalov*, 217.

Byudzhet na IA „Glavna inspektsia po truda" za perioda ot 2018 do 2021 g. (2021). Gli.gov. https://www.gli.government.bg/sites/default/files/upload/archive/docs/2019-01/B__dzet_2019_g.pdf

Dinev, M. (1999). *Kontrol v sotsialnoto upravlenie*. TrakiaM.

Godishen doklad za deynostta na Izpalnitelna agentsia Glavna inspektsia po Truda. (2021). Gli.gov. https://www.gli.government.bg/sites/default/files/upload/documents/2022-04/godishen-doklad-2021.pdf

Integriran narachnik po upravlenie saglasno BDS EN ISO/IEC 27001. (2014). Gli.gov. https://www.gli.government.bg/sites/default/files/upload/archive/docs/2015-09/Integriran_nar__cnik_po_upravlenie_IA_GIT_versi___5.pdf

NaredbaN. (2022). *Наръчник За Инспекторите По Труда.* Международно Бюро По Тру. http://ohrananatruda.com/files/documents/252.pdf

Nedyalkova, P. (2019). Government Supervision – A Factor for Business Development. *Journal of Management Policy and Practice, Atlanta, Georgia, USA: North American Business Press, 20*(2), 114–120.

Nedyalkova, P. (2020). Quality of Internal Auditing in the Public Sector: Perspectives from the Bulgarian and International Context. Cham: Springer Nature Switzerland.

Nedyalkova, P. (2020). Empirical Study of the VAIA Metric (Value Added of Internal Audit) and Determination of the Internal Audit Quality for Shumen Municipality for the Period 2011–2016. *Contributions to Management Science, 2020*, 171–185. doi:10.1007/978-3-030-29329-1_11

Nedyalkova, P. (2020). Presentation of the Dependence Between the Chosen Internal Audit Approach and the Methods for Assessing the Quality of the Internal Audit in the Public Sector. *Contributions to Management Science, 2020*, 105–114. doi:10.1007/978-3-030-29329-1_8

Nedyalkova, P. (2020). Types of Control Assessments Applied in Control Practice. *Contributions to Management Science, 2020*, 23–30. doi:10.1007/978-3-030-29329-1_3

Nedyalkova, P., Dimitrova, D., & Bogdanov, H. (2022). New Features in the Bulgarian Legal Framework and Financial Control Practice for Compliance with Labour Legislation in the Age of Globalization. Redefining Global Economic Thinking for the Welfare of Society: [Monography]. IGI Global Publ.

Sharma, M. (2020). Types of Control Methods: Top 3 Types. *Business Management*. https://www.businessmanagementideas.com/management/controlling/types-of-control-methods-top-3-typesmanagement/7981

Strategicheski plan za deynostta na IA „GIT" - https://www.gli.government.bg/sites/default/files/upload/archive/docs/2019-08/StrategicheskiPlanGIT_2018_2021.pdf

Zhao, B., Zhao, Z., Huang, M., Zhang, X., Li, Y., & Wang, R. (2021). Model Predictive Control of Solar PV-Powered Ice-Storage Air-Conditioning System Considering Forecast 246 Uncertainties. *IEEE Transactions on Sustainable Energy*, *12*(3), 1672–1683. doi:10.1109/TSTE.2021.3061776

Chapter 10
Testing and Defining the Effectiveness of the Supervisory Institution Executive Agency "General Labour Inspectorate"

Plamena Nedyalkova
University of Economics, Varna, Bulgaria

ABSTRACT

The approach known until now in the organizations of the private/busines / sector was applied in order to test the effectiveness of the control in a budgetary organization, such as the executive agency "General Labor Inspectorate." The main conclusion reached is that the methodology of testing and determining control effectiveness for the non-public sector is also applicable to public sector organizations. The analysis should not be applied solely as a means for follow-up control. It should be applied on an ongoing basis in order to identify the weaknesses and problems during the relevant current period based on the current data and the current status of the factors that have impacted on the change of economic effectiveness.

DOI: 10.4018/978-1-6684-9067-9.ch010

INTRODUCTION

In order to determine whether the controlling inspections performed have been effective, efficient and corresponding to the requirements for economy, it is necessary to:

1. First evaluate the performance itself, which should focus on: Testing and defining whether the process has been lawful; identification of the influence of the controlling activity implemented by the controlling inspectors on the object under control; furthermore, testing the link between the human resources management in the respective controlling institution of Executive Agency "General Labour Inspectorate" and the final results from the control inspections performed.
2. Testing and defining the professional competence and qualification of the controlling inspectors.
3. Testing and checking whether the pre-defined criteria the respective controlling procedure should meet have been fulfilled in order to determine whether it has been effective and efficient.

We believe that in order to achieve efficiency, the test for lawfulness of the process of control needs to be performed both by the controlling inspectors themselves and by the internal auditors of the Agency. During the internal audit, the procedures for inspection activity, their lawful application and establishment will be tested. The work of the inspectors themselves, on the other hand, will focus on testing the process of control at the current moment. One weakness of the current practice is that it focuses on the identification of the current status of the object and its change as compared to the effective legislation defining the relevant deviations of the object from the current legal provisions. During the ongoing process of control, the inspectors do not have the time needed to apply all methods and means for analysis, so that they can determine not only the status of the object under control, but also analyse the entire controlling process as such.

Different researchers have been testing the effectiveness based on the theory of performance management and the measurement and evaluation of effectiveness are the most important things in the application of this theory. A study by Ilgen & Schneider conducted as early as in 1991 has concluded that in order to determine the effectiveness of performance (i.e. the performance of the controlling process), the measurement needs to be quantitative, where the evaluation of performance needs to be made based on the evaluation activity, based on which "the value or quality of the quantified performance" should be derived. Some researchers, such as Maya Lambovska, Rastislav Rajnoha and Jan Dobrovic, offer a modern approach for defining the performance, particularly through the performance management theory, which is based on the fuzzy logic and fuzzy sets.

The new model for measuring performance suggested by Maya Lambovska, Rastislav Rajnoha and Jan Dobrovic and presented in fig. 4 examines the evaluation as the last stage of the controlling process of an organisation. The model first evaluates the overall understanding of the controlling persons about the achievements and effectiveness of the controlling process and also evaluates the achievements of control and the effectiveness of the responsibility centres of the supervisory institution. The responsibility centres are subdivisions of the relevant supervisory institution used by the directors for achieving specific results. The main factors that influence the development of such centres, especially in Anglo-Saxon countries, are as follows: the organisation's strategy; the management structure; the policy of decentralisation and delegation of rights and responsibilities by management level; the level of control on all expenses and revenues of the organisation; the extent to which the selected evaluation criteria for the activity stimulate the management and the other staff to perform better. Each organisation defines different types of responsibility centres under the influence and impact of the factors described above. For the supervisory institutions, including the Executive Agency "General Labour Inspectorate", the types of responsibility centres are different, such as internal audit unit, risk management centre, etc.

The model of Maya Lambovska, Rastislav Rajnoha and Jan Dobrovic is presented below in fig. 1:

The suggested ***model for measuring performance*** goes through 3 stages:

1. Standardisation.
2. Evaluation of responsibility centres' achievements, which are a prerequisite for achieving control.
3. Evaluation of the responsibility centres' work.

During the first step, the respective controlling process is put in the general legal framework, with elimination of the characteristic features of the object under control. In this way, general standardisation is achieved, which can help for the testing of each controlling process, so as to achieve comparability and

Figure 1. Model for measuring performance of Maya Lambovska, Rastislav Rajnoha and Jan Dobrovic

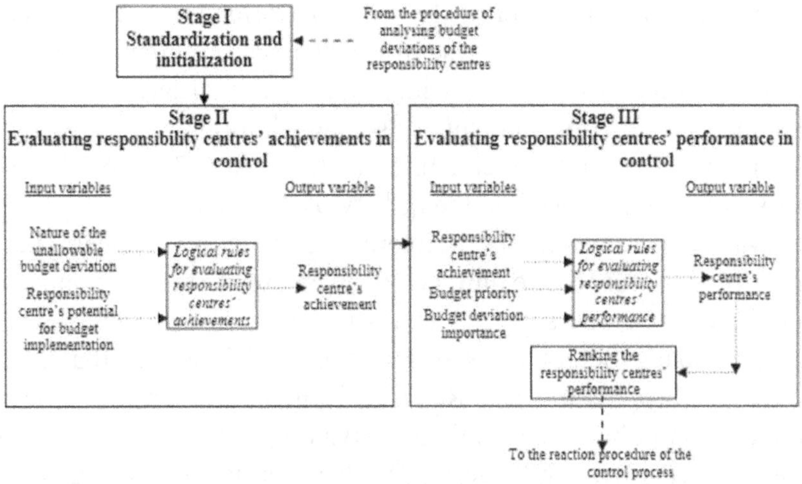

make a more precise comparative analysis between the different controlling processes. Using the fuzzy sets, the evaluation procedure is performed in two stages: the first stage is the transformation of the measurements derived (quantitative and qualitative) from the agency's activity into the two input variables. The second stage is to evaluate the agency's achievements as a supervisory institution together with the subjective evaluation from two different input variables (i.e. the so-called "stress" test is performed) by transforming them into output measurements. The transformation is performed based on other logical rules and the main purpose of this transformation is to present the subjective aspect of the agency in the annual reporting of the strategic objectives achieved.

The second stage of the proposed model may not be fully applicable yet for our practice in the field of control. It can be assumed that the suggested model is more suitable for enterprises from the private sector where the individual management responsibility centres function according to their purpose. In the public sector, particularly with respect to the supervisory institutions in Bulgaria, including Executive Agency "General Labour Inspectorate", the achievements of the individual units are not subject to evaluation yet. The supervisory institutions have the obligation to report their activity on an annual basis by accounting for the level of achievement of the predefined objectives and tasks, however, they do not have any statutory obligation to perform evaluation of achievements. The achievements of the supervisory institutions should be examined outside the planned objectives and tasks defined in their annual strategic plans. The summary reports from the activity of the supervisory institutions describe the level of the work performed, i.e. the planned and unplanned inspections and the system weaknesses and infringements of the objects under control that have been identified. The internal audit units, which are established in the relevant supervisory institutions when they meet the requirements of the Public Sector Internal Audit Act (ZVOPS), have direct statutory obligation to evaluate the quality of the activity.

The evaluation determined by the internal audit units only concerns the scope and activity of the respective unit, i.e. it can be used to measure and evaluate the activity of the entire supervisory institution as a structural organisation where individual structural units are functioning. We assume that the model suggested by Maya Lambovska, Rastislav Rajnoha and Jan Dobrovic is very suitable for non-public organisations (private sector enterprises) where the responsibility centres are well-defined with respect to their management. The model could be also applicable to the public sector, however, further tests and, particularly, legal changes are necessary for this to happen.

We believe the fuzzy sets theory is suitable for testing and defining the effectiveness not just for a certain controlling process, but also for the activity of the entire supervisory institution. The suggestion and construction of a suitable current model for defining the effectiveness is a complex process not just from the perspective of the significance of this indicator, but also because of the uncertainty of the criteria for defining the level of its application (Bogdanov, 2010). Grouping these criteria in a certain class/group will be different for each supervisory institution. The fuzzy sets theory allows to test different versions of random criteria, which allows the relevant criteria to be tested with respect to the supervisory institution. A fuzzy set shows that the elements comprising a certain set and having a common property can have this property to a different extent and therefore can belong to the respective set to a different extent.

According to Maya Lambovska, Rastislav Rajnoha and Jan Dobrovic, the first stage of the applied model requires standardisation of the output data and this stage undergoes four main procedures (Pr). During the first procedure it should be determined what the unacceptable deviation will be. The model allows us to define two types of unacceptable deviations – from the fuzzy sets and from the fuzzy numbers. If the deviations are described by using the fuzzy numbers, one should proceed to the third procedure of the presented model. If the results are derived through the fuzzy sets, then the second procedure should be implemented "within which fuzzy sets describing the unacceptable deviations are transformed into symmetric fuzzy triangular numbers with the same area and nature of the deviations"(M. Lambovska, R. Rajnoha, J. Dobrovic, 2019), which are unfavourable for the achievement of the predefined effectiveness objectives. The entire procedure under the model ends by representing the fuzzy numbers of unacceptable deviations "in a discrete (crisp) form through their normalised distance by Hamming called "Hamming's number" (Kaufman & Gil-Aluja, 1990).

The fuzzy sets theory is considered analogical to the probability theory applied to the processing of information based on subjective, qualitative evaluations under uncertainty (Kaufman & Gil-Aluja, 1990; Živković et al, 2016). When studying the controlling activity of *Executive Agency "General Labour Inspectorate"*, the parties that are directly affected by the effectiveness of the controlling activities are society, the controlling inspectors and the agency's internal auditors. The examination of the performance effectiveness of controlling activity is performed into three individual testing procedures. The study covers the period from 2018 to 2021 and the empirical data have been derived from:

1. Strategic plan of the agency operations for the period 2018–2021.
2. Annual national plans of the agency operations for the period 2018–2021.
3. Annual reports (accounts) on the activity of Executive Agency "General Labour Inspectorate" for the period 2018–2021.
4. Reports from a survey on the user satisfaction from the administrative services provided by Executive Agency "General Labour Inspectorate" over the period 2020-2021.
5. The annual budgets of Executive Agency "General Labour Inspectorate" for the period 2018–2021.
6. Reports on the results from the controlling activities performed in the period between 2018 and 2021.

In the new model for testing the efficiency of control, it is necessary to determine the input variable, which comprises of the *results from the controlling practice* in this study. The following characteristics have been identified in the suggested model, which are used for defining the results from the controlling practice, particularly: the annual objectives of Executive Agency "General Labour Inspectorate" that have been achieved; the controlling inspectors' satisfaction with the controlling inspections performed; the satisfaction of society and the agency's management staff with the results obtained from the controlling inspections. The suggested model is based on the model for control on teams proposed by *Maya Lambovska*. The originality of the model is related to "a combination of managerial concepts and mathematical theories of fuzzy logic and fuzzy sets. In addition to the team control model, the author suggests a set of instruments for measurement and evaluation of the team performance" (Lambovska, 2018).

All 28 directorates of Executive Agency "General Labour Inspectorate" participated in the study, namely the directorates from Blagoevgrad, Varna, Vidin, Gabrovo, Kardzhali, Lovech, Pazardzhik, Pleven, Razgrad, Silistra, Smolyan, Sofia, Targovishte, Shumen, Burgas, Veliko Tarnovo, Vratsa, Dobrich, Kyustendil, Montana, Pernik, Plovdiv, Ruse, Sloven, Sofia District, Stara Zagora, Haskovo and Yambol. 30 surveyed people out of 80 people with provided questionnaires from the respective territorial directorates participated in the survey. The results from this type of survey are divided into 2 primary groups, where the division was based on the time of carrying out the surveys. The survey questionnaire was composed of specific questions (attached to the paper) seeking specific responses to the problems and matters studied. The summary results from the survey are presented in Table 1, namely:

The data presented in table 1 shows that based on the empirical study conducted among 30 participants in the survey from the respective territorial directorates of Executive Agency "General Labour Inspectorate" it is concluded that the standard deviation from the pre-defined values for control effectiveness is 1.140 units. The deviation is not significant and is within the interval from 1 to 5. If it were above 5, then it would be assumed that the deviation is significant and it would be necessary to find the cause for that deviation. The best result is achieved when this deviation is within the range between 0 and 1. This deviation is standard, it is within the allowable limits and means that the achievements of the inspectors' work and their objectives have reached the preliminary estimates for effectiveness. Practically, it is very difficult to achieve these values within the interval between 0 and 1, because this would mean that the inspection controlling activity has been performed entirely based on the planned activity.

It is also possible to obtain negative values of the deviation into practice, which means that the preliminary estimation of the effectiveness is much higher than the assessment actually achieved and derived. In the studied case, the deviation values are not negative, which means that there have been no significant deviations from the predefined planned values in the period between 2018 and 2022. It should be noted here that the unplanned inspections can be either included in or excluded from the estimated value. This depends mainly on the time when this estimation is derived. When the estimation about the

Table 1. Empirical study of the effectiveness of control

Types of territorial directorates tested	First evaluation from the performed study on the effectiveness of control	Second evaluation on the effectiveness of control from the survey	Estimated evaluation of effectiveness	Actual progress in the achievement of the control objectives	Estimated progress/ achievement of objectives	Deviation in progress/ achievement of objectives
	1	2	4	5=2-1	6=4-1	7= 5-6
"Labour Inspectorate – Blagoevgrad" Directorate	0.7712	0.8918	0.8801	0.1206	0.1089	0.0117
"Labour Inspectorate – Varna" Directorate	0.9218	0.9909	0.9853	0.0691	0.0635	0.0056
"Labour Inspectorate – Vidin" Directorate	0.5421	0.6081	0.5829	0.066	0.0408	0.0252
"Labour Inspectorate – Gabrovo" Directorate	0.6322	0.7727	0.7701	0.1405	0.1379	0.0026
"Labour Inspectorate – Kardzhali" Directorate	0.4339	0.5068	0.4929	0.0729	0.059	0.0139
"Labour Inspectorate – Lovech" Directorate	0.5524	0.5963	0.5616	0.0439	0.0092	0.0347
"Labour Inspectorate – Pazardzhik" Directorate	0.7727	0.7802	0.8106	0.0075	0.0379	-0.0304
"Labour Inspectorate – Pleven" Directorate	0.4455	0.5519	0.5098	0.1064	0.0643	0.0421
"Labour Inspectorate – Razgrad" Directorate	0.6767	0.9811	0.8788	0.3044	0.2021	0.1023
"Labour Inspectorate – Silistra" Directorate	0.0698	0.3511	0.3441	0.2813	0.2743	0.007
"Labour Inspectorate – Smolyan" Directorate	0.1022	0.3377	0.3242	0.2355	0.222	0.0135
"Labour Inspectorate – Sofia" Directorate	0.2325	0.4212	0.4114	0.1887	0.1789	0.0098

continued on following page

Table 1. Continued

Types of territorial directorates tested	First evaluation from the performed study on the effectiveness of control	Second evaluation on the effectiveness of control from the survey	Estimated evaluation of effectiveness	Actual progress in the achievement of the control objectives	Estimated progress/ achievement of objectives	Deviation in progress/ achievement of objectives
	1	2	4	5=2-1	6=4-1	7= 5-6
"Labour Inspectorate – Targovishte" Directorate	0.1918	0.9717	0.9077	0.7799	0.7159	0.064
"Labour Inspectorate – Shumen" Directorate	0.8802	0.9909	0.8992	0.1107	0.019	0.0917
"Labour Inspectorate – Burgas" Directorate	0.8993	0.9202	0.9009	0.0209	0.0016	0.0193
"Labour Inspectorate – Veliko Tarnovo" Directorate	0.6534	0.8521	0.8039	0.1987	0.1505	0.0482
"Labour Inspectorate – Vratsa" Directorate	0.6036	0.8624	0.8529	0.2588	0.2493	0.0095
"Labour Inspectorate – Dobrich" Directorate	0.6216	0.7276	0.7073	0.106	0.0857	0.0203
"Labour Inspectorate – Kyustendil" Directorate	0.6309	0.8683	0.8409	0.2374	0.21	0.0274
"Labour Inspectorate – Montana" Directorate	0.7217	0.7654	0.7331	0.0437	0.0114	0.0323
"Labour Inspectorate – Pernik" Directorate	0.4401	0.5505	0.4981	0.1104	0.058	0.0524
"Labour Inspectorate – Plovdiv" Directorate	0.6705	0.8498	0.7388	0.1793	0.0683	0.111
"Labour Inspectorate – Ruse" Directorate	0.7879	0.7919	0.7099	0.004	-0.078	0.082
"Labour Inspectorate – Sliven" Directorate	0.6692	0.7823	0.6907	0.1131	0.0215	0.0916

continued on following page

Table 1. Continued

Types of territorial directorates tested	First evaluation from the performed study on the effectiveness of control	Second evaluation on the effectiveness of control from the survey	Estimated evaluation of effectiveness	Actual progress in the achievement of the control objectives	Estimated progress/ achievement of objectives	Deviation in progress/ achievement of objectives
	1	2	4	5=2-1	6=4-1	7= 5-6
"Labour Inspectorate – Sofia District" Directorate	0.7978	0.8562	0.7919	0.0584	-0.0059	0.0643
"Labour Inspectorate – Stara Zagora" Directorate	0.2122	0.4349	0.3798	0.2227	0.1676	0.0551
"Labour Inspectorate – Haskovo" Directorate	0.3215	0.5985	0.5144	0.277	0.1929	0.0841
"Labour Inspectorate – Yambol" Directorate	0.4409	0.6567	0.6078	0.2158	0.1669	0.0489
Total						*1.140*

effectiveness has been done at the beginning of the period, there is no way it can include the unplanned inspections. When the estimation is done at a later stage, i.e. at some time interval, such as the first quarter, the second quarter, etc., it is possible to include part of these unplanned inspections in the estimation for the remaining part of the period of the year studied. Usually, this is done by including these unplanned inspections as results from the total controlling activity performed over the past period, thus reducing the margin of the deviation between the expected/estimated assessments and the assessments of the objectives and results achieved actually derived. This is the main role of analysers – to determine the causal link of the results.

According to M. Dinev, "the effectiveness of control is further measured by indicators that reflect the revenues from the inspections performed and the losses resulting from failure to exercise control or improper control" (Dinev, 1986). With the technological development and digitalisation of the processes, today it is much easier to define the actual direct losses from failure to exercise control or improper control. The results from the court rulings where Executive Agency "General Labour Inspectorate" is a party to the proceedings demonstrate the presence of improperly performed controlling procedures. The controlling procedures can be appealed against in two stages:

1. Administrative procedure
2. Court procedure

In the case of disagreement with the findings mentioned in the official statement, the affected party (i.e. the entity under control) can express their disagreement immediately in the presence of the inspectors and can enter their objections in the relevant space in the official statement intended for that purpose. The second option for objection based on the administrative procedure is applicable to the cases where we disagree with the instructions given or when we want to object to the amount of the administrative penalty (a fine or a sanction) imposed. In such case of a disagreement, an appeal should be submitted within 14 days of the date of being handed the order via the relevant territorial directorate. The appeal should be addressed to the executive director of the General Labour Inspectorate. The administrative appeal does not give rise to suspension of the order and the latter continues to be effective until a final decision on the contested part of the order is issued. The appeal submitted can be accompanied by documents proving the statements made by the appellant, which are used to prove the elimination of the infringement. The executive director should issue a reasoned decision, which can be appealed against within a period of 14 days before the relevant administrative court. In the cases where the executive director has made a tacit rejection of the appeal submitted, the appellant has the right to dispute this within one month after the expiration of the period for issuing an administrative decision.

For the overall procedure of identification of the infringement, the general provisions of the ***Administrative Infringements and Penalties Act (ZANN)*** shall be applied. The procedure for identification of the administrative infringement is part of the enforcement proceeding of Executive Agency "General Labour Inspectorate". An administrative infringement "in the field of employment relations is a deed that can be committed both in the form of an action and in the form of omission. A special feature of these infringements that can be identified is related to their danger to society" (Adneeva and Yolova, 2008). When studying the effectiveness of control, one should also consider this stage of the proceedings and the subsequent appeal against the administrative official statements based on the administrative and court procedure. In the proceedings exercised by the inspectors from Executive

Agency "General Labour Inspectorate", they have the right to draft an official statement of administrative infringement (OSAI) on the spot at the site during the inspection itself or they can draft the official statement at a later stage (after leaving the site). In the second case, the inspectors need to schedule a specific date and time with the person under inspection when the person should show up at the respective territorial division to sign the official statement and receive it. In this case the invitation should be sent to the person in writing, otherwise, in the case of subsequent appeals, Art. 40, para. 2 of ZANN may be applied, which may result in cancellation of the procedure. To avoid this legal possibility, Art. 43 of ZANN has explicitly described and regulated the entire procedure for serving the official statement when the procedure of serving the official statement is in the absence of the employer.

The legislation states that where the official statement cannot be served in person, it shall be sent via registered mail with return receipt to the registered address of the inspected company. If no representative of the company is found at the relevant address, an official notification shall be placed at the special places designated for that purpose in the territorial directorate and the official statement will be considered served after expiration of a period of 7 days.

The inspectors of EA "General Labour Inspectorate" should aim at drafting the official statements in the presence of the offender, however, sometimes the offender might not be present at the inspection and in this case the official statement can be drafted in the presence of witnesses. There may be exceptions to this rule in the following cases:

- when it is clear who the offender is, but they cannot be found;
- when there are no witnesses present during the infringement or establishment of infringement, in which case the inspectors may resort to other witnesses, where these circumstances must be explicitly described.

In the case of improperly performed controlling activities, the entire proceedings will be cancelled with the administrative appeal before the executive director of the General Labour Inspectorate. In the case of appeals filed to the court, the purpose of appealing against the relevant official statements is to either dismiss the official statement in its entirety or contest part of its content so as to dismiss the entire criminal liability or achieve partial dismissal of the infringement, which reflects on the amount of the sanctions and fines. In these cases it can be assumed that the infringements have been improperly or failed to be established. According to M. Dinev, when there is information about such situations and cases of control (and these are quite common in the practice of control), the effectiveness of control should be determined by using the following formula:

E = 1 – (Ex/Ey), where

Ex – the amount of the expenses incurred for control;
Ey – the amount of losses from failure to exercise control or improper control.

The amounts of the expenses incurred for control during the studied period between 2018 and 2022 have been presented in table 2, where the main expenses of EA "General Labour Inspectorate" are staff expenses (i.e. expenses for the work performed by the controlling inspectors and the administrative staff). The total payroll staff of EA "General Labour Inspectorate" is 495, with no changes in the payroll staff during the period between 2018 and 2021. These are the so-called direct expenses that have impact on the controlling process, whereas the indirect expenses include the expenses for supporting the entire agency and other overhead expenses.

Table 2. Operating expenses for the controlling activity of EA "GLI"

Operating expenses for controlling activity of EA "GLI"	year 2018/BGN	year 2019/BGN	year 2020/BGN	year 2021/BGN
Staff	9261000	9470000	9317000	12197000
Support and other overhead expenses	767000	847000	932000	1432000
Total	***10028000***	***10317000***	***10249000***	***13629000***

For the purpose of the empirical study, the court rulings for decreasing the amount of the financial sanctions and fines imposed or for entire dismissal of the penalties, which have entered into force in the period between 2018 and 2021, have been reviewed. In addition, for the purpose of studying the effectiveness of control over the period between 2018 and 2021, the official summary reports about the results from the controlling activity of Executive Agency "General Labour Inspectorate" have been also taken into account. Table 3 presents the results from the controlling activity during the studied period between 2018 and 2021, particularly:

Table 3. Results from the controlling activity of EA "GLI"

Results from control	2018	2019	2020	2021
Total number of inspections performed	43 958	40 216	37 145	40 788
Total number of companies inspected	32 309	31 412	29 919	33 177
including companies with up to 9 employees	19 645	18 746	17 503	20 008
including companies with 10 to 49 employees	8 518	8 363	8 082	8 983
including companies with 50 to 249 employees	3 141	3 297	3 388	3 205
including companies with 250 to 499 employees	443	453	435	445
including companies with more than 500 employees	562	553	511	536
Average payroll staff in the inspected companies	1 484 092	1 466 412	1 439 029	1 416 948
Infringements of the labour law and the Employment Promotion Act identified	174 318	171 826	153 760	187 712
Administrative enforcement measures imposed - total	165 921	164 538	147 556	181 323
including instructions issued in accordance with Art. 404, para. 1, subsection 1 of the Labour Code	160 706	156 887	140 643	175 258
including machines stopped, workplaces closed, etc. in accordance with Art. 404, para. 1, subsection 3 of the Labour Code	305	293	263	261
including instructions issued in accordance with Art. 404, para. 1, subsection 5 of the Labour Code	36	87	24	42
including under Art. 78, para. 1 of ZNZ	212	132	159	167
Official statements for infringements of the labour law and the Employment Promotion Act issued	9 958	9 649	7 606	8 557
Penalty orders issued and agreements signed	9 874	9 109	7 577	8 544
Amount under the penalty orders that have entered into force and the agreements approved	15 799 560	12 938 160	11 622 325	10 531 810
Work permits granted to people under the age of 16	205	222	133	200
Work permits granted to people aged between 16 and 18	8 033	9 185	4 526	7 758
Permits granted under Art. 333 of the Labour Code	319	411	375	223

Based on the data in table 3 it is concluded that a significant number of inspections have been carried out in the period between 2018 and 2021. These inspections were 43 958 in 2018, 40 216 in 2019, 37 145 in 2020 and a total number of 40 788 inspections in 40 788. Based on these inspections, a total number of 174 318 infringements were identified in 2018, 171 826 infringements in 2019, 153 760 infringements found and identified in 2020 and 187 712 infringements found and identified in 2021. The total number of official statements issued were 9958 in 2018, 9649 official statements in 2019, 7606 official statements were issued in 2020 and 8557 official statements were issued in 2021. These data show that not all inspections have resulted in the issuance of official statements for administrative infringements. A significant part of the inspections resulted in instructions that the inspected entities took into account and rectified any irregularities and deviations from the statutory norms in due time. The penalty orders issued by EA "GLI" were 9874 in 2018, 9109 in 2019, 7577 in 2020 and 8544 penalty orders issued in 2021. The administrative penalty is imposed with a penalty order imposed by the director of the respective directorate of the "General Labour Inspectorate" within one month of receiving the file on the order.

The data in table 3 further show that the total amount under the penalty orders that entered into force in 2018 was BGN 15 799 560, it was BGN 12 938 160 in 2019, BGN 11 622 325 in 2020 and the amount under the penalty orders that entered into force in 2021 was BGN 10 531 810. Based on the information provided by Executive Agency "General Labour Inspectorate", part of the penalty orders were contested, which resulted in partial or full dismissal of the penal liability or reduction or cancellation of the fines or sanctions imposed. In terms of figures, the penal orders dismissed or reduced

Table 4. Effectiveness of control over the period between 2018 and 2021

Effectiveness	2018	2019	2020	2021
E = 1 – Ex/Ey, where: *Ex* – the amount of the expenses incurred for control; *Ey* – the amount of losses from failure to exercise control or improper control.	1-10028000/26320 = - **380**	1-10317000/35540 = - **289.29**	1-10249000/36780 = - **277.66**	1-13629000/24970 = - **544,82**

amount to BGN 26 320 in 2018, BGN 35 540 in 2019, BGN 36 780 in 2020 and BGN 24 970 in 2021.

Based on these data, the effectiveness of control identified over the period between 2018 and 2021 by applying the formula indicated above is as follows:

Based on the data presented in table 4 it is concluded that the values of the effectiveness of control between 2018 and 2021 are negative. According to K. Donev, this means that its "factual complex value is lower than one and that the supervisory institution does not function normally, i.e. it is not within the positive norms" (Donev, 1984). The expenses for control are significant in the studied case and therefore, after applying this specific method for defining the effectiveness of control, the results turn out to be negative. It is necessary to conduct more in-depth studies for the application of this particular methodology for defining the effectiveness of control, which would require more data due to the need to test each and every object under control (i.e. each enterprise) and the need to test and define the impact of the subject (i.e. the supervisory institution EA "GLI") on the respective object. It is recommended to perform this test on the different forms of control exercised by Executive Agency "General Labour Inspectorate". We assume this method is suitable for the purposes and needs of internal control, because the supervisory institution has the entire documentation from each inspection and could easily determine the direct result from the impact. In the case of external analyses, the external person (analysers) do not have access to a large part of the information and due to this reason we assume that not all methods are applicable for the purpose of external analysis. Many of the methods and indicators that have established themselves in practice have much more weight and significance for the fulfilment of the internal managerial objectives and tasks.

The problem with the timing of the study and review in the field of control has been discussed by K. Donev as early as in 1984. He has also touched another problem, particularly the issue about the form of control (Donev, 194). The three forms of control, that is, preliminary, ongoing and follow-up control also need to be considered as a factor relevant to the conduct of the respective study. Depending on the moment of performing the study, the status of the object and the subject of the study is different depending on the form of the relevant controlling process. In all three forms, the object of control is developing and changing, especially when it is carrying out business as a going concern and strives to be creative and innovative under the new conditions. The subject of control tries to have impact on the object. The impact of each supervisory institution, including Executive Agency "General

Labour Inspectorate", focuses on improving the activity of the object under control and identifying any weaknesses and infringement so as to avoid any further infringements. This means that the form and scope of impact can differ, too. There may be normal impact, regulating impact, supervisory impact, etc. Thus, "the timing of the object's conduct and the timing of the subject's impact will fully or partially coincide, whereas in other cases there will not coincide at all" (Donev, 1984). This also affects the achievement of effectiveness of control and the final result is opposing the object under control to the philosophy of the controlling inspection.

The results from the study presented in table 4 refer to the entire controlling institution Executive Agency "General Labour Inspectorate", however, this study does not cover a specific controlling activity or object. This study proves again that the methodology for testing the effectiveness of a specific object under control is different from the methodology for testing the effectiveness of the entire supervisory institution. It is possible for the controlling procedure implemented to be ineffective, inefficient and uneconomical for a certain object under control that is subject to a controlling impact and influence. This does not mean that the entire supervisory institution as such has not fulfilled its objectives and tasks. Therefore it is necessary to examine each specific case, which is a prerequisite for a change in the status of the supervisory institution.

It is possible for a certain structural unit from the respective supervisory institution to achieve its economic efficiency by decreasing its expenses (i.e. decreasing the payroll staff in a certain unit/department, and, respectively reducing the administrative costs for supporting a certain unit/department, etc.) and thus achieve the overall objectives of the unit, whereas another structural unit might not succeed in achieving the planned results for effectiveness. After a review of the overall results for the entire organisation, consolidated for all structural units, one might say that the overall objectives and tasks have been achieved at organisational level, however, the analysis should not end here with the conclusions so derived. In strategic management, it is necessary to apply a specific policy on the relevant structural units in the long term, which should be customised based on the respective problems within the units. In this regard, K. Donev believes it is necessary to make a clear distinction between the internal and external economic effectiveness for a given supervisory institution, including in the case of analysing the effectiveness of the controlling activity (Donev, 1980).

According to B. Sokolov, a given supervisory institution can achieve internal economic effectiveness (Sokolov, 2006) in the following way:

1. The supervisory institution should create the necessary conditions for exercising internal control with respect to all objects. This requirement can be achieved by establishing an internal control system to cover all objects within the enterprise, including human resources management.
2. It needs to identify the criteria and define the extent to inadmissible deviations for which liability will be sought from the offenders.
3. It should not allow internal control to be exercised by just one person, where this particular person has significant influence on the management of the respective supervisory institution. It is considered that this may give rise to allowing more infringements because of the single-rule management.
4. The management of the organisation needs to show understanding and engagement in the case of problems and it should act for their adequate and timely resolution.
5. Competence, diligence and ethics on the part of the persons exercising internal control.
6. The internal methodologies, programmes and procedures should be adapted to an adequate and operational internal control system.
7. Preventing any repeated or parallel exercising of the same type of control on one and the same object under control.

No matter whether the economic effectiveness is studied with respect to the activity and the results of the internal structural units of the respective supervisory institution or with respect to the external assessment of external stakeholders about the results and actions of the overall controlling activity exercised by the respective supervisory institution, from a methodological perspective it is suitable to measure effectiveness by using a system of indicators. This will provide a complex assessment about the status of the supervisory institution and of the overall controlling activity it exercises.

From the point of view of the controlling process, the system of indicators can be different for the different types of control, for example with indicators for defining the economic effectiveness of the internal control and indicators for defining the economic effectiveness of the external control. This means that it is necessary to divide the indicators into groups based on two main characteristics, particularly – based on ***the scope of use*** (for defining the effectiveness of the specific controlling activity, for defining the effectiveness of the individual structural unit, etc.) and based on ***the level of universality*** (for the entire supervisory institution, for defining the effectiveness of internal or external control, etc.). Using a system of indicators rather than just a single indicator will help study more factors that have impact on the change of effectiveness and will help determine the reasons for the unwanted deviations.

When building the system of indicators used to derive general data or partial data for a specific secondary object studied (i.e. a specific activity, structural units, etc.), the following groups of indicators are used:

1. Indicators characterising the full scope of the activity of the supervisory institution. These are the indicators for the total revenues from the activity of the supervisory institution.
2. Indicators characterising the net result from the controlling activity of the respective supervisory institution. These indicators are calculated by deducting the direct expenses incurred (for materials, labour, etc.) for exercising the controlling activity from the total revenues.

Table 5 presents the system of indicators, particularly:

Table 5. System of indicators for defining the effectiveness of control

System of indicators for defining the effectiveness of control with respect to the level of universality	***System of indicators for defining the effectiveness of control with respect to the scope of use***
I. Indicators for defining the total return on resources and absorption of resources as a result of the control **RCc = Rt/Rs** RCc – return on resources as a result of the control Rt – the results from the activity (total number of inspections) Rs – the advance resources of the relevant supervisory institution **RSC = Rs/Rt** RSC – absorption of resources as a result of the control The average rate of change of the result for a given period is: $\mathbf{RC}_{\mathbf{t\ weighted\ average}} = \Sigma\ \mathbf{RC}_{\mathbf{t}} / \mathbf{n} = (RC_{t1} + RC_{t2} + RC_{t3} + RC_{tn}) / n$ n – number of units in the period (years, months, etc.) $\mathbf{RSC}_{\mathbf{t\ weighted\ average}} = \Sigma\ \mathbf{RSC}_{\mathbf{t}} / \mathbf{n} = (RSC_{t1} + RSC_{t2} + RSC_{tn}) / n$ n – number of periods	I. Indicators for defining the return of labour from a specific controlling activity $\mathbf{R_{LC} = RT / L}$ RT – results from the activity (i.e. results from a specific controlling inspection) L – number of staff (inspectors engaged in a specific controlling inspection)
II. Indicators for defining the total return on costs and absorption of costs as a result of the control $R_{TCC} = Rt / TC$ R_{TCC} – return on costs as a result of the control Rt – results from the activity TC – total costs **TCC = TC/ RT** TCC – total absorption of costs with respect to the total revenues from the activity of the supervisory institution	II.*Indicators for defining the labour intensity of the controlling activity* TLc = T/RT T – number of staff engaged in a specific inspection RT – results from the activity T – number of inspectors engaged in a specific inspection

The proposed system of indicators developed based on testing the direct and indirect resources and costs incurred expresses the absorption of resources and costs (intensity) of the controlling activity. The proposed approach for studying the effectiveness of control based on two aspects – the level of use with respect to the level of universality, the methods considered and the grouping of the relevant indicators based on their characteristics has its own research and practical purpose.

The control exercised by Executive Agency "General Labour Inspectorate" combines state control with social and public control. This is primarily manifested in the contribution of the agency's controlling activity focusing, on the one hand, on strengthening lawfulness and the rule of law with respect to compliance with labour law and, on the other hand, on the establishment of the moral, unwritten rules characterising the relationships between the employers and their employees/workers and the relationship between the state authorities and society as a whole, and this is particularly evident in the application of preventive measures for avoiding infringements of labour law. The methods of factual and documentary control provide the agency with the opportunity to make a final evaluation on the lawfulness and rule of law with respect to compliance with labour law in different economic sectors and industries. This is what determines the specifics of the agency's activity and the measures it can undertake and impose on the objects under control in order to rectify any offences, propose the elimination of specific activities and suggest improvements in the working environment in accordance with the Occupational Health and Safety Act, the Employment Promotion Act and the Labour Code. The agency also has the power to file an application to the competent court for declaring insolvency of enterprises in accordance with the provisions of Art. 625 of the Commercial Act. According to the provisions of this law, the agency has the power to initiate insolvency proceedings when the employer owes wages and has "payables for more than two months for wages and salaries to at least one third of the workers and employees of the company". In the cases where the insolvency proceedings are initiated by the labour inspectorate, the latter, as the initiator, has to collect the necessary evidence and exercise procedural representation on behalf of the Agency through the "Legal and Inspection Activity" Directorate in the insolvency proceedings with respect to the relevant enterprises.

After the amendments to the Commercial Act that took place in 2018, the number of unfair employers that delay the payment of remuneration to their workers and employees decreased significantly. For instance, in 2018 the labour inspectors checked about 250 companies that had problems paying their workers during certain periods over the past three years. According to information from the agency, as a result of the inspections "some of the companies inspected paid what they owed to their workers and employees". The agency further reported that during its inspections in 2018 there were companies that owed "salaries for previous periods, however, they had paid their workers and employees regularly as of 2018, due to which no consistent insolvency could be proven. The controlling authorities of the Agency continue exercising control with respect to those companies so that the workers can receive their delayed salaries for previous periods". In 2018, "after the interference of the Labour Inspectorate, BGN 8.7 million of delayed salaries were paid. The amount of delayed salaries identified, for which measures for their repayment in accordance with the law have been undertaken, is BGN 8 million".

Table 6 shows the court rulings for declaring insolvency of enterprises in

Table 6. Number of proceedings for declaring insolvency of commercial companies in the period between 2018 and 2021

Year	Number of initiated proceedings for declaring insolvency of commercial companies (enterprises)
2018	*34 court rulings*
2019	*38 court rulings*
2020	*37 court rulings*
2021	*22 court rulings*

accordance with Art. 625 of the Commercial Act that have entered into force as a result of proceedings initiated by Executive Agency "General Labour Inspectorate", particularly:

Regarding the information in Table 7, a distinction needs to be made between insolvency proceedings that have been initiated and court rulings that have entered into force. The main information provided officially by Executive Agency "General Labour Inspectorate" through their website is the information about the proceedings initiated. Not all court rulings for opening an insolvency proceeding end with a final ruling for declaring the respective enterprise insolvent. Additional evidence may be provided in the course of the court proceedings proving that the company is capable of continuing its business, that it is not insolvent and that its financial indicators (such as liquidity and profitability) are satisfactory. In the cases

Table 7. Number of court rulings for declaring insolvency of the commercial companies that have entered into force in the period between 2018 and 2021

Year	Number of court rulings for declaring insolvency of commercial companies (enterprises) that have entered into force
2018	*27 court rulings*
2019	*26 court rulings*
2020	*30 court rulings*
2021	*15 court rulings*

where the final court rulings confirms the long-term indebtedness and insolvency of the company, workers and employees have the right to refer to the "Guarantee of Employment Claims" Fund to receive compensation for the salaries due by their employers. Furthermore, based on this final ruling, the court can terminate the company business and serve an attachment order with respect to the property of the debtor in order to guarantee the repayment of their obligations.

Some of the enterprises declared insolvent are of major importance to society due to their activity in favour of the citizens and society, such as: ***Diagnostic and Consulting Centre "Eskulap-Citomed"*** OOD, pursuant to Ruling No. 20 of 1 October 2021 of Pazardzhik District Court; ***"KALIAKRA FOOTBALL CLUB" ASSOCIATION***", pursuant to Ruling No. 260068 of 17 May 2021 of Dobrich District Court, entered in the Register of Non-Profit Legal Entities on 1 June 2021 has an open insolvency proceeding; ***the travel operator*** "***Astral Holidays BG" EPPD***, pursuant to Ruling No. 260081 of 16 October 2020 of Plovdiv District Court; "***TELECOM SERVICE BULGARIA"*** EOOD, Unified Identification Code 175260600, pursuant to Ruling No. 1960 of 2 October 2018 of Sofia City Court, entered in the commercial register on 2 October 2018, and others.

The results from the activity of Executive Agency "General Labour Inspectorate" prove its consistency in its work and fulfilment of its main objectives as a supervisory institution of the executive power. It is more important to determine the extent to which the results achieved meet the defined objectives, i.e. to determine the overall effectiveness and also the economic effectiveness of the agency by comparing the results achieved from the activity with the resources invested (used) for achieving them.

The annual report on the activity of Executive Agency "General Labour Inspectorate" for 2021 states that the agency's long-term priorities are set out in the Strategic Plan of the Agency for the period from 2018 to 2021 and the idea of effective and efficient operation of the Labour Inspectorate is reflected in the Agency's strategic objective To improve the quality of the activity of EA "GLI"", which is achieved by fulfilment of the following five operational objectives:

1. Exercising effective control on compliance with the legislation in the field of employment, public service and labour mobility.
2. Prevention for the purpose of compliance with labour law.
3. Increasing the Agency's administrative capacity and the labour inspectors' professional capacity.
4. Enhancing and strengthening of the institutional image of the Labour Inspectorate.
5. Active international activities;

This annual plan for the activity of Executive Agency "General Labour Inspectorate" further states that "To build its institutional capacity and improve the overall management of the quality of its activity focusing on the effective and efficient achievement of the strategic and annual objectives, EA "General Labour Inspectorate" introduced a Common Assessment Framework (CAF)". The CAF model is a relatively new management instrument. According to some other documents, CAF is not a model, but a "framework for assessment of the quality of public administrations in Europe". The framework was approved through the European Public Administration Network (EUPAN) and the European Commission and its purpose is to provide an overview of all public administrations "by applying a holistic approach to the analysis of organisational performance". The general concept of CAF is to apply a unified approach and common method for assessment of the quality of the public administration and the services it offers. Therefore, the model for self-assessment in public administration proposed with the CAF framework is not designed to identify the economic effectiveness, but rather to assess the quality of the service offered by the public administration.

The administrative services provided by Executive Agency "General Labour Inspectorate" are as follows:

1. Issuing a preliminary authorisation or a refusal for dismissal of certain categories of workers and employees that are subject to special protection.
2. Issuing an order for termination of an employment contract with a worker or employee in the case where the worker or employee cannot submit

their written declaration for termination of the employment contract to the employer.

3. Issuing an authorisation for performing special explosive works.
4. Issuing a new service book.
5. Entry of industrial collective bargaining agreements and supplementary agreements (annexes) thereto in a special register.
6. Issuing an authorisation for performing technological (repeated) explosive works.
7. Entry of collective bargaining agreements of enterprises and supplementary agreements (annexes) thereto in a special register.
8. Issuing a duplicate of a service book that has been lost or destroyed.
9. Issuing an authorisation to organise and conduct qualification courses for the main staff working with explosive materials.
10. Issuing an authorisation for use of newly developed explosive materials, equipment and facilities designed for the explosive machines and technologies.
11. Verification of certificates for work with explosive materials issued to explosives workers, heads of warehouses for explosive materials, assistants in warehouses for explosive materials, laboratory workers dealing with explosive materials, testers of explosive materials, pyrotechnicians, sorting operators and for operation of charging machines or devices for explosive substances.
12. Issuing an authorisation for design of special explosive works.
13. Issuing an authorisation for use of explosive materials, equipment and facilities designed for the explosive machines and technologies.
14. Issuing an authorisation for industrial tests on newly developed explosive materials, equipment and facilities designed for the explosive machines and technologies.
15. Verification of certificates for work with explosive materials issued to first and second grade designers, explosive works managers, explosive materials production managers and senior pyrotechnicians.
16. Issuing an authorisation for work to minors.
17. Issuing a certificate for the presence or lack of penalty orders or court rulings for infringements of labour law that have entered into force.

The internal self-assessment of the abovementioned 17 administrative services offered by Executive Agency "General Labour Inspectorate" can be tested by using the CAF model (Common Assessment Framework - CAF). The model is suitable for analysis of the organisational performance of the administrative services offered by a public sector organisation. We believe that a study focusing on the quality of the services offered by public sector organisations by using the CAF model (Common Assessment Framework - CAF) requires an in-depth analysis based on a good empirical database. Therefore, we believe such a study should be the subject of a separate research and not part of another study.

Based on what has been detailed above, it can be assumed that the approach suggested in table 15 for defining the effectiveness of the overall activity of Executive Agency "General Labour Inspectorate" is acceptable in terms of comprehensiveness and completeness. Testing of public sector organisations, particularly for defining the effectiveness of their activity, especially at national or local level, is performed in several different ways. These differ "in their complexity, the work responsibilities and the employees' workload. The fulfilment of certain tasks requires that the employees are highly qualified. This necessitates allocation of the labour used (input) into several categories of complexity, with an assessment of results performed for each one of them" (Xristov, 2005). According to Hr. Hristov, "the most widely used indicators to measure the results of the activity of public organisations are: the volume of production (services provided), the number of workers and employees and

Table 8. Advance resources for the period between 2018 and 2021

Indicator	year 2018/BGN	year 2019/BGN	year 2020/BGN	year 2021/BGN
Advance resources (Rs)	BGN 9 020 000	BGN 9 317 000	BGN 8 920 000	BGN 12 150 000

the costs incurred" (Xristov, 2005). The advance resources for performance of the controlling activities of Executive Agency "General Labour Inspectorate" are as follows:

By using the data from table 8 of the advance resources and the data from table 16, the total return on resources and absorption of resources of Executive Agency "General Labour Inspectorate" as a result of the control during the period from 2018 and 2021 was calculated, particularly:

Based on the data in table 16, the following major conclusions can be inferred:

Table 9. Coefficients for defining the total return on resources and absorption of resources as a result of the control

Coefficients	*2018*	*2019*	*2020*	*2021*
Return on resources **RCc = Rt/Rs * 100** Rt – total inspections performed Rs – advance resources	0.48%	0.44%	0.42%	0.34%
Absorption of resources **RSC = Rs/Rt** Rt – total inspections performed Rs – advance resources	205.19	231.67	240.14	297.88

1. The result coverage as compared to the advance costs for the period between 2018 and 2020 is 0.48% for 2018, 0.44% for 2019, 0.42% for 2020 and 0.34% for 2021, i.e. the cost of 1 inspection was BGN 205.19 in 2018, BGN 231.67 in 2019, BGN 240.14 in 2020 and BGN 297.88 in 2021.
2. For a more detailed analysis of the effectiveness of the activity of Executive Agency "General Labour Inspectorate", it is necessary to consider the influence and impact of two more factors, particularly – the number of inspecting persons involved in the specific controlling inspections and the duration of the controlling inspections.
3. The data from table 10 show that Executive Agency "General Labour Inspectorate" maintains the same level of coverage of the number of inspections performed as compared to the advance resources. Furthermore, it was found that there has been no significant change in the total amount of the advance resources as compared to the total number of inspections during the period between 2018 and 2021. A significant increase in the advance resources was observed in 2021, however, the number of inspections performed during that year did not change significantly as compared to the previous years studied, e.g. the total number of inspections was 40 788 in 2021, 37 145 in 2020, 40 216 in 2019 and 43 958 in 2018.

When analysing the effectiveness of control, it is necessary to consider the ratio between the costs incurred and the revenues obtained from the activity. Two coefficients are used for that purpose in order to determine the return on costs and the absorption of costs as a result of the controlling activity. Table 10 presents the data about the total costs incurred by Executive

Table 10. Revenues and costs of EA "GLI" during the period from 2018 to 2021

Indicators of revenues and costs	year 2018/BGN	year 2019/BGN	year 2020/BGN	year 2021/BGN
Amount of the penalty orders that have entered into force and the agreements approved	BGN 15 799 560	BGN 12 938 160	BGN 11 622 325	BGN 10 531 810
Total costs	BGN 10 028 000	BGN 10 317 000	BGN 10 249 000	BGN 13 629 000

Agency "General Labour Inspectorate" and the amount (i.e. the revenues) of the total penalty orders that have entered into force and the agreements approved, particularly:

The study of the effectiveness based on the coefficients for return on costs and absorption of costs is presented in Table 11, particularly:

Table 11. Coefficients of return on costs and absorption of costs during the period between 2018 and 2021

Coefficients	***year 2018/BGN***	***year 2019/BGN***	***year 2020/BGN***	***year 2021/BGN***
Return on costs as a result of the control RTCC = Rt / TC RTCC – return on costs as a result of the control Rt – the results from the activity (revenues from the activity) TC – total costs	1.58	1.25	1.13	0.77
Absorption of costs as a result of the control **TCC = TC/ RT** TCC – total absorption of costs with respect to the total revenues from the activity of the supervisory institution	0.63	0.80	0.88	1.29

The two indicators listed above define the so-called economic effectiveness of Executive Agency "General Labour Inspectorate". The indicator for return on costs allows to determine the amount of revenues received by the agency from its direct activity from using a unit of costs for the same activity. For the agency, it is favourable to have the return on costs indicator increased, however, the data in table 18 show that this indicator is decreasing. This is the result of the fact that the amount under the penalty orders issued by EA "GLI" that have entered into force during the period between 2018 and 2021 is decreasing. There were contested orders during this period and this is one of the reasons for the decrease in the amount. Another reason for this decrease may also be the fact that the administrative sanctions imposed might have been within the range of medium to low sanctions instead of the highest sanctions possible under the law.

For instance, according to Art. 413 of the Labour Code, in case of a failure to ***provide*** occupational health and safety, the company will be punished with a fine ranging between BGN 100 and BGN 500, unless it is subject to a stricter penalty. Para. 2 of Art. 413 of the Labour Code specifies that "an employer who fails to fulfil their obligations to provide occupational health and safety, shall be punished with a property sanction or a fine amounting to BGN 1500 to BGN 15 000, unless it is subject to a stricter penalty, whereas the culpable officer shall be punished with a fine of BGN 1000 to BGN 10 000, unless it is subject to a stricter penalty." Para. 3 of Art. 413 of the Labour Code states that in the case of a repeated infringement under para. 1, a fine of BGN 500 to BGN 1000 shall be imposed, whereas in the case of a repeated infringement under para. 2, a property sanction or fine of BGN 20 000 to BGN 30 000 shall be imposed, or, respectively, a fine between BGN 5000 and BGN 20 000.

The other coefficient is the absorption of costs, which shows how much costs have been incurred per unit of revenue. Based on the general rules and if the methodologies of the analysis have been complied with, it is assumed that this coefficient should be decreasing if the relevant enterprise functions properly. In the studied case it was concluded that the coefficient is increasing during the period between 2018 and 2021. The reason for this increase is that the total costs have been increasing over the studied period, with the costs for salaries being the most significant increase in the total costs.

The study requires an in-depth factor analysis to be able to determine to what extent and how the relevant factors influence the change in the total effectiveness of Executive Agency "General Labour Inspectorate". For this purpose, we will apply the generally accepted factor analysis methodology

(Kostova, 2010) by first analysing the impact of the factors on the coefficient of effectiveness of return on costs and then making a factor analysis on the change of the coefficient of cost absorption. When performing factor analysis, the factors for the previous year are compared to the ones for the current year

Table 12. Factor analysis of the coefficient of return on costs for 2019 as compared to 2018

Indicators	*Number of row*	*Calculation method*	*Data*
1. Costs in BGN			
a) for the previous year 2018	1	*	*BGN 10 028 000*
b) for the current year 2019	2	*	BGN 10 317 000
c) change	3	2-1	BGN 289 000
2. Revenues in BGN			
a) for the previous year 2018	4	*	*BGN 15 799 560*
b) for the current year 2019	5	*	BGN 12 938 160
c) change	6	5-4	-2 8614 000
3. Coefficient of return on costs			
A) for the previous year 2018	7	1/4	0.63
B) for the current year 2019	8	2/4	0.80
C) change	9	7-8	-0.1009
4. Absolute change in the effectiveness of revenues	10	9-7	-0.5291
5. Factor analysis			
A) Impact of changes on the amount of costs	11	8-7	0.17
B) Impact of changes on the amount of revenues	12	9-8	-0.9009
C) Cumulative impact of factors on the absolute change of the revenue effectiveness coefficient	13	11+12	-0.7309

and this is used to determine the change in the factor.

Table 12 presents the factor analysis of the coefficient of return on costs for 2018 as compared to 2019, particularly:

The data on table 12 show that the impact of the change in costs in 2019 as compared to 2018 is BGN 0.17, whereas the changes in the amount of revenues are negative, i.e. there is a decrease. This means that Executive Agency "General Labour Inspectorate" has implemented its tasks by not fully covering the amount of expenses with the amount of revenues received from the penalty orders that had entered into force and the agreements approved. The fluctuations in the changes to the effectiveness of costs are not significant, which did not create major problems during the studied period of 2019 as compared to 2018, however, it would be good to perform a systematic and ongoing analysis of the costs so as to prevent situations that are not favourable for the development of the organisation.

Table 13. Factor analysis of the coefficient of return on costs for 2020 as compared to 2019

Indicators	***Number of row***	***Calculation method***	***Data***
1. Costs in BGN			
a) for the previous year 2019	1	*	*BGN 10 317 000*
b) for the current year 2020	2	*	*BGN 10 249 000*
c) change	3	2-1	***BGN -68 000***
2. Revenues in BGN			
a) for the previous year 2019	4	*	*BGN 12 938 160*
B) for the current year 2020	5	*	*BGN 11 622 325*
C) change	6	5-4	BGN ***-1 315 835***
3. Coefficient of return on costs			
A) for the previous year 2019	7	1/4	BGN 0.80
B) for the current year 2020	8	2/5	BGN 0.88
C) change	9	7-8	BGN -0.08
4. Absolute change in the effectiveness of revenues	10	9-7	BGN -0.88
5. Factor analysis			
A) Impact of changes on the amount of costs	11	8-7	BGN 0.08
B) Impact of changes on the amount of revenues	12	9-8	BGN -0.96
C) Cumulative impact of factors on the absolute change of the revenue effectiveness coefficient	13	11+12	BGN -0.88

The impact of factors on the efficiency for 2020 as compared to 2019 are shown on table 12 and those for 2021 as compared to 2020 are shown on table 13:

Table 14. Factor analysis of the coefficient of return on costs for 2021 as compared to 2020

Indicators	*Number of row*	*Calculation method*	*Data*
1. Costs in BGN			
a) for the previous year 2020	1	*	*BGN 10 249 000*
b) for the current year 2021	2	*	BGN 13 629 000
c) change	3	2-1	BGN 3,380,000
2. Revenues in BGN			
a) for the previous year 2020	4	*	*BGN 11,622,325*
B) for the current year 2021	5	*	BGN 10,531,810
C) change	6	5-4	BGN -1,090,515
3. Coefficient of return on costs			
A) for the previous year 2020	7	1/4	BGN 0.88
B) for the current year 2021	8	2/5	BGN 1.29
C) change	9	7-8	BGN -0.41
4. Absolute change in the effectiveness of revenues	10	9-7	BGN -1.29
5. Factor analysis			
A) Impact of changes on the amount of costs	11	8-7	BGN 0.41
B) Impact of changes on the amount of revenues	12	9-8	BGN -1.70
C) Cumulative impact of factors on the absolute change of the revenue effectiveness coefficient	13	11+12	BGN -1.29

Based on the data presented in table 13 and 14 it is concluded that the cumulative impact of the factors on the absolute change of the coefficient of revenues is negative. Therefore, based on what has been detailed above, it can be concluded that:

1. The economic effectiveness of the agency is not very good over the studied period between 2018 and 2022.
2. The revenues are not significant as compared to the amount of costs, i.e. they do not cover all costs associated with the controlling activities implemented.
3. The trend of a moderately negative absolute effectiveness has been maintained over the studied period between 2018 and 2021, which means

that mechanisms to reduce the costs and increase the revenues should (i.e. the amount under penalty orders that have entered into force and agreements approved) be considered.

4. It is necessary to analyse certain inherent risks for the organisations, which are a prerequisite for incurring costs due to the need of resources to cover for those risks. This creates further unfavourable conditions for the functioning of the agency has has impact on the loss of its financial balance.
5. It is necessary to perform systematic analysis and seek the possible mechanisms, approaches and activities to improve the operation of the agency so that it can achieve effectiveness.

Research can also be directed to the intellectual history and traditional environmental factors such as economic, social, demographic and political/ management perspectives in the development of labor - legal activity, which problems are explored by Turner, M., & Hulme, D. (1997); Nunberg, B. (1999); Drechsler, W. (2005); Randma-Liiv, T., & Drechsler, W. (2017), et al. These authors have each explored the problem in great detail from the perspective of their field. In the book, we do not cover the political problems that are the main ones for the development of state power and the implementation of state control, since these problems in Bulgaria are influenced by various factors and the discussion on them can shift the main focus of the research.

The analysis should not be applied solely as a means for follow-up control. It should be applied on an ongoing basis in order to identify the weaknesses and problems during the relevant current period based on the current data and the current status of the factors that have impact on the change of economic effectiveness.

REFERENCES

Andreeva, A., Yolova, G. (2008). *Nakazatelnopravna zashtita na trudovite i osiguritelni pravootnoshenia*. Izvestia, Varna.

Bogdanov, Hr. (2011). Podhodi za opredelyane efektivnostta na danachnia kontrol. // Predizvikatelstvata pred schetovodstvoto i kontrola. Sbornik dokladi. Varna: Nauka i ikonomika, 2011, s. 329-334.

Dinev, M. (1986). *Kontrol i regulirane na ikonomicheskite sistemi*. Partizdat.

Donev, K. (1980). Efektivnost na kontrolno-revizionnata deynost i faktori za neynoto povishavane. *Izv. na VINS – Varna*, *1980*(3), 103–110.

Donev, K. (1984). *Stopanski i finansov kontrol*. Sofia: Nauka i izkustvo, 1984, s. 40.

Drechsler, W. (2005). The re-emergence of "Weberian" public administration after the fall of new public management: The central and eastern European perspective. *Halduskultuur*, *6*(1), 94–108.

Ilgen, D. (1991). Schneider, J. Performance Measurement: A Multidiscipline View. *International Review of Industrial and Organizational Psychology*, *6*, 71–10.

Kaufmann, A., & Gil-Aluja, J. (1990). *Laz matematicas del azar y de la incertidumbre*. Ediciones Graficas Ortega.

Kostova, N. (2010). *Finansovo-schetovoden analiz*. Aktiv – K OOD.

Lambovska, M. (2018). Control on teams: A model and empirical evidence from Bulgaria. *Serbian Journal of Management*, *13*(2), 311–322. doi:10.5937jm13-14633

Lambovska, M., Rajnoha, R., Dobrovic, J. (2019). From Quality to Quantity and Vice Versa: How to Evaluate Performance in the Budgetary Control Process. *Journal of Competitiveness, 3,* 1.

Nunberg, B. (1999). *The state after communism: administrative transitions in Central and Eastern Europe*. World Bank Publications. doi:10.1596/0-8213-4205-3

Randma-Liiv, T., & Drechsler, W. (2017). Three decades, four phases: Public administration development in Central and Eastern Europe, 1989-2017. *International Journal of Public Sector Management*, *30*(6-7), 595–605. doi:10.1108/IJPSM-06-2017-0175

Sharma, M. (2020). Types of Control Methods: Top 3 Types. *Business Management*. https://www.businessmanagementideas.com/management/controlling/types-of-control-methods-top-3-types-management/7981

Timchev, M. (1999). *Finansovo-stopanski analiz*. Trakia .

Tomov, Y., Krumov. K. (2007). *Stopanski, finansov i danachen kontrol*. Svishtov, Akad. izd. Tsenov.

Turner, M., & Hulme, D. (1997). *Governance, administration and development: Making the state work*. Macmillan. doi:10.1007/978-1-349-25675-4

Zhao, B., Zhao, Z., Huang, M., Zhang, X., Li, Y., & Wang, R. (2021). Model Predictive Control of Solar PV-Powered Ice-Storage Air-Conditioning System Considering Forecast Uncertainties. *IEEE Transactions on Sustainable Energy*, *12*(3), 1672–1683. doi:10.1109/TSTE.2021.3061776

Živković, Ž., Nikolić, D., Mihajlović, I., & Djordjević, P. (2016). Dependability assessment of supplier performance based on fuzzy sets theory. Pál Michelberger (Ed.), Management, Enterprise and Benchmarking in the 21st century. Óbuda University, Keleti Faculty of Business and Management.

Conclusion

The conducted interdisciplinary study of the state control of compliance with labour legislation is aimed at realizing the goal set by the authors, which is achieved through the complex application of legal and economic methods. Doctrinally and theoretically, the authors have analyzed the control mechanisms for compliance with labor legislation, examining them through the prism of normative systematics and in the aspect of their economic effects on traditional and alternative forms of employment.

The conclusions and recommendations that are drawn in the individual parts of the work are in response to the specific research tasks. Here they are summarized and will be presented in the two main axes of the study, namely legal and economic aspects of the issues.

As a result of the first axis, around which the research was conducted, namely the legal aspects of state control, the set objective for the analysis of the national legislation on the control of compliance with labour rights, as well as for the examination of the new actual moments in the legal regulation on the transposition of European norms in the field of control of compliance with labour legislation in Bulgaria is realized.

The historical part of the study traces the genesis in the development of the legal institut of control in Bulgarian labour law, as the periodization corresponds to the historical stages from the liberation of the country to the present day. This chronological order shows not only the dependence of control on social relations, but also traces its place and role in the protection of labour rights during the different stages.

In addition, on the basis of the analysis of the current legal framework, in the aspect of general and special acts regulating the control activity, it can be summarized that structurally and systematically develops and consolidates in our legislation a coherent approach in the consolidation of the external specialized form of guarantee of fair and decent working conditions and the related various methods of sanctioning in cases of illegality, at the same time - building on the principles of individual freedom in the exercise of the right to work and related subjective labour rights.The systematics of the legal acts regulating the control of compliance with labour legislation establish a broad system of authorities and competences concerning different aspects of the implementation of national legislation. The regulated scope of competences and the diverse nature of the object of control obviously aim at a comprehensiveness of the supervision of correctness and lawfulness which in practice leads to a legally guaranteed, stable and functioning system of labour relations. On the other hand, the dynamics of the development of labour relations and the related need to rethink the functions of supervision and the need to expand their comprehensiveness and detail necessitate a rethinking of the structuring of the activity, in which aspect is also the proposed Draft of the new Regulations of the Executive Agency "General Labour Inspectorate" (23.06.2022). This establishes a lasting tendency to detail the functions of control activity, as well as to strengthen the control effects and means in detailed areas and corresponding competences, allowing for a regular, continuous and, above all, qualitative and preventive control mechanism.

The book provides a sufficiently large number of literary sources over 190 from different researchers, and also presents numerous legal acts that regulate the rights and obligations between employers and soldiers/employees. Numerous issues and problems with the application of labor legislation are discussed, as well as the most common violations are presented. The references used in this manuscript are sufficient, relevant and up-to-date for their time. In one manuscript, viz. in a book it is good to have references, but they should not be too many, and they should not lose the author's opinion. In this book, the references are in moderate number, so the readers can feel the author's opinions and the author's theses, which preserves the authenticity of the development and its originality. Readers can feel the different style of each author and thus prove the originality of the book, the applicability of the book in scientific circles and its relevance for its time.

In continuation of this and as a result of the analysis of the control powers of the EA GLI, the following specific conclusions and summaries can be made regarding the applicable legislation concerning the issues under consideration:

First, the provision of labour in the modern context requires the creation of legal guarantees to respect the rights arising from the provision of labour. The existing legal framework must define the limits within which the reciprocal rights and obligations under the employment relationship can be realised in the context of an employee's dependent position on the employer. The regulation of the right to work, including its constitutional recognition as a fundamental right, demonstrates its function and importance for society and for the individual;

Second, the administrative control of the EA GLI performs an important social function in relation to employees and at the same time has a disciplinary function towards the unfair and unscrupulous employers. These two functions of the administrative control of compliance with labour legislation justify the positive assessment of the legal framework under study;

Thirdly, the protection of the right to work requires the continued active influence of the state through the updating of relevant legislation. Contemporary social conditions pose new challenges to the legislator, requiring administrative law protection of fundamental labour rights. In this sense, administrative control and administrative violations liability provided for in labour legislation are of great practical importance. The recent amendments to the Labour Code aim at more effective implementation of control activities and better prevention in relation to the provided administrative sanctions in case of violation of labour legislation. This demonstrates once again the role and importance of administrative law protection in ensuring the necessary level of protection of the right to work.

In summary, it can be concluded that both inspections for compliance with labour legislation and compulsory administrative measures are an effective means of preventing violations of employees' labour rights. The effectiveness of the administrative coercion imposed under the Labour Code is also enhanced by the provision of Article 405(2) of the Labour Code, according to which an appeal does not suspend the enforcement of the compulsory administrative measure. Through the acts of the Labour Inspectorate bodies, an active impact is sought for the protection of the labour rights affected, in order to guarantee the legitimate interests of employees. It is the will of the legislator to introduce promptness in the elimination of violations of labour legislation, given the social importance of the regulated legal relations.

The foregoing shows that the control of compliance with the rights arising from the employment is subject to very dynamic regulation. As a result of the analysis of the new moments in the legal framework and, in particular, the transposition of the European norms in the sphere of control of compliance with the labour legislation in Bulgaria, the following conclusions, summaries and recommendations can be made regarding the applicable legal framework concerning the issues under consideration:

- There is a tendency to expand the powers of the EA GLI both in terms of the types of coercive measures and the intensity of administrative control. This demonstrates the role and importance of administrative legal protection in ensuring the appropriate level of protection of the right to work;

- The current societal conditions of globalisation and digitalisation pose new challenges to the legal framework requiring administrative law protection of fundamental labour rights (e.g. health and safety at work, right to remuneration, right to rest and leave, etc.). The new social relations after the democratic changes in the country are, on the one hand, related to the transition from a planned to a market economy and the development of private economic activity and, on the other hand, stem from Bulgaria's realised EU membership. The national legal framework, which transposes the European norms in the area of control of compliance with the labour rights of employees, is one of the main factors influencing the control procedures for compliance with labour legislation;
- Despite the significant impact of European acts on the development of our national law, the EU does not have exclusive competence in the field of labour law. The exercise of administrative control over compliance with labour law is a matter for national authorities. In this sense, the role of the EA GLI is very important. Unfortunately, the Labour Code adopted in 1986, despite its repeated amendments and additions, is not fully capable of responding to the changes that have taken place in modern social relations. In view of this, a proposal can be made to the legislator for the drafting and adoption of a new Labour Code which would comprehensively regulate all labour law norms and institutes in accordance with the current development of social relations. Of course, it should be taken into account that the adoption of a code in the field of labour law is not an easy task. It is one of the major branches of law regulating not only the legal relations that arise in the provision of working force and the employment of labour, but also a number of other relations directly related to labour, including the control of compliance with labour legislation.

The second axis of research in the work are the economic aspects of the issues of the effectiveness of control over compliance with labour legislation. Accordingly, the following final conclusions and generalizations can be made:

1. The control exercised by the Executive Agency "General Labour Inspectorate" combines both state control and social and public control.

This is mainly expressed in the contribution of the control activities of the Agency, aimed on the one hand at strengthening the legality and legal order regarding compliance with the labour legislation, and on the other hand at strengthening the moral, unwritten norms characterizing the relations between employers and their employees/workers, and the relations between the state authority and the society as a whole, and especially manifested in the implementation of preventive measures to prevent violations of the difficult legislation.

2. There is a need to systematically analyse and seek possible mechanisms, approaches and activities to improve the Agency's performance in order to achieve its effectiveness.
3. Analysis should not be applied solely as a means of subsequent control. It needs to be applied on an ongoing basis in order to identify weaknesses and problems in the relevant current period, based on current data and the current status of the factors that influence changes in economic efficiency.
4. The proposed system of indicators, which is based on the testing of direct and indirect resources and incurred costs, express the resource- and cost-absorption (capacity) of the control activity. The proposed approach to the study of the effectiveness of control from two aspects, namely according to the level of use and according to the degree of generality, in relation to the methods considered and the grouping of the relevant indicators according to the relevant indicators have their scientific - practical purpose.

It is clear that there are different approaches to determining the effectiveness and efficiency of the control activities of the EA GLI. When assessing the activities of budget support organisations, the approach to determining the results of their activities is different from that applied in enterprises with a business activity.

In the approach adopted in the study, indicators are compiled that link the results of the control activity in a certain respect to the objectives of the agency and the resources with which the control activity is carried out.

Assuming that one of the main objectives of the control activity of the EA GLI is related to the control of compliance with labour legislation and occupational health and safety for employees in organizations, then we can argue that the more employees in the country are covered by the control, the more effective it is. The study calculated such an indicator for the period 2017 - 2019, through which it was found that the effectiveness of control activity was highest in 2017, and subsequently remained at a slightly lower level for the period 2018 - 2021.

The efficiency of the control activity of the EA GLI is defined as the ratio of the results achieved and the resources invested in it.

Several efficiency indicators have been examined as follows:

- efficiency of controls, for the period 2019-2021. Efficiency in terms of the budget required to carry them out is found to be deteriorating in the period 2019-2021;
- efficiency in the use of human resources. This efficiency is found to decrease in the period 2017 - 2020, improving in 2021;
- efficiency of the final stage of control by the EA GLI. The efficiency is found to be at a good level throughout the study period from 2017 to 2021.

Labour law is among the branches of law with a pronounced protective function, respectively called to secure and guarantee the lawful application of the right to work. In all stages of the development of the legal sector, an important role has been assigned to the monitoring of compliance with the legislation. Through this study, the legal and economic aspects of this important state control activity are presented in a different relationship. It is not only a challenge for the legislator, who has to update the norms of control with the most current tendencies, but also for the doctrine, as well as for the parties to the employment relationship, who, given the dynamics in the legal matter, are not infrequently hindered in its application in practice.

Appendix

Abbreviations Used

AEAV: Act to establish an administrative violation

APC: Administrative Procedure Code

BCP: Bulgarian Communist Party

CM: Council of Ministers

CPC: Civil Procedure Code

CRB: Constitution of the Republic of Bulgaria

CT: Labor Code

CWC/GWC: Committees/groups on working conditions

DPR: Decree of the President of the Republic

EU: European Union

HSWC: Healthy and safe working conditions

IA GIT/EA MLI: Executive Agency “Main Labor Inspectorate”

ILO: International Labor Organization

INTOSAI: (lat. INTOSAI) international organization of supreme audit institutions (SAIs), respectively - audit chambers

ISVP/ISIM: Information system of the internal market

LAVP: Law on Administrative Violations and Penalties

LHSW: Law on Health and Safety at Work

LIA: Labor Inspection Act

LIAPS: Law on Internal Audit in the Public Sector

LWCL: Law on Women’s and Child Labor

Ministry of Interior: Ministry of Internal Affairs

MLSP: Ministry of Labor and Social Policy

NRA: National Revenue Agency

SAC: Supreme Administrative Court

SG: State Gazette

Compilation of References

Adams-Prassl, J., & Risak, M. (2016) Uber, Taskrabbit, & Co: Platforms as Employers? Rethinking the Legal Analysis of Crowdwork. *Comparative Labor Law Policy Journal, Oxford Legal Studies Research Paper, 8.* https://ssrn.com/abstract=2733003.

Adato, A. (2022). Factors Affecting Internal Audit Effectiveness: Evidence from Microfinance Institutions Operating in Hawassa, Sidama Region, Ethiopia. *American Journal of Theoretical and Applied Business*, *8*(2), 19–29.

Administrativni uslugi na Izpalnitelna agentsia Glavna inspektsia po Truda. (n.d.). Gli.cov. https://www.gli.government.bg/bg/node/6367

Ahmed, N., Gore, E., & Langford, N. (2020). *Pandemic and Precarity: rethinking what it means to be precarious under COVID 19.* Sheffield Political Economy Research Institute. http://speri.dept.shef.ac.uk/2020/04/30/pandemic-and-precarity-rethinking-what-it-means-to-be-precarious-under-covid-19/ [Accessed 30.01.2022].

Aleksandrov, A. (2016). Prakticheski problemi na trudovoto pravo, svarzani s kontrola za spazvane i administrativnonakazatelnata otgovornost za narushenia na trudovoto zakonodatelstvo. *Trud i pravo , 11*, 10-15.

Aleksandrov, A. (2020). Administrativna i izvansadebna zashtita na individualnite subektivni trudovi prava. Ot: Andreeva, A., Yolova, G., Blagoycheva, H., Aleksandrov, A., Banov, H., Yordanov, Z. Zashtita za individualnite subektivni trudovi prava (na rabotnika ili sluzhitelya). Varna: Nauka i ikonomika.

Aleksandrov, A. (2016). Prakticheski problemi na trudovoto pravo, svarzani s kontrola za spazvane i administrativnonakazatelnata otgovornost za narushenia na trudovoto zakonodatelstvo. *Trud i pravo*, (11), 10–15.

Aleksandrov, A. (2017). Mitove i fakti v trudovoto pravo – Za inspektsiyata po truda. *Trud i pravo*, (12), 13–17.

Aleksandrov, N. G. (1959). *Sovetskoe trudovoe pravo*. Gosyurizdat.

Alonso Soto, D. (2020). *Technology and the future of work in emerging economies: What is different*. OECD Working Papers No. 236.

Andreeva, A. & Yolova, G. (2011). *Yuridicheska otgovornost i kontrol za spazvane na trudovoto i osiguritelno zakonodatelstvo*. Varna: Univ. izd. Nauka i ikonomika.

Andreeva, A. & Yolova, G. (2018). *Predizvikatelstva i tendentsii pred sotsialnata zashtita v usloviyata na digitalnoto obshtestvo. Izvestiya Sp. Ikonomicheski universitet*. Varna: Nauka i ikonomika.

Andreeva, A. (2009). *Normativni promeni v kontrola za spazvane na trudovoto i osiguritelno zakonodatelstvo. Izvestia na Ikonomicheski universitet*. Varna.

Andreeva, A. (2010). Vliyanie na ikonomicheskata kriza varhu prekratyavaneto na trudovoto pravootnoshenie. Svetovnata kriza i ikonomicheskoto razvitie. Varna: Nauka i ikonomika.

Andreeva, A. (2016). Zakonodatelni reshenia v balgarskoto trudovo pravo obusloveni ot vrazkata mu s ikonomikata. Pravnata nauka i biznesat – zaedno za ustoychivo razvitie na ikonomikata. Varna: Nauka i ikonomika.

Andreeva, A. (2018). Normativni merki za garantirane na trudovoto vaznagrazhdenie pri nesastoyatelnost na rabotodatelya. *Izvestia na IU* . Varna.

Andreeva, A. (2019). Neprikosnovenost na lichnia zhivot na rabotnitsite v konteksta na digitalizatsiyata. Izv. na Sayuza na uchenite . *Ser. Humanitarni nauki*. Varna: Sayuz na uchenite.

Andreeva, A. (2020). Digitalization as a Factor for the Development of the Modern Labour Legislation. *Digital Economy: Azerbaijan at the New Stage of Economic Development: Conference Proceedings of the International Scientific-Practical Conference*. Baku Business University

Andreeva, A. (2020). Digitalization as a Factor for the Development of the Modern Labour Legislation. *Digital Economy: Azerbaijan at the New Stage of Economic Development: Conference Proceedings of the International Scientific-Practical Conference*. Baku Business University.

Andreeva, A. (2020). i dr. Zashtita za individualnite subektivni trudovi prava (na rabotnika ili sluzhitelya). *Varna: Nauka i ikonomika*.

Andreeva, A. (2020). Otrazhenie na digitalizatsiyata varhu trudovia protses – riskove i perspektivi. Ikonomicheska nauka, obrazovanie i realna ikonomika: razvitie i vzaimodeystvia v digitalnata epoha: Sbornik s dokladi ot Yubileyna mezhdunarodna nauchna konferentsia v chest na 100 god. ot osnovavaneto na IU. Varna.

Andreeva, A. (2020). Otrazhenie na digitalizatsiyata varhu trudovia protses - riskove i perspektivi. Ikonomicheska nauka, obrazovanie i realna ikonomika: razvitie i vzaimodeystvia v digitalnata epoha: Sbornik s dokladi ot Yubileyna mezhdunarodna nauchna konferentsia v chest na 100 god. Varna, Varna: Nauka i ikonomika.

Andreeva, A. (2021). Rabota v pandemichna obstanovka i nyakoi predizvikatelstva za stranite po trudovoto pravootnoshenie. Pravoto i biznesat v savremennoto obshtestvo: Sbornik s dokladi ot 4-ta natsionalna nauchna konferentsia. Varna: Nauka i ikonomika.

Andreeva, A., & Dimitrova, D. (2019). Spetsifiki na kontrola na Izpalnitelna agentsia Glavna inspektsia po truda, v konteksta na garantsiite za izplashtane na trudovoto vaznagrazhdenie. Godishnik na Burgaskia svoboden universitet, 40, 243 – 258.

Andreeva, A., & Dimitrova, D. (2019). Spetsifiki na kontrola na Izpalnitelna agentsia Glavna inspektsia po truda, v konteksta na garantsiite za izplashtane na trudovoto vaznagrazhdenie. Godishnik na Burgaskia svoboden universitet.

Andreeva, A., & Yolova, G. (2008a). Administrativno-nakazatelna otgovornost za narushenia na trudovoto i osiguritelno zakonodatelstvo. Godishnik na Ikonomicheski universitet. Varna.

Andreeva, A., & Yolova, G. (2017). Tendentsii i predizvikatelstva pred trudovoto i osiguritelnoto zakonodatelstvo - deset godini sled chlenstvoto na R. Bulgaria v ES. *Nauchni trudove na Instituta za darzhavata i pravoto*. Sofia: BAN.

Andreeva, A., & Yolova, G. (2018). Harmonizirane na balgarskoto trudovoto i osiguritelno zakonodatelstvo s evropeyskite printsipi. Sabiedrība un kultūra. Rakstu krājums, Liepāja: Liepājas universitāte izglītības zinātņu i nstitūts socioloģisko pētījum u centrs vadības un sociālo z inātņu fakultāte, 20, 334 - 341.

Andreeva, A., & Yolova, G. (2018). Za nyakoi osobenosti na administrativnia kontrol i administrativnonakazatelnata otgovornost za narushavane na zdravoslovnite i bezopasni uslovia na trud. Administrativno pravo – savremenni tendentsii v pravorazdavaneto i doktrinata: Sbornik doklad., Varna: Nauka i ikonomika.

Andreeva, A., & Yolova, G. (2018). Za nyakoi osobenosti na administrativnia kontrol i administrativnonakazatelnata otgovornost za narushavane na zdravoslovnite i bezopasni uslovia na trud. Administrativno pravo – savremenni tendentsii v pravorazdavaneto i doktrinata: Sbornik dokladi, Varna.

Andreeva, A., & Yolova, G. (2019). The Right to Work in a Digital Society: Evolution and Trends. Mezhdunarodni klasterni politiki: Balgaro-kitayski forum: Sbornik s dokladi ot mezhdunarodna konferentsia, Varna: Nauka i ikonomika.

Andreeva, A., & Yolova, G. (2019). The Right to Work in a Digital Society: Evolution and Trends. Mezhdunarodni klasterni politiki: Balgaro-kitayski forum: Sbornik s dokladi ot mezhdunarodna konferentsia. Varna: Nauka i ikonomika.

Andreeva, A., & Yolova, G. (2020). Pravni aspekti na balansa mezhdu lichen i profesionalen zhivot. Pravoto i biznesat v savremennoto obshtestvo: Sbornik s dokladi ot 3-ta Natsionalna nauchna konferentsia. Varna: Nauka i ikonomika.

Andreeva, A., & Yolova, G. (2020a). Rabotodatelskiyat kontrol v konteksta na digitalizatsiyata. Upravlenie na choveshkite resursi v erata na digitalnite predizvikatelstva: Sbornik s dokladi ot Mezhdunarodna nauchno-prakticheska konferentsia, organizirana ot IU. Varna.

Andreeva, A., & Yolova, G. (2020d). Trudovo i osiguritelno pravo. 2. prerab. i dop. izd. Varna: Nauka i ikonomika.

Andreeva, A., & Yolova, G. (2021). Za funktsiite na trudovoto i osiguritelnoto pravo v usloviyata na pandemia. Problemi na trudovoto i osiguritelnoto pravo: Sbornik s dokladi ot Natsionalnata nauchna konferentsia v pamet na prof. d-r Atanas Vasilev po povod na 70 g. ot rozhdenieto mu. Sofia: Izd.

Andreeva, A., Yolova, G. (2008). *Nakazatelnopravna zashtita na trudovite i osiguritelni pravootnoshenia.* Izvestia, Varna.

Andreeva, A., Yolova, G. (2011). *Yuridicheska otgovornost i kontrol za spazvane na trudovoto i osiguritelno zakonodatelstvo.* Varna: Nauka i ikonomika.

Andreeva, A., Yolova, G., Dimitrova, D., (2004). *Osnovi na publichnata administratsiya.* Varna: s.n.

Andreeva, A.; Yolova, G. (2008b). Nakazatelnopravna zashtita na trudovite i osiguritelni pravootnoshenia. *Izvestia na Ikonomicheski universitet.* Varna.

Andreeva, A.; Yolova, G. (2009). Normativni promeni v kontrola za spazvane na trudovoto i osiguritelno zakonodatelstvo. *Izvestia na Ikonomicheski universitet.* Varna.

Andreeva, A.; Yolova, G. (2011). Yuridicheska otgovornost i kontrol za spazvane na trudovoto i osiguritelno zakonodatelstvo. *Univ. izd. Nauka i ikonomika.* Varna.

Andreeva, A., & Yolova, G. (2019). *Administrative Penal Liability for Violations of the Labour Migration and Labour Mobility Act. Globalization, the State and the Individual: International Scientific Journal* (Conference Edition 2019). Free University of Varna.

Andreeva, A., & Yolova, G. (2020b). Transformatsia na pravnata vrazka rabotodatel – rabotnik v rezultat na vliyanieto na digitalizatsiyata. *De Jure (Durban), 1*(20), 11–18.

Aussilloux, V. (2017). Testing novel approaches: Two takes on individual activity accounts. *A lever for more inclusive social protection.* European Political Strategy Centre (EPSC). https://medium.com/reaffirming-social-values-in-uncertain-times/testing-novel-approaches-two-takes-on-individual-activity-accounts-beab1281fc78

Balabanova, H. (2004). Administrativen kontrol: kontrolna kompetentnost na izpalnitelnata vlast. Varna: Varnenski svoboden universitet Chernorizets Hrabar.

Baltadzhieva, R., & Todorov, I. (2012). *Vzaimodeystvie mezhdu evropeyskoto i balgarskoto administrativno pravo.* Siela.

Banov, H. (2016). Evropa 2020. i trudoviyat dogovor za obuchenie po vreme na rabota. *Pravna misal, 4,* 47 – 64.

Banov, H. (2020). Istorichesko razvitie na individualnite subektivni trudovi prava v balgarskoto pravo. ot: Andreeva, A., Yolova, G., Blagoycheva, H., Aleksandrov, A., Banov, H., Yordanov, Z. Zashtita za individualnite subektivni trudovi prava (na rabotnika ili sluzhitelya). Varna: Nauka i ikonomika.

Barbieri, P., Bozzon, R., Schere, S., Grotti, R., & Lugo, M. (2015). The rise of a Latin model? Family and fertility consequences of employment instability in Italy and Spain. *European Societies*, *17*(4), 423–446. doi:10.1080/14616696.2015.1064147

BarriosJ.HochbergY.YiH. (2018) The Cost of Convenience: Ridesharing and Traffic Fatalities. . doi:10.2139/ssrn.3259965

Blagoycheva, H. (2016). Employment and the Working Poor; Phenomenon in the EU. *International Journal of Economics and Business Administration (IJEBA)*. Piraeus: GNU Public License.

Blagoycheva, H. (2018). Employers and Employees – on Both Sides of the 'Minimum Wages' Barricade. *International Scientific Journal Fundamental and Applied Researches in Practice of Leading Scientific Schools, Hamilton, Canada: Accent Graphics Communications, 28*(4), 9 – 15. https://doi.org/https://doi.org/10.33531/farplss.2018.4.02

Blagoycheva, H. (2019). Sotsialnata (ne)sigurnost na raboteshtite prez tsifrovi platformi. Pravoto i biznesat v savremennoto obshtestvo: Aktualni pravni predizvikatelstva v ikonomikata: Sbornik s dokladi ot 1-va Natsionalna nauchna konferentsia. Varna: Nauka i ikonomika.

Blagoycheva, H. (2020). Predizvikatelstvata pred sotsialnata zashtita na litsata s nestandartna zaetost. Ikonomicheska nauka, obrazovanie i realna ikonomika: razvitie i vzaimodeystvia v digitalnata epoha: Sbornik s dokladi ot Yubileyna mezhdunarodna nauchna konferentsia v chest na 100 god. Varna, Varna: Nauka i ikonomika.

Blagoycheva, H. (2020). Predizvikatelstvata pred sotsialnata zashtita na litsata s nestandartna zaetost. Ikonomicheska nauka, obrazovanie i realna ikonomika: razvitie i vzaimodeystviya v digitalnata epoha. *Sbornik s dokladi ot Yubileyna mezhdunarodna nauchna konferentsiya v chest na 100 god. ot osnovavaneto na IU.* Varna: Nauka i ikonomika.

Blagoycheva, H. (2021). Robotizatsia, izkustven intelekt i ochakvani transformatsii na pazara na truda. Pravoto i biznesat v savremennoto obshtestvo: Sbornik s dokladi ot 4-ta natsionalna nauchna konferentsia. Varna: Nauka i ikonomika.

Blagoycheva, H. (2016). Employment and the 'Working Poor' Phenomenon in the EU. International Journal of Economics &amp [IJEBA]. *Business Administration (London)*, *4*(3), 3–18.

Blagoycheva, H., Andreeva, A., & Yolova, G. (2019). Obligation and Responsibility of Employers to Provide Health and Safety at Work – Principles, Current Regulation and Prospects. *Economic Studies*, *28*(2), 115–137.

Bogdanov, Hr. (2011). Podhodi za opredelyane efektivnostta na danachnia kontrol. // Predizvikatelstvata pred schetovodstvoto i kontrola. Sbornik dokladi. Varna: Nauka i ikonomika, 2011, s. 329-334.

Bogomilova, Zh. (2016). Kontrol i administrativnonakazatelna otgovornost vav vrazka s pravilata za trudova zaetost na chuzhdi grazhdani v Republika Bulgaria. Trud i pravo, 7.

Bonev, K., Lalova, N., & Ivanov, A. (1989). Matematichesko modelirane. G. *Bakalov*, 217.

Byudzhet na IA „Glavna inspektsia po truda“ za perioda ot 2018 do 2021 g. (2021). Gli.gov. https://www.gli.government.bg/sites/default/files/upload/archive/docs/2019-01/B__dzet_2019_g.pdf

Card, D., & Krueger, A. (2015). *Myth and measurement: the new economics of the minimum wage*. Princeton University Press. doi:10.2307/j.ctv7h0s52

Causa, O., & Cavalleri, M. C. (2020). How non-standard workers are affected and protected during the Covid-19 crisis: stylised facts and policy considerations. CEPR, VOXeu. https://voxeu.org/article/how-non-standard-workers-are-affected-and-protected-during-covid-19-crisis.

CEPS. (Centre for European Policy studies). (2018). Online Talent Platforms, Labour Market Intermediaries and the Changing World of Work. CEPS. https://www.ceps.eu/ceps-publications/online-talent-platforms-labour-market-intermediaries-and-changing-world-work/.

Chastichna predvaritelna otsenka na vazdeystvieto. (n.d.). Public Consultants. https://www.strategy.bg/PublicConsultations/View.aspx?lang=bg-BG&Id=6918

CherryM. A. (2016) Beyond Misclassification: The Digital Transformation of Work. *Comparative Labor Law Policy Journal*. https://ssrn.com/abstract=2734288.

Cherry, M., & Aloisi, A. (2017). ‘Dependent Contractors’ in the Gig Economy: A Comparative Approach. American University Law Review, 66(3), 365–689. doi:10.2139srn.2847869

Chesalina, O. (2018) Access to social security for digital platform workers in Germany and in Russia: a comparative study. *Spanish Labour Law and Employment Relations Journal*, 1(7) pp. 17-28. doi:10.20318/sllerj.2018.4433

Countouris, N., Deakin, S., Freedland, M., Koukiadaki, A., & Prassl, J. (2016). *Report on temporary employment agencies and temporary agency work*. International Labour Office.

Danailov, D. (1987). Kodeksat na truda i kontrolat za spazvane na trudovoto zakonodatelstvo. Kodeksat na truda v deystvie. Materiali ot nauchno-prakticheska konferentsia. Sofia. *Profizdat, 1987*, 210–215.

Däubler, W. (2016). Challenges to Labour Law. *Pravo. Zhurnal Vysshey shkoly ekonomiki 1*, pp. 189-203. . doi:10.17323/2072-8166.2016.1.201.215

Davidov, G., Freedland, M., & Countouris, N. (2015) The Subjects of Labor Law: 'Employees' and Other Workers, in Finkin, M. & Mundlak, G. (eds.), *Research Handbook in Comparative Labor Law,* Edward Elgar. https://papers.ssrn.com/sol3/papers.cfm?abstract_id=2561752.

De La Rica, S., & Iza, A. (2005). Career planning in Spain: Do fixed-term contracts delay marriage and parenthood? *Review of Economics of the Household*, *3*(1), 49–73. doi:10.100711150-004-0979-8

Deganis, I., Tagashira, M., & Yang, W. (2021). *Digitally enabled new forms of work and policy implications for labour regulation frameworks and social protection systems*. United Nations Department of Economic and Social Affairs. https://www.un.org/development/desa/dspd/2021/09/digitally-enabled-new-forms-of-work-and-policy-implications-for-labour-regulation-frameworks-and-social-protection-systems/.

Dermendzhiev, I., Kostov, D., & Hrusanov, D. (2010). *Administrativno pravo na Republika Bulgaria: obshta chast*. Sibi.

Deutscher Bundestag. (2016). *Arbeit 4.0 – Arbeitswelt von morgen gestalten*. Deutscher Bundestag Drucksache 18/10254. https://dipbt.bundestag.de/dip21/btd/18/102/1810254.pdf.

Dimitrova, D. (2010). Oblastniyat upravitel kato organ na izpalnitelnata vlast: Disertatsia za prisazhdane na obrazovatelna i nauchna stepen "doktor", nauchna spetsialnost Administrativno pravo i administrativen protses, shifar. Sofia: Sofiyski universitet.

Dimitrova, D. (2019). Savremenna rolya na Izpalnitelna agentsiya; za zashtita na pravata na stranite po trudovite pravootnosheniya. Pravoto i biznesat v savremennoto obshtestvo: *Sbornik s dokladi ot 2-ra Natsionalna nauchna konferentsiya, 8*. Varna, Nauka i ikonomika.

Dimitrova, D. (2019a). Savremenna rolya na Izpalnitelna agentsia "Glavna inspektsia po truda" za zashtita na pravata na stranite po trudovite pravootnoshenia. Pravoto i biznesat v savremennoto obshtestvo: Sbornik s dokladi ot 2-ra Natsionalna nauchna konferentsia. Varna: Nauka i ikonomika

Dimitrova, D. (2019b). Savremenni tendentsii v administrativnoto zakonodatelstvo na Bulgaria. Pravoto i biznesat v savremennoto obshtestvo: Sbornik s dokladi ot 2-ra Natsionalna nauchna konferentsia. Varna: Nauka i ikonomika.

Dimitrova, D. (2020). Bezopasnite i zdravoslovni uslovia na trud – angazhiment na rabotodatelya i kontrol za spazvane. *Ikonomicheskata nauka, obrazovanie i realna ikonomika: razvitie i vzaimodeystvia v digitalnata epoha. Sbornik dokladi.* Varna: Nauka i ikonomika.

Dimitrova, D. (2020). Bezopasnite i zdravoslovni usloviya na trud - angazhiment na rabotodatelya i kontrol za spazvane. *Ikonomicheskata nauka, obrazovanie i realna ikonomika: razvitie i vzaimodeystviya v digitalnata epoha: Sbornik s dokladi.* Varna, Nauka i ikonomika .

Dimitrova, D. (2020). Po nyakoi vaprosi na administrativnopravnata zashtita na pravoto na trud. *Pravoto i biznesat v savremennoto obshtestvo*. Sbornik dokladi Varna: Nauka i ikonomika.

Dimitrova, D. (2020). Po nyakoi vaprosi na administrativnopravnata zashtita na pravoto na trud. Pravoto i biznesat v savremennoto obshtestvo: Sbornik s dokladi ot 3-ta Natsionalna nauchna konferentsia. Nauka i ikonomika.

Dimitrova, D. (2020). Po nyakoi vaprosi na administrativnopravnata zashtita na pravoto na trud. Pravoto i biznesat v savremennoto obshtestvo: Sbornik s dokladi ot 3-ta Natsionalna nauchna konferentsia. Varna: Nauka i ikonomika.

Dimitrova, D. (2020). *Sivata ikonomika – aktualni merki za protivodeystvie v KT. Pravoto i biznesat v savremennoto obshtestvo: Sbornik s dokladi ot 3-ta Natsionalna nauchna konferentsiya*. Varna, Nauka i ikonomika.

Dimitrova, D. (2022). Vidove prinuditelni administrativni merki po chl. 404, al. 1 ot Kodeksa na truda. *Trud i pravo, 31*, 59-66.

Dimitrova, D., Mateeva, Z., & Dimitrova, D. (2020). *Administrativno pravo i protses*. Varna: Nauka i ikonomika.

Dimitrova, D. (2021). Istoricheski traditsii na kontrola za spazvane na trudovoto zakonodatelstvo. *De Jure (Durban)*, *2*(21), 192–202.

Dimitrova, D. (2022). Current Trends in the Field of Control over Compliance with Labour Legislation. Economics and Computer Science: Varna. *Knowledge and Business*, *8*, 14–20.

Dimitrov, D. (1994). *Administrativno pravo*. Sofiya.

Dinev, M. (1986). *Kontrol i regulirane na ikonomicheskite sistemi*. Partizdat.

Dinev, M. (1999). *Kontrol v sotsialnoto upravlenie*. TrakiaM.

Doklad otnosno Proekt na Postanovlenie na Ministerskia savet za priemane na Ustroystven pravilnik na Izpalnitelna agentsia. (n.d.). Public Consultants. https://www.strategy.bg/PublicConsultations/View.aspx?lang=b g-BG&Id=6918

Donev, K. (1984). *Stopanski i finansov kontrol*. Sofia: Nauka i izkustvo, 1984, s. 40.

Donev, K. (1980). Efektivnost na kontrolno-revizionnata deynost i faktori za neynoto povishavane. *Izv. na VINS – Varna*, *1980*(3), 103–110.

Drechsler, W. (2005). The re-emergence of "Weberian" public administration after the fall of new public management: The central and eastern European perspective. *Halduskultuur*, *6*(1), 94–108.

Eurofound (2020b). COVID-19: Policy responses across Europe, Publications Office of the European Union, Luxembourg.

Eurofound. (2015). *New forms of employment*. Publications Office of the European Union, Luxembourg.

Eurofound. (2020a). New forms of employment: 2020 update, New forms of employment series, Publications Office of the European Union, Luxembourg.

Eurofound. (2022). Living and working in Europe 2021, Publications Office of the European Union, Luxembourg.

European Commission. (2016). A European Agenda for the Collaborative Economy. Communication from the Commission to the European Parliament, the Council, the European Economic and Social Committee and the Committee of the Regions. European Commission, Brussels. Available at: https://eur-lex.europa.eu/legal-content/EN/TXT/PDF/?uri=CELEX:52016DC0356&from=EN [Accessed 18.03.2022].

European Commission. (2021). Questions and answers: Improving working conditions in platform work. Brussels, 9 December 2021. Available at: https://ec.europa.eu/commission/presscorner/detail/en/qanda_21_6606 [Accessed 18.03.2022].

European Commission. Digital labour platforms: The COLLEEM research project. Available at: https://joint-research-centre.ec.europa.eu/digital-labour-platforms-colleem-research-project_en

European Parliament. (2016). The Situation of Workers in the Collaborative Economy. Directorate General for Internal Policies, Policy Department A: Economic and Scientific Policy October 2016. Available at: https://www.europarl.europa.eu/RegData/etudes/IDAN/2016/587316/IPOL_I DA(2016)587316_EN.pdf [Accessed 21.03.2022].

FudgeJ. (2006). Fragmenting Work and Fragmenting Organizations: The Contract of Employment and the Scope of Labour Regulation. Osgoode Hall Law Journal, Vol. 44, No. 4. Available at SSRN: https://ssrn.com/abstract=974916

Godishen doklad za deynostta na Izpalnitelna agentsia Glavna inspektsia po Truda. (2021). Gli.gov. https://www.gli.government.bg/sites/default/files/upload/documents/2022-04/godishen-doklad-2021.pdf

Hristoforov, V. G. (1966). Darzhavnite uchrezhdenia – pravna sashtnost i administrativno-praven rezhim. Sofia: Nauka i izkustvo.

Ilgen, D. (1991). Schneider, J. Performance Measurement: A Multidiscipline View. *International Review of Industrial and Organizational Psychology*, *6*, 71–10.

ILO. (2006). The employment relationship. International Labour Conference, 95th Session, Report V (1). Available at: https://www.ilo.org/global/publications/ilo-bookstore/order-online/books/WCMS_PUBL_9221166112_EN/lang--en/index.htm. [Accessed 11.02.2022].

ILO. (2016). Non-standard employment around the world: Understanding challenges, shaping prospects. International Labour Office – Geneva. Available at: https://www.ilo.org/global/publications/books/WCMS_534326/lang--en/index.htm. [Accessed 11.12.2021].

ILO. (2018). Report II: Statistics on Work Relationships. 20th International Conference of Labour Statisticians, 10-19 October 2018, International Labour Office, Geneva. Available at: https://www.ilo.org/wcmsp5/groups/public/---dgreports/---stat/documents/publication/wcms_644596.pdf. [Accessed 11.12.2021].

ILO. (2019). Work for a brighter future. Report of the Global Commission on the Future of Work. https://www.ilo.org/global/publications/books/WCMS_662410/lang--en/index.htm.

ILO. (2022) World Employment and Social Outlook. *Trends 2021*. https://www.ilo.org/global/research/global- reports/weso/trends2021/WCMS_795453/lang--en/index.htm[Accessed 04.10.2022].

Integriran narachnik po upravlenie saglasno BDS EN ISO/IEC 27001. (2014). Gli.gov. https://www.gli.government.bg/sites/default/files/upload/archive/docs/2015-09/Integriran_nar__cnik_po_upravlenie_IA_GIT_versi___5.pdf

Ivanova, P. (2020). *Novite tendentsii v trudovite otnoshenia. Izvestia Sp. Ikonomicheski universitet.* Varna.

Kaltner, J. (2018). Employment Status of Uber and Lyft Drivers: Unsettlingly Settled. *Hastings Women's Law Journal*, *29*(1), 29–54. https://repository.uchastings.edu/cgi/viewcontent.cgi?article=1403&context=hwlj

Kässi, O., & Lehdonvirta, V. (2018). Online labour index: Measuring the online gig economy for policy and research. *Technological Forecasting and Social Change*, *137*, 241–248. doi:10.1016/j.techfore.2018.07.056

Kaufmann, A., & Gil-Aluja, J. (1990). *Laz matematicas del azar y de la incertidumbre*. Ediciones Graficas Ortega.

Kingsley, S., Gray, M., & Suri, S. (2015). Accounting for Market Frictions and Power Asymmetries in Online Labor Markets, Policy &amp. *Policy and Internet*, *7*(4), 383–400. doi:10.1002/poi3.111

Kostova, N. (2010). *Finansovo-schetovoden analiz*. Aktiv – K OOD.

Lambovska, M., Rajnoha, R., Dobrovic, J. (2019). From Quality to Quantity and Vice Versa: How to Evaluate Performance in the Budgetary Control Process. *Journal of Competitiveness, 3,* 1.

Lambovska, M. (2018). Control on teams: A model and empirical evidence from Bulgaria. *Serbian Journal of Management*, *13*(2), 311–322. doi:10.5937jm13-14633

Mevorah, N., Lidzhi, D. I., & Farhi, L. (1926). Komentar na Zakona za zadalzheniyata i dogovorite. Chast II. Sofia: Pechatnitsa.

MLSP. (2020) Doklad: Analiz na ochakvanite promeni v organizatsiyata na truda i zaetostta v Balgariya, porodeni ot novovaznikvashtite „novi formi na trud". Available at: https://www.mlsp.government.bg/uploads/1/lm-report-v3.pdf

Mrachkov, V. (1978). *Balgarskoto trudovo zakonodatelstvo i mezhdunarodnite trudovi konventsii i preporaki.* Sofia: s.n.

Mrachkov, V. (1985). *Kontrol za spazvane na trudovoto zakonodatelstvo i otgovornost za negovoto narushavane.* Sofia: Izdatelstvo na Balgarska akademia na naukite, 1985.

Mrachkov, V. (2008). Sto godini Inspektsiya po truda. *Yuridicheski svyat, 1,* 94.

Mrachkov, V. (2010). *Trudovo pravo, Sedmo izdanie*. Sofya: Sibi.

Mrachkov, V. (2008). Sto godini inspektsia po truda. *Yuridicheski svyat*, (1), 77–102.

Mrachkov, V. (2016). *Kontrol za spazvane na trudovoto zakonodatelstvo i administrativnonakazatelna otgovornost za negovoto narushavane. // Mrachkov, V., Sredkova, K., Vasilev, A. Komentar na Kodeksa na truda*. Sibi.

Mrachkov, V. (2018). *Trudovo pravo (deseto preraboteno i dopalneno izdanie)*. Sibi.

Mrachkov, V. (2020). Sotsialni prava na balgarskite grazhdani. Sofia. *Siela*, *2020*, 40.

Mrachkov, V., Sredkova, K., & Vasilev, A. (2016). Komentar na Kodeksa na truda, 12-to preraboteno i dopalneno izdanie, Sofia. *Sibi*, *2016*, 1148.

NaredbaN. (2022). *Наръчник За Инспекторите По Труда*. Международно Бюро По Тру. http://ohrananatruda.com/files/documents/252.pdf

Nedyalkova, P. (2019). Government Supervision – A Factor for Business Development. Journal of Management Policy and Practice. Atlanta, Georgia, USA: North American Business Press.

Nedyalkova, P. (2020). Quality of Internal Auditing in the Public Sector: Perspectives from the Bulgarian and International Context. Cham: Springer Nature Switzerland.

Nedyalkova, P., Dimitrova, D., & Bogdanov, H. (2022). New Features in the Bulgarian Legal Framework and Financial Control Practice for Compliance with Labour Legislation in the Age of Globalization. IGI Global Publ.

Nedyalkova, P., Dimitrova, D., & Bogdanov, H. (2022). New Features in the Bulgarian Legal Framework and Financial Control Practice for Compliance with Labour Legislation in the Age of Globalization. Redefining Global Economic Thinking for the Welfare of Society: [Monography]. IGI Global Publ.

Nedyalkova, P. (2019). Government Supervision – A Factor for Business Development. *Journal of Management Policy and Practice, Atlanta, Georgia, USA: North American Business Press, 20*(2), 114–120.

Nedyalkova, P. (2020). Empirical Study of the VAIA Metric (Value Added of Internal Audit) and Determination of the Internal Audit Quality for Shumen Municipality for the Period 2011–2016. *Contributions to Management Science*, *2020*, 171–185. doi:10.1007/978-3-030-29329-1_11

Nedyalkova, P. (2020). Presentation of the Dependence Between the Chosen Internal Audit Approach and the Methods for Assessing the Quality of the Internal Audit in the Public Sector. *Contributions to Management Science*, *2020*, 105–114. doi:10.1007/978-3-030-29329-1_8

Nedyalkova, P. (2020). Types of Control Assessments Applied in Control Practice. *Contributions to Management Science*, *2020*, 23–30. doi:10.1007/978-3-030-29329-1_3

Nunberg, B. (1999). *The state after communism: administrative transitions in Central and Eastern Europe*. World Bank Publications. doi:10.1596/0-8213-4205-3

OECD. (2008). *OECD Employment Outlook 2008*. OECD Publishing. doi:10.1787/empl_outlook-2008-

OECD. (2014). *OECD Employment Outlook 2014*. OECD Publishing. doi:10.1787/empl_outlook-2014-

OECD. (2018a). *Tax Challenges Arising from Digitalisation – Interim Report 2018: Inclusive Framework on BEPS*. OECD Publishing. doi:10.1787/9789264293083-

OECD. (2018b). *The Future of Social Protection: What works for non-standard workers?* OECD Publishing. doi:10.1787/9789264306943-

OECD. (2019a). *Policy Responses to New Forms of Work*. OECD Publishing. doi:10.1787/0763f1b7-

OECD. (2019b). *OECD Employment Outlook 2019: The Future of Work*. OECD Publishing. doi:10.1787/9ee00155-

OECD. (2019c). *Preparing for the Changing Nature of Work in the Digital Era, March 2019*. OECD. https://dokumen.tips/documents/preparing-for-the-changing-nature-of-work-in-the-digital-preparing-for-thechanging.html?page=1.

OECD. (2020). *OECD Employment Outlook 2020: Worker Security and the COVID-19 Crisis*. OECD Publishing. doi:10.1787/1686c758-

Pedersini, R. (2002). Economically dependent workers', employment law and industrial relations. *Eurofound*. https://www.eurofound.europa.eu/publications/report/2002/economically-dependent-workers-employment-law-and-industrial-re
lations.

Pesole, A., M., Urzí Brancati, C., Fernández-Macías, E., Biagi, F., & González Vázquez, I. (2018). Platform Workers in Europe. *Publications Office of the European Union, Luxembourg., JRC112157*. Advance online publication. doi:10.2760/742789

Popova, Zh. (2011). Pravo na Evropeyskia sayuz. Sofia. *Siela*, *2011*, 396.

Proekt na Ustroystven pravilnik na izpalnitelna agentsia. (n.d.). Public Consultants. https://www.strategy.bg/PublicConsultations/View.aspx?lang=bg-BG&Id=6918

Pvd, A. (2017) Een Verbonden Samenleving - Verkiezingsprogramma 2017. *Partij van de Arbeid*. https://www.pvda.nl/wp-content/uploads/2017/02/PvdAVerkiezingsprogramma2017EenVerbondenSamenleving.pdf

Rachev, R., Andreeva, A., Yolova, G., & Vladova, V. (2008). Trudovo i osiguritelno pravo. Varna: Nauka i ikonomika.

Radoilski, L. (1957). *Trudovo pravo, istorichesko razvitie*. Sofia: Nauka i izkustvo,

Randma-Liiv, T., & Drechsler, W. (2017). Three decades, four phases: Public administration development in Central and Eastern Europe, 1989-2017. *International Journal of Public Sector Management, 30*(6-7), 595–605. doi:10.1108/IJPSM-06-2017-0175

Ross, H. (2015). Ridesharing's House of Cards: O'Connor v. Uber Technologies, Inc. and the Viability of Uber's Labor Model in Washington, Washington. *Law Review, 90*, 1431–1469. https://digital.law.washington.edu/dspace-law/bitstream/handle/1773.1/1489/90WLR1431.pdf

Sabev, S., & Doncheva, M. (2021). Pandemiyata ot COVID-19 kato yuridicheski fakt. Reformata v administrativnoto nakazvane ot 2020 g., 17 may 2021: Sbornik dokladi, Sofia: Univ. izd. Sv. *Kliment Ohridski*, 93–102.

Schoukens P. (2020) Digitalisation and social security in the EU. The case of platform work: from work protection to income protection? *European Journal of Social Security*, 1–18. . doi:10.1177/1388262720971300

Serafimova, D. (2021). Corporate social responsibility – trends andinnovative practices in the labour market and the higher education sector. *Izvestiya. Journal of the University of Economics.*

Serafimova, D. (2021). Korporativna sotsialna otgovornost – tendentsii i inovativni praktiki na pazara na truda i v sektora na vissheto obrazovanie. Izvestia. Varna: Nauka i ikonomika.

Serafimova, D. (2021). *Interdisciplinary Educational Models for Creating CSR and Sustainability Culture in European Business Schools. 2021 Sustainable Leadership and Academic Excellence International Conference (SLAE).* IEEE. https://doi.org/doi, doi:10.1109/SLAE54202.2021.9788104

Sharma, M. (2020). Types of Control Methods: Top 3 Types. *Business Management.* https://www.businessmanagementideas.com/management/controlling/types-of-control-methods-top-3-typesmanagement/7981

Sharma, M. (2020). Types of Control Methods: Top 3 Types. *Business Management.* https://www.businessmanagementideas.com/management/controlling/types-of-control-methods-top-3-types-management/7981

Shi, L., Li, S., & Fu, X. (2020). The Fourth Industrial Revolution, Technological Innovation and Firm Wages: Firm-level Evidence from OECD Economies. *Revue d'Economie Industrielle, 1*(69), 89–125. https://journals.openedition.org/rei/8798?lang=en. doi:10.4000/rei.8798

Shirvanyan, M. (2021). Spetsifiki v rezhima na trudovata zlopoluka v balgarskoto zakonodatelstvo. Varna. *Steno, 2021*, 106–107.

Sivkov, Ts. (2021). *Izmeneniyata v ZANN ot kraya na 2020 g. – stapka po posoka na priemaneto na Kodeks za administrativni narushenia i nakazania.* Reformata v administrativnoto nakazvane ot. Sbornik dokladi, Sofia: Univ. izd. Sv. Kliment Ohridski.

Spasova, S., Ghailani, D., Sabato, S., Coster, S., Fronteddu, B., & Vanhercke, B. (2021). *Non-standard workers and the self-employed in the EU: social protection during the Covid-19 pandemic.* ETUI. https://etui.org/publications/non-standard-workers-and-self-employed-eu.

Sredkova, K. (2007). *Balgarskoto trudovo zakonodatelstvo – 100 godini i sled tova. // Aktualni problemi na trudovoto i osiguritelno pravo. T. II. Sofia: Sv.* Kl. Ohridski.

Staykov, I. (2021). Razvitieto na trudovoto pravo na Evropeyskia sayuz prez 2019 godina – novi iztochnitsi i novi perspektivi za po-nadezhdna pravna uredba na trudovite otnoshenia. Chast parva: Evropeyski organ po truda – sazdavane i pravna harakteristika. Sofia: Izdatelstvo na Nov balgarski universitet.

Staynov, P. (1952). *Administrativnite aktove i pravnata sistema na Narodna republika Bulgaria.* BAN.

Stoychev, S. (2002). *Konstitutsionno pravo.* Siela.

Strategicheski plan za deynostta na IA „GIT" - https://www.gli.government.bg/sites/default/files/upload/archive/docs/2019-08/StrategicheskiPlanGIT_2018_2021.pdf

Timchev, M. (1999). *Finansovo-stopanski analiz.* Trakia .

Tokushev, D. (2008). *Istoria na novobalgarskata darzhava i pravo 1878–1944.* Sibi.

Tomov, Y., Krumov. K. (2007). *Stopanski, finansov i danachen kontrol.* Svishtov, Akad. izd. Tsenov.

Turner, M., & Hulme, D. (1997). *Governance, administration and development: Making the state work.* Macmillan. doi:10.1007/978-1-349-25675-4

UNECE. (2021) New forms of employment and quality of employment: Implications for official statistics. *Working Paper Series on Statistics, 8.*

Urzi Brancati, M. C., Pesole, A., & Fernandez Macias, E. (2020). New evidence on platform workers in Europe. Results from the second COLLEEM survey Luxembourg. *Publications Office of the European Union, JRC118570.* doi:10.2760/459278

World Economic Forum. (2020). *The Promise of Platform Work: Understanding the Ecosystem.* WEF. https://www.weforum.org/whitepapers/the-promise-of-platform-work-understanding-the-ecosystem/

Yanulov, I. (1948). *Trudovo pravo.*

Yolova, G. (2020). Subektivnite trudovi prava - evolyutsia vav filosofiyata, normativnata uredba i doktrinata. Ot Andreeva, A., Yolova, G., Blagoycheva, H., Aleksandrov, A., Banov, H., Yordanov, Z. Zashtita za individualnite subektivni trudovi prava (na rabotnika ili sluzhitelya). Varna: Nauka i ikonomika, pp. 21 – 47.

Zhao, B., Zhao, Z., Huang, M., Zhang, X., Li, Y., & Wang, R. (2021). Model Predictive Control of Solar PV-Powered Ice-Storage Air-Conditioning System Considering Forecast 246 Uncertainties. *IEEE Transactions on Sustainable Energy*, *12*(3), 1672–1683. doi:10.1109/TSTE.2021.3061776

Živković, Ž., Nikolić, D., Mihajlović, I., & Djordjević, P. (2016). Dependability assessment of supplier performance based on fuzzy sets theory. Pál Michelberger (Ed.), Management, Enterprise and Benchmarking in the 21st century. Óbuda University, Keleti Faculty of Business and Management.

About the Authors

Andriyana Andreeva is an Associate Professor at the Department of Legal Studies at the University of Economics in Varna, Bulgaria and a certified mediator listed in the Unified Register of Mediators. She is also a member of the Bulgarian Association of Labour Law and Social Insurance. She has extensive research experience in the field of labour law and public insurance, practical legal experience as a consultant, including as an auditor on European projects. Over the years she has been a guest lecturer at a number of foreign universities.

Galina Yolova is Associate Professor at the Legal Studies Department, Economic University of Varna, Bulgaria, PhD in Criminal Law. Deputy Head of the Department of Legal Studies, with over 26 years of teaching and research experience. She has over 120 scientific publications and her research interests are in the field of Labour Law, Social-Security Law, Healthcare insurance, Digitalization, Artificial intellect, eHealth. Member of Union of Scientists – Varna, and member of the Bulgarian association of Labour law and social security.

Darina Dimitrova is a Doctor of Law, Senior Assistant Professor at the University of Economics - Varna, Department of Legal Studies. She has 25 years of teaching experience. Her research interests are in the field of administrative law. She participates in the organizing committees of all scientific conferences held by the Department of Legal Studies, two of which she has chaired. Darina Dimitrova performs the functions of Scientific Secretary of the Department of Legal Studies and, in this regard, makes contacts with specialized libraries of related scientific organizations and universities. She has co-authored a number of interdisciplinary publications exploring the interrelationship between labour and administrative law aspects of labour law compliance, labour migration and labour mobility.

Hristina Blagoycheva is Doctor of Economics, Associated professor at the Finance Department, University of Economics – Varna, Varna, Bulgaria. Since 2019 she is a Dean of the Faculty of Finance and Accounting, University of Economics – Varna. Member of the Union of Scientists in Bulgaria and Member of the Scientific and Technical Unions - Varna, "Finance" section. She writes and presents on issues of social security, corporate social responsibility and social innovations. She has been invited as a lecturer at various Bulgarian universities and as a social security consultant in the business. She is an author of 99 publications in Bulgaria and abroad with more than 220 citations of her publications.

Plamena Nedyalkova is the chief assistant at the Department of Accounting, Economic University of Varna, Bulgaria and a certified internal auditor at the Ministry of Finance. Also a member of the Institute of Internal Auditors in Bulgaria, she has gathered extensive professional experience as an accountant, chief accountant, and assistant auditor. Since 2014, she has been a certified internal auditor in the public sector at the Ministry of Finance in Bulgaria. Over the years, she has been a guest lecturer at numerous foreign universities. Works with various non-governmental organizations to support society.

Hristosko Bogdanov is a lecturer in the Department of Accounting at the University of Economics - Varna. He has a private practice as an accountant. An expert is in the District Court - Varna.

Index

L

M

N

O

P

Q

R

S

www.ingramcontent.com/pod-product-compliance
Lightning Source LLC
LaVergne TN
LVHW080650011026
849160LV00014B/1373